Fat Cats & Lucky Dogs

How to leave (some of) your estate to your pet

Barry Seltzer

B.A. LL.B., TEP (Preferred area of practice – estate law)
Barrister and Solicitor

Gerry W. Beyer

J.S.D., LL.M., J.D., B.A. (Professor of Law)

Edited by
Jim Bee

Prism
Publishing Inc.

Toronto, Ontario, Canada • Delray Beach, Florida, U.S.A.

Prism Publishing Inc.
9140 Leslie Street, Ste. 204
Richmond Hill, Ontario, Canada L4B 0A9
prismmpub@hotmail.com

ISBN 978-0-9664313-5-3

Book Design by Ledden Design
www.leddendesign.com

Cover Illustration by Janet McLeod

A Note on the Type
This book was set in ITC Esprit, which was designed
by calligrapher and type designer Jovica Veljovic
for the International Typeface Corporation in 1985.
ITC Esprit incorporates old style characteristics
with calligraphic features.

This book is printed on FSC paper.
Supporting responsible use of forest resources.

Other Publications by the authors:

Seltzer, Barry

No One Should Have an Unplanned Death,
   Wills, Powers of Attorney, Taxes, Estate Administration. – 1st edition

Beyer, Gerry, W.

Wills, Trusts, and Estates – Examples and Explanations (4th edition 2007)

Modern Dictionary for the Legal Profession (4th edition 2008)

Wills, Trusts, and Estates for Legal Assistants (3rd edition 2009)
   (co-authored with John C. Hanft)

Beyer's Texas Property Code Annotated – 2008 – 2009 Edition

West's Legal Forms – Real Estate Transactions – Residential
   –Volumes 19 & 19A (4th edition 2008)

Texas Wills and Estates: Cases and Materials (6th edition 2008)

Texas Estate Administration: Cases and Materials (2008)

West's Texas Forms – Administration of Decedents' Estates and Guardianships
   –Volumes 12, 12A, & 12B (3rd edition 2007)
   (co-authored with Aloysius Leopold)

Texas Estate Planning Statutes with Commentary (2008) (Aspen Publishers)

Texas Trust Law: Cases and Materials (2007)

Teaching Materials on Estate Planning (3rd edition 2005)

Texas Law of Wills – Volumes 9 & 10 of Texas Practice Series (3rd edition 2002)

To contact the authors:

Barry Seltzer

Barrister and Solicitor
B.A. LL.B., TEP

9140 Leslie Street, Unit 204
Richmond Hill, Ontario
Canada, L4B 0A9

Tel: 905-475-9001
       416-880-2837

Fax: 905-475-9004

barry@barryseltzer.com

Professor Gerry W. Beyer

Governor Preston E. Smith
Regents Professor of Law
Texas Tech University School of Law
1802 Hartford Street
Lubbock, Texas 79409-0004 U.S.A.

Tel: (806) 742-3990, ext. 302
Fax: (978) 285-7941

gwb@professorbeyer.com

Quantity discounted orders available for groups. Please make enquiries to 905-475-9001.
Internet e-mail: prismmpub@hotmail.com

Acknowledgements

We want to gratefully acknowledge and thank the following people for their contributions to the book:

Toronto tax and estate lawyer Phil Friedlan, who read through the manuscript and made a number of significant comments and suggestions; research assistants Adam Fulkerson and Kyle Wolf of Lubbock, Texas; and Ruth Cohen, who assisted in expediting the project through the design and printing stage.

TABLE OF CONTENTS

On August 20, 2007, Leona Helmsley, a reclusive billionaire hotel operator and real estate investor, died of congestive heart failure at her home in Greenwich, Connecticut, at the age of 87.

In life, Ms. Helmsley was a flamboyant woman with an alleged despotic personality that earned her the nickname Queen of Mean. Some of her employees complained that even the slightest mistake might be grounds for firing.

An often-cited example of her meanness occurred after her only son died in 1982. She sued his estate for money and property that she claimed he had borrowed from her. Her son's widow, and the mother of her four grand-children, received an eviction notice for one of the disputed properties. The widow ruined herself financially fighting her mother-in-law in court.

Seven years later, the United States government convicted Ms. Helmsley of federal tax evasion and other white-collar crimes, sentencing her to 16 years in prison. She was released after serving only 19 months.

In 2001, a Chicago Sun-Times article portrayed her as living alone with her little Maltese dog, *Trouble*, who remained her constant companion for the rest of her life. At the time, she was estranged from her grand-children and had few friends.

Despite her unsavory reputation, Ms. Helmsley was generous in her charitable donations. She gave $5 million to help families of New York firefighters after the attacks of September 11, 2001, and another $5 mil-lion to hurricane Katrina relief. In addition to other contributions, she gave $25 million to New York's Presbyterian Hospital for medical research and millions in the 1990s to help rebuild African-American churches that had been burned in the South.

In death, Ms. Helmsley left most of her estate – estimated at $5-8 billion – to her family charitable trust, which appears to be dedicated to the care of dogs. Two of her four grandchildren received $5 million in trust and another $5 million outright, provided they visited their father's grave once each calendar year. Her other two grandchildren received nothing for reasons that they apparently well knew. She also left $100,000 to her chauffeur.

But the real blockbuster in her will was the $12-million trust fund she left for the care of little *Trouble*.

Like many of us, Ms. Helmsley wanted to make certain that her dog – perhaps her only friend in her later years – would not be ignored, forgotten, or simply disposed of after her death.

Because she was rich and famous (or infamous, take your pick) she was able to provide a very large trust fund for her pet – large enough to make the international media sit up and take notice. The tale of the $12-million dog was a major story around the world for several days. It therefore served several purposes:

- It reminded us that many people consider their pet animals more than inanimate objects that can be casually discarded when their owners die or become incapacitated.
- It reminded pet owners that, in the event of their death or incapacitation, they can and should make some type of arrangements for the long-term care of their pets.
- It reminded the legal profession that people who want to set up provisions to provide for their pets need to be taken seriously.

Unfortunately for Ms. Helmsley and *Trouble*, disgruntled relatives and a cooperative judge managed to undo the trust agreement by reducing it to $2 million and awarding $6 million to each of the two disinherited grandsons – all on the basis that their grandmother was not of sound mind when she concocted her will and trust agreements.

Ms. Helmsley had asked in her will that either her brother, Alvin, or her grandson, David, take the dog and use the $12 million for its care. Any money remaining in the trust after the dog's death would go to the family charitable trust. Because Alvin was already inheriting $15 million, and had no need for any additional funds, he passed on caring for *Trouble*, as did David, who also had his own inheritance and little interest in an animal that was reputedly as mean as its former mistress.

By early 2009, the little dog was being cared for by Carl Lekic, the general manager of the Helmsley Sandcastle Hotel. Mr. Lekic says the $2 million left to look after *Trouble* is more than sufficient for her care over the remainder of her life. He, of course, collects a caregiver fee.

As of September 2009, the case regarding the bulk of Ms. Helmsley's estate remained unsettled, with the courts deciding that the trustees were free to give the money to whichever charitable causes they saw fit, rather than primarily to organizations that cared for dogs. Three leading charities said they would try to have this aspect of the court ruling overturned. The case goes on.

So despite some bumps along the way, Ms. Helmsley did manage to ensure the ongoing care of her canine companion. Had there been no trust provision, *Trouble* would likely have been in real trouble, considering no one really wanted her.

 **FACTOIDS**

- **Spoiling Fido and Fifi.**
  The wealthy can find plenty of high-end items with which to spoil their pets, including faux mink coats for cold weather outings, feathered French day-beds for afternoon naps, designer bird cages, botanical fragrances, and even rhinestone tiaras.

- **The well-groomed pet.**
  Some of the new products and services available for keeping pets well-groomed include mouthwashes and electric toothbrushes for dogs and pedicures (some with nail polish) and special cage perches for birds. In addition, there are litter boxes that flush automatically, cleaning cloths that imitate baby wipes for dirty paws, and special air fresheners to eliminate pet odors.

And that is the focus of this book – to point out the pitfalls involved in setting up ongoing care for pets when their owners can no longer provide it, and to establish ways to counter these pitfalls.

This book is intended only as a vehicle for sharing information and ideas; for providing guidance to those who would like to explore various possibilities; and for stimulating pet owners to take action while they are able to do so. It is not intended to replace sound legal advice from a practicing lawyer in your particular part of the world.

While this book was largely written for pet owners in the United States and Canada, it should also be useful in other jurisdictions where the legal system is based on English common law, including Great Britain, Australia, New Zealand and parts of the Caribbean.

That said, even within national borders, the laws governing estate affairs and animals vary from state to state, province to province, and municipality to municipality. Wherever you live, you will need local legal advice before taking any action that may affect your estate plan and your pet's future.

If you have comments, questions or concerns regarding the information in this book, please pass them along to us, either by e-mail or regular mail. Our addresses may be found at the front of this book.

A note on terminology

We use the term *pet owners* to describe people who keep animals for companionship and out of affection for them (rather than for commercial purposes, such as breeding or racing). We refer to the animals they keep as *pets*, a term that can include almost any type of animal, from small rodents, fish and snakes to ferrets, cats, dogs, birds and horses.

Animal rights groups use the term *companion animal* rather than *pet*. And they substitute *animal guardian* for *pet owner*, in part because they reject the notion of animals as property. We are sympathetic, but we have to work within the context of the law as it stands and, in this respect, animals are currently considered property in almost all jurisdictions.

We use the term *caregiver* to describe the person or institution in whose care a pet is left by its original owner.

In this book, the term *companion animal* is used in sample paragraphs that may be inserted into a will where we want to make it clear that, in the event of an emergency, specific pets are left to the care of others as *companions*, not as working animals, caged captives or as property to be sold, traded or given away to third parties.

Otherwise, we avoid substituting the term *companion animal* for *pet* in the text of the book because we believe most people take the term to mean a mammal, specifically a dog or cat. Many people have difficulty thinking of birds, rodents and reptiles as companions. Yet, for the purpose of this book, we want readers to feel they can, and should, include members of these other groups of living beings in their estate plans, or in informal arrangements with friends and relatives, even though they may not fit the public perception of a *companion animal*.

INTRODUCTION

*P*ets have been important to humans for many thousands of years. Dogs, for example, were domesticated in Mesolithic times (more than 10,000 years ago in the Middle Stone Age) by our hunter-gatherer forefathers – likely for very practical purposes – guarding camps, hauling sleds and the like. But if early dogs were anything like their modern counterparts, they soon ingratiated themselves as friends and loyal companions.

Our ancestors took a fancy to other animals as well. Cheetahs were first tamed by the Sumerians and were kept by the ancient Egyptians. In later times, they were companions to a number of historical giants, including Genghis Khan, Akbar the Great and Charlemagne. Hawks and falcons were also tamed and trained as hunters and hunting companions to generations of men throughout prehistoric and historic times.

The common house cat has been with us for four or five millennia. The ancient Egyptians frequently embalmed them, perhaps to keep their human owners company in the afterlife.

In later times, the Prophet Muhummad reportedly once cut off the sleeve of his robe so he wouldn't wake his sleeping cat, *Muezza*, when he was called to prayer. The 18th century English writer, Samuel Johnson, would personally fetch oysters for his favorite cat, *Hodge*, so his servants would not come to dislike the animal from having to serve it themselves.

In more recent times, many of our villains and heroes have been pet lovers. Josef Stalin was apparently a cat fancier; Adolf Hitler liked large dogs; United States President Franklin D. Roosevelt owned a Scottish terrier named *Fala*; and his successor, Harry Truman, had a pet goat named *Dewey's Goat*.

Winston Churchill adored a cat named *Nelson* and kept an entire menagerie that included lambs, pigs, cattle, swans and, at one point, a leopard. In fact, a clause in Churchill's will states that his home at Chartwell is to be occupied by a ginger cat in perpetuity.

And in a January 19, 2004, feature that appeared in a British tabloid, the *Daily Mirror*, reporter Bill Barrows revealed that Churchill's pet parrot, *Charlie*, had just turned 104.

In the article, Barrows writes:

> **"Her favorite sayings were 'F*** Hitler' and 'F*** the Nazis.' And even today, 39 years after the great man's death, she can still be coaxed into repeating them with that unmistakable Churchillian inflection."**

The tradition of pets in the corridors of power continues to this day. In the United States, for example, all recent United States presidents have had First Pets, generally cats or dogs.

President Bill Clinton's family had a Labrador retriever named *Buddy* and a cat named *Socks*, who died in 2009. George W. Bush brought a Scottish terrier named *Barney*, an English springer spaniel named *Spot*, and a cat called *India* (nicknamed *Willie*) into the White House. On his ranch in Crawford, Texas, President Bush kept a longhorn cow named *Ofelia*, named after someone who worked with him when he was the governor of Texas.

President Barak Obama and his family selected a Portuguese water dog named *Bo* as the White House pet – and subsequently triggered a surge of interest in the breed across North America and the United Kingdom.

But some earlier American presidents and their families were far more flamboyant when it came to pets. The wife of John Quincy Adams (Louisa Catherine), the 6th president, kept silkworms. Herbert Hoover, the 31st president, had an opossum. And Calvin Coolidge, the 30th president, walked a raccoon named *Rebecca* on a leash. Theodore Roosevelt, the 26th president, was famous for his many pets. And his six children were said to have kept snakes, dogs, cats, a badger, birds, guinea pigs and more.

For many people in less exalted positions, their pets are also their favorite companions. Several years ago, the American Animal Hospital Association conducted a survey of 1,019 pet owners to determine the role their pets played in their lives. Some 57% said they would want a pet as their only companion if they were stranded on a deserted island; 55% considered themselves a parent to their pets; and 80% selected companionship as the main reason for having pets.

Since people feel so strongly about their pets, it stands to reason they would want to provide for their pets if they predecease them. Consequently, estate planners, especially in the United States, are drafting more trusts to provide care for clients' pets. A number of states have even passed legislation relaxing the technicalities of trust creation, making it easier for pet owners to provide for pets. If a pet owner does not name a person to enforce a trust, the courts can appoint someone to act on the animal's behalf.

One state, Wisconsin, recognizes trusts for pets as valid, but does not provide for their enforcement should the trustee decide not to implement them.

 FACTOIDS

- **Keeping reptiles in Australia.** In Australia, all native reptiles are protected by law and cannot be collected from the wild. Some Australian states even require pet owners to obtain a license to keep store-bought reptiles. In Western Australia, it is actually illegal to own reptiles (and insects) as pets.

- **Orphans.** The organization 2nd Chance 4 Pets estimates that more than 500,000 pets are orphaned each year in the U.S. due to the death or disability of their human companions. This is the first organization to focus its efforts on this issue.

- **Dogs see some colors.** It was commonly believed that dogs are color blind, but research indicates they can see some color, just not as vividly as humans. And they may not see red or green.

- **The devil, you say.** One of Cardinal Richelieu's many cats was named *Lucifer*.

At the time of writing, about 40 states plus the District of Columbia recognize pet trusts in some form. As the demand for pet protection increases, however, other states will come on board. You can check in *Appendix H* of this book, on the Internet, or with your lawyer to find out whether the state in which you live recognizes and provides for the creation of pet trusts, or whether such recognition is under consideration.

In states and in countries where such trusts are not permitted, attorneys are setting up trusts that are more obliquely designed to protect pets. These trusts name a pet *caregiver* as the beneficiary who can receive monies from the trust, provided an animal is cared for according to terms spelled out in the trust.

Both types of trusts are increasingly popular as more people ponder the fate of their pets after their death. No one wants to think of *Fido* or *Fluffy* winding up on death row at the local pound. Attorneys in some United States jurisdictions report that, when asked, 90% of their pet-owning clients want to make provisions for their animals, either through trusts or some other mechanism.

Trusts are often the most useful instrument available for clients who have few relatives or friends, or who have pets, such as horses or parrots, that are more difficult to care for than a dog or cat. In some cases, where people are largely alone in the world, their pets are the children for whom they must provide.

We hope you find this book informative and enjoyable and that it encourages you to include your animal companion in your long-range financial planning activities.

Message from a pet whose owner did not make plans

> This morning I woke up feeling great. Ran to the door and found my best friend waiting for me. We went for our usual morning walk. My friend does most of the talking, but I am happy just to be listening. My best friend's words are always soothing and comforting. After our walk, we went back home and had breakfast together. I got kissed on my nose and my best friend went off to work. Now comes my boring time. I walk around the house making sure everything is safe and secure, then I just lay on the couch or the bed or the easy chair waiting for my best friend to come home.

> Today is different. Night has fallen. My friend normally is home by now. It is getting late. I'm starting to worry. I hope she gets home soon. I'm starting to get hungry. You know I don't care if I get to eat or not. I don't complain. Please come home. I miss you. I am so tired now. Why is it getting light out again? This is so strange. I need to get on the bed. I can smell my friend was here. This is where I feel safe. Wait! I hear someone at the door – it must be her, No, it is someone I don't know. Who are you? Why are you coming in here?

Are you going to hurt me? Rob my friend's home? What am I supposed to do? I know. I will act mean. I will growl, bark, defend my friend's home the best that I can. They have just put a leash on me. They are trying to talk calmly to me, but I don't trust them. I will still act mean. I just heard them say my friend's name and something about a fatal heart attack. Now I am in a small cement barred area. This is not the food I normally eat. These are not the smells I normally smell. I am so scared. I still need to act mean. I know my friend must be trying to find me. I have been here for about a week now. I hear people talking about me being aggressive. Wait. They are opening my door.

They are putting that leash on me again. My friend must be here. Now I am in the exam room. Oh I see the needle again. My friend always told me the needles will help keep me healthy. I felt the pinch-this needle is different. Something is happening. I feel very sleepy…where is my friend?

(Reprinted by permission of Amy Shever, Director of 2nd Chance 4 Pets.)

*Footnote: Although the above message may seem a little emotional, consider the fate of American writer Dorothy Parker's last little dog, which she had named **C'est Tout** (That's All).*

*When Parker died in her Manhattan apartment in June 1967, **C'est Tout** was found whimpering beside her body, heartbroken and loyal to the end.*

*In her will, Parker left the bulk of her modest estate to the National Association for the Advancement of Colored People (NAACP). She had made no provision for her dog, however. Poor little **C'est Tout** went to the local pound and was never heard of again.*

C'est Tout!

CHAPTER 1

The growing importance of pets

OVERVIEW

- Pets are increasingly important in western society.
- According to the American Pet Products Association Inc., pet ownership in the United States is growing. In its 2007-08 survey, some 63% of U.S. households (71.1 million households) owned a pet, up from 56 million in 1988.
- American pet owners spent an estimated $45.4 billion in 2009 to care for, feed, spoil, amuse and pamper their pets.
- Similar trends are apparent in Canada, Australia, New Zealand and Great Britain.
- We owe it to our pets to do what they cannot – ensure their well-being if we are no longer mentally or physically able to do so.

The notion that pets are becoming more important in our lives today is borne out by recent research, which shows that 75% of American dog owners view their animals as family members and more than 50% of cat owners feel the same. About 20% of pet owners have actually changed romantic relationships because of disputes over pets. Nearly 40% of pet owners carry pet pictures in their wallets and more than 30% have taken time off work because of sick pets. A majority of pet dogs and cats sleep indoors, most on their owner's bed or on a blanket or pet bed. A recent survey revealed that more pet owners would rather be stranded on a desert island with their pets than their spouse.

Furthermore, lifestyles in many western countries are changing: more people are choosing to remain single or to live without human companionship. They acquire pets to become their friends and companions.

"I once decided not to date a guy because he wasn't excited to meet my dog. I mean, this was like not wanting to meet my mother."
– **BONNIE SCHACTER**, FOUNDER OF THE SINGLE PET OWNER'S SOCIETY SINGLES GROUP

"Love me, love my dog." – JOHN HEYWOOD
(149?-1580), ENGLISH PLAYWRIGHT

In Canada, a 2001 IPSOS-REID pet ownership study (Paws & Claws) found that:

"Eight in ten of the pet owners ... (83%) consider their pet to be a family member; only 15 percent said they love their pet as a pet rather than as a family member.

"This perception of the pet as family translates into 'parental' behavior for many pet owners: seven in ten (69%) pet owners allow their pets to sleep on their beds and six in ten have their pet's pictures in their wallets or on display with other family photos. Almost all pet owners (98%) admit to talking to their pets."

Another indication of the growing status and importance of pets is the rise of pet-friendly travel outfitters. Instead of packing *Fido* off to a boarding kennel for a couple of weeks, more people are choosing to take him on vacation with them. One such company, Dog Paddling Adventures (www.dogpaddlingadventures.com) of Markham, Ontario, Canada, for example, offers cross-country skiing, hiking and canoeing expeditions for pets and their owners. Dog Paddling Adventures claims its business has quadrupled since it opened in 2000.

Or you could take your dog on a guided tour of Provence in France or Napa Valley in California through the Europaws division of California-based vacation packager Europeds www.europeds.com.

Of course, there have been pet-friendly motels and hotels for years, but today there are hotels that even provide room service for cats and dogs. And if you and your dog book into the *Las Ventanas al Paraiso* resort in Los Cabos, Mexico (www.lasventanas.com), *Buster* can look over some of the chef-prepared menus for doggie guests, while the two of you enjoy side-by-side massages.

Recently in California, a seven-year-old black Labrador retriever named *Daisy* enjoyed a two-week stay at the luxurious Paradise Ranch Country Club for Dogs in Sun Valley, California, complete with swimming pool and a bedroom with TV, for $45 a night. This came after she had served as a *bridesmaid* at her mistress' wedding in a fetching collar wreathed in flowers. *Daisy* got the doggie country club treatment while the newlyweds honeymooned in Italy.

Traveling by air? Check to see if your airline gives frequent-flyer miles for animals. Some do.

And then there are the magazines – not just the ordinary pet magazines that expound the virtues of a particular type of pet, or a breed of cat or dog, but specialty publications such as *Fido Friendly* (www.fidofriendly.com), which bills itself as the travel magazine for you and your dog. It offers a complete guide to dog-friendly accommodations across the United States and Canada.

And then there is the fact that nearly one in five U.S. companies now allows pets at work, according to a survey by the American Pet Products Manufacturers Association. The survey also showed that a majority of those polled believe there are benefits to having pets at work – relieving stress, improving relationships with co-workers, making for a happier workforce and creating a happier work environment.

What other evidence suggests the increasing importance of pets in our lives? For one thing, shared pet ownership is becoming more common among divorced and separated couples who can't bear the thought of losing *Felix* or *Buster*. Shared custody only works, however, when civility dominates a break-up. Fighting couples will be unlikely to reach a shared custody arrangement.

 FACTOIDS

- **Why some cats don't come when called.** Almost all white cats with two blue eyes are born deaf. White cats with only one blue eye, however, are deaf only in the ear closest to the blue eye.

- **Pampered doggies.** In Colombia, Bogota's well-to-do send their pampered doggies on a bus to the countryside to run, swim, play and take obedience classes at a canine camp in the village of Cajica. The dogs return home exhausted.

- **Pigeons.** People have been keeping pigeons as pets for centuries, but they have also used the birds to carry messages in wartime for just as long. Pigeons have been known to fly at speeds of more than 80 mph. Of the 289 species of pigeons, two-thirds live in the Orient and Australasia.

- **Sacred dogs.** Pekingese dogs, one of the oldest breeds, were sacred in China for more than 2,000 years.

In the United States, bitter custody disputes over pets are becoming more common and are often costly. A California couple's fight in 2000 over *Gigi*, their pointer-greyhound adopted from a shelter, cost more than $100,000 in legal fees. The three-day trial included testimony from animal experts, who were called on to determine which home would better suit *Gigi*. Eventually, the wife was granted full custody after a day in the life video of the dog was played in court.

And in 2003, a Kentucky woman went to jail for 30 days rather than obey a court order to turn her two cats over to her ex-husband.

"I love them both like they're kids," said the woman. "I will fight and fight and fight until I get [them] back." She was jailed after lying under oath that the cats had run away. A private investigator, hired by her husband, found the cats hidden at a local business.

> *"A cat is a pygmy lion who loves mice, hates dogs, and patronizes human beings."* – OLIVER HERFORD (1863-1935)
> ENGLISH AUTHOR & ILLUSTRATOR

> *"In ancient times cats were worshipped as gods; they have not forgotten this."* – TERRY PRATCHETT,
> BRITISH FANTASY AUTHOR

In Canada, an Alberta truck driver was ordered to pay his ex-wife $200 a month in dog support starting in 2004 – plus a $2,000 retroactive payment. Under the ruling, the truck driver was ordered to reimburse his ex-wife for the food, health bills and general caregiving for their St. Bernard, *Crunchy*. It was believed to be the first court order of its kind in Canada, and perhaps in North America. Visitation rights were not included.

While much of the to-do surrounding the importance of pets in our lives centers on dogs and cats, other creatures are gaining ground. *The New York Times Magazine* of May 2, 2004, ran an article entitled *Fixing Nemo* by Rebecca Skloot about veterinarians who are earning a good living performing operations on pet fish – mostly fancy goldfish and koi, the Japanese pond fish. Many of the operations involved fixing buoyancy problems.

Why would anyone spend good money to fix a fish? While a koi's average lifespan ranges between 40 and 70 years, certain varieties may live for more than 100 years and be handed down from one generation of human caretakers to the next. Koi fanciers will part with thousands of dollars for a fancy or unique mature specimen. So the investment in a specialist to fix a buoyancy problem may be well worth the money. And then there's the sentimental value of a fish that was purchased as a fingerling by granddad so long ago.

Whatever the reason, our pets – regardless of species – are important to us. We become attached to them and we want to make sure that they remain safe and happy, even when we have bowed out of their lives.

How many Americans own pets?

The 2007-2008 National Pet Owners Survey conducted by the American Pet Products Association Inc. (APPA) reveals that some 63% of U.S. households (71.1 million households) owned a pet, up from 56 million in 1988.

APPA's survey data shows that Americans own 88.3 million cats, 74.8 million dogs, 24.3 million small animals, 16.0 million birds, 13.4 million reptiles, 9.6 million saltwater fish and 142 million fresh-water fish. Figures published by other animal organizations, such as the American Society for the Prevention of Cruelty to Animals (ASPCA) and the American Veterinary Medical Association (AVMA), vary slightly, but not substantially.

The survey also showed that American pet owners spent $45.4 billion in 2009 to care for, feed, amuse and pamper their pets.

Past and present APPA surveys have also revealed that:

- Dogs and cats are found in at least one out of three U.S. households.
- Seven out of 10 fish owners say keeping fish generates a relaxing environment and helps relieve stress.
- Households that have the most pet birds are located in the southern and western regions of the U.S.A.
- Turtles/tortoises are the most popular reptile owned by U.S. households with children.
- *Companionship, love, company and affection* along with *fun to have in a household* are top benefits associated with pet ownership.
- The majority of U.S. pet owners have purchased a gift for their companion animals within the last 12 months.

"When a cat adopts you there is nothing to be done about it except to put up with it until the wind changes."
– **T.S. ELIOT** (1888-1965), AMERICAN POET

A global phenomenon

In Australia, The Petcare Information and Advisory Service Australia Pty Ltd (PIAS), an organization committed to promoting socially responsible pet ownership, reveals that:

- 12 million Australians were associated with pets in 2002.
- 64% of the 7.5 million households in Australia owned pets.
- Australia had one of the highest incidences of pet ownership in the world.
- 91% of pet owners reported feeling *very close* to their pet, reinforcing the idea that pets are integral members of the family unit, however constituted.
- Pets were a normal part of childhood for more than 83% of Australians.
- Of the Australians who do not currently own a pet, 53% would like to do so in the future.

PIAS statistics reveal that Aussies own about 3.9 million dogs, 2.4 million cats, 8.7 million birds, 12.2 million fish and 2.1 million other species, such as horses, rodents and reptiles.

In the U.K., pets – dogs, cats, rabbits, snakes, spiders and other critters – reside in just under half of all households. Dogs and cats have traditionally been the most popular British pets, but dogs are dropping in popularity in favor of more cats and fish, according to a recent study by market analysts Mintel International Group Ltd.

Mintel cites the increasing popularity of computer games and television programs among children in the U.K. as a major contributing factor in the decreasing demand for domestic animals.

"Children are now growing up in an age of electronic gadgetry with games consoles, computers, mobile phones and even virtual pets all demanding their attention," Katy Child, senior retail analyst at Mintel, told the BBC in June 2005.

According to the 2001 IPSOS-REID Canadian pet ownership study, more than half of all Canadian households owned a cat or a dog, with one third of households owning cats and one-third owning dogs. One in 10 households (13%) owned both cats and dogs. These results suggested that there were more than seven million cats and more than five million dogs living in Canadian homes.

Canadian government statistics show that, in 2004, Canadians spent some CDN$3.5 billion on food, accessories, toys and health care for their pets.

> *"A house without either a cat or a dog is the house of a scoundrel."* – PORTUGUESE PROVERB
>
> *"Anyone who hates dogs and kids can't be all bad."*
> – **W.C. FIELDS** (1879-1946), AMERICAN COMEDIAN & FILM STAR

It stands to reason that if our pets are important to us, we owe it to them to do what they cannot – ensure their well-being when we are no longer mentally or physically able to take care of them. In this book, we cover a range of options to provide for our pets' future under such circumstances. We also discuss a number of related topics, such as pet retirement homes, pre-planning after-death arrangements for pets, and working around special problems associated with exotic pets.

Note: *While there is every indication that pets are becoming increasingly important in our lives, to some degree, they have occupied a special place in our hearts in centuries past as well – especially among those who could afford to keep and indulge them. (See **Appendix A** for a series of vignettes about pampered pets of the past.)*

CHAPTER 2

What we owe our pets

OVERVIEW

- Pets can contribute greatly to the quality of our lives. Some can also provide us with a number of practical services.
- In return, our pets rely on us to keep them happy, healthy and out of harm's way for the duration of their lives, even if they outlive us.
- For a variety of reasons, many of us do not make plans for the continued care of our pets should we fall ill or die.
- Pet owners are able to make provisions to provide for their pets in their estate plans.
- An estate plan will likely include, among other documents, a will and perhaps powers of attorney and trusts. Provisions for pets may be covered by any or all of these components.
- Preparing a comprehensive estate plan that includes the relevant documents requires the services of an attorney, and possibly a certified public or chartered accountant.
- It is important to keep your estate plan current.

Depending on the type of animal a person chooses, pets can be fun, fascinating and loving. They can serve as our friends and companions. They can be our children's playmates and protectors. They can accompany us into old age and provide comfort and company. And they can double as home security systems and pest control agents.

Pets contribute to our well being in other ways too. Medical research shows they can help lower our blood pressure, reduce stress and depression, lessen the risk of heart disease, shorten recovery times in hospital, and improve overall mental attitude. Indeed, many hospitals and nursing homes have recognized the role pets can play in helping the sick and elderly, and have instituted policies and programs that allow their patients access to pets, usually dogs and cats.

A recent study at Memorial University of Newfoundland demonstrated that friendly dogs have a positive effect on most sick children. An evaluation of pediatric dog visitation programs in 10 children's hospitals across Canada showed that dog visits to hospitalized children produced happier kids, less anxiety and stress, greater compliance with medical regimes, and a reduction in heart rate and blood pressure. Some kids even required less pain medication.

Other research programs indicate that, in the future, dogs may play a much more interventionist role in keeping us healthy. Apparently, some of our canine friends can detect bladder cancer (through scent perception) at an early stage in humans. And in 2005, there were published reports of dogs that are able to help diabetics by detecting dangerous shifts in blood sugar levels. Scientists are currently investigating the abilities of dogs to detect other ailments and abnormalities in humans.

So, we know what humans get out of their relationship with pets, but what's in it for the animals? They are innocent, trusting and vulnerable. They rely on their human companions to feed and house them, to look after their emotional and medical needs, and to protect them from harm. Can we deliver?

Once we accept the responsibility of pet ownership, that responsibility includes making sure our charges are cared for in our absence. Responsible pet owners wouldn't dream of leaving their pets alone for extended periods of time without arranging for someone to look after them. Yet, many pet owners enter long-term medical care facilities, or go to their graves, with no arrangements for the care of their pets. They have nothing written down; they have made no reasonable plans, not even informal ones.

You may be one of the people who think such plans are unnecessary for one or more of the following reasons:

My dog is already quite old, so I will surely outlive her. Some pet owners who died in New York City on September 11, 2001, may have sadly believed the same thing. The fact is, we cannot predict the time

FACTOIDS

- Cheetahs are easily tamed and can even be taught to play games like fetch. But they cannot be housebroken; even a wild cheetah will soil its resting place, since it is very mobile and has no true lair. Sportsmen once used them for coursing – hunting by sight, as opposed to scent. Typically, the hooded cheetah was carried on horseback or in a cart. When the hunted animal came near, the hood was removed and the cheetah released. If the cheetah then caught the animal, it was rewarded with some small part of the prey or a dish of blood.

of our death, as any traffic cop, firefighter, emergency services worker, lifeguard, or health care provider will tell you. Anything from a major catastrophe, such as 9/11, to a highway accident, can snatch away your life. Furthermore, you may outlive your pet in a nursing home or other extended care facility where you will be unable to take care of it.

When I die or enter a nursing home, my pets will go to the local animal shelter. They will soon be found new homes. A study by the National Council on Pet Population Study and Policy (www.petpopulation.org) found that 64% of all types of pets that entered the participating shelters between 1994 and 1997 were euthanized.

Recent estimates concerning only dogs and cats are no more heartwarming. Of the roughly four million dogs that enter shelters each year, half are put to sleep; an even greater percentage of cats are euthanized.

Older pets have almost no chance of being adopted: adopters want puppies and kittens. Exotic pets, which may include cute-looking animals such as raccoons, badgers and wallabies, will likely be killed as a matter of policy. (See *Chapter 13.*) And even if your pet is adopted, there is no guarantee it will go to a good home.

Indeed, animal shelters are refuges of last resort – for all of the reasons above and also because of a practice known as *pound seizure*, which refers to the practice of taking cats and dogs from shelters and pounds to feed the biomedical research industry. (See *Appendix B* for more information on this practice.)

I have stated in my will that I am leaving my cat, *Tabby*, to a dear friend, who agreed several years ago to take care of him if I died or had to go into a long-term care facility. If you have a will, you are in the minority, at least in the United States. Seven out of 10 people die without one. In Canada, it is estimated that half of all adults die without a will.

If you do have a will, putting something in it to cover your pet is an important first step, but remember, your will may not be read right away. The first person who enters your home after you die may not know about your arrangement with your dear friend and may send your cat to the local animal shelter. By the time your will is read, your cat may be gone. Also, if your will needs to be probated (validated by the court), that process can take considerable time in some jurisdictions.

Who will look after your cat in the interim? And what if your friend can no longer accept the cat?

Something else to remember: if you haven't named a caregiver in your will or trust document, your pet will likely go to the residual beneficiary of your will (the person who inherits everything that's not taken care of by the rest of the will). If you die without a will, the pet will go to your next of kin, as determined by the laws of your jurisdiction. In either instance, the person who will legally receive your pet may not be someone you would have chosen. The new owner will be free to give or sell your pet to someone else, or drop it off at the local animal shelter.

I'm sure someone in my family will adopt *Rex*. Please don't count on it. While you may assume that your brother or your daughter will take care of your pet after you die, they may not. Instead, they may dispose of your pet because they:

- worry that veterinarian bills will become a burden if the pet gets sick;
- have their own pets and feel there would be conflicts, or that costs would become too great;
- despise your pet (but never had the heart to tell you);
- recently moved into an apartment or condo complex that prohibits pets;
- have no interest in owning a pet.

When I die, I will have no estate to speak of, so there will be no funds for *Smokey's* care. Perhaps you know someone who would be glad to take *Smokey*, even if you cannot provide money for his care. If not, investigate life insurance programs that would fund your pet's future. If you are insurable, for a tiny monthly premium, you may be able to work around your lack of funds.

When I die, I will have no one to whom I can leave my pet. Some people, particularly those who are elderly and alone, may not have anyone who can, or will, look after their pet if it outlives them. Often, these people have survived most of their friends and relatives and may see little of their neighbors. Many elderly people won't get another pet, despite their therapeutic effects, because they know they would be unable to find a caretaker, should anything happen to them.

If you are in that position, and if you are insurable and can afford it, consider buying an insurance policy on your life with a lump sum payout to an animal sanctuary, veterinarian school or animal shelter. In a similar fashion, perhaps you have a retirement plan annuity or similar arrangement in which you could name such an organization to receive a payout upon your death.

You would, of course, need to have an agreement with the organization you choose to look after your pet, stating that it would take care of the animal over its entire life in exchange for receiving the payout. You would likely find an organization even more agreeable to the idea if the payout significantly exceeded the expected cost for looking after your pet. That way, the sanctuary would have money left over for its own use.

My lawyer will laugh at me if I ask to have *Smokey* looked after in my estate plan. Some lawyers might be callous (or dumb) enough to ridicule a client who wants to include a pet in his or her estate plan, but their numbers are dwindling rapidly.

Writing in the Canadian newsletter *Estate Planner*, lawyer Robert Spenceley notes: "...all too often, pet owners encounter professionals who are ill-equipped to meet their needs in this regard and who are directly or indirectly dismissive of their desires to make sure their pets receive adequate care."

If you do encounter some negative attitude, remind your estate planners that *they* work for *you*, not the other way around. That will likely end any opposition. If not, make certain they understand that if they can't deal with your wishes, there are others who can and will.

To summarize, you can safeguard your pet's future. Start by considering your existing state of affairs and, in particular, your estate plan.

"If having a soul means being able to feel love, loyalty and gratitude, then animals are better off than a lot of humans."
– **JAMES HERRIOT** (PEN NAME OF U.K. VETERINARIAN AND AUTHOR JAMES ALFRED WIGHT)

"Animals...in a world far older than ours, finished and complete, gifted with extensions of the senses we have lost or never attained...live by voices we shall never hear."
– **HENRY BESTON** (1928-1968), AMERICAN AUTHOR, WHOSE BEST KNOWN WORK IS **THE OUTERMOST HOUSE**

An overview of a basic estate plan

If you don't have an estate plan, this would be a great time to prepare one, because you can include arrangements for your pet right from the onset. If you do have an estate plan, you can modify it to include your pet. And don't let the term estate plan intimidate you. Estate plans are not just for the rich. Almost all of us have estates. Our estates include all that we own – even if it is only a baseball card collection.

A reasonably complete estate plan might include the following documents:

- last will and testament;
- trusts (including living or *inter vivos* trusts, testamentary trusts, charitable trusts, insurance or wealth replacement trusts);
- durable power of attorney for financial matters;
- power of attorney for health care matters (sometimes known as powers of attorney for personal care, medical powers of attorney, or advance directives);
- directive to physicians in the event you are in a terminal condition and cannot express your treatment desires (often called living wills); and
- body disposition desires (such as anatomical gifts and burial or cremation instructions).

Of course, if your estate is composed solely of a baseball card collection, your estate plan documents might include only a power of attorney for health matters (to give someone the authority to act for you if you become too sick or disabled to act for yourself), and a last will and testament (naming the person or organization to whom you are gifting your baseball card collection). If the collection is valuable, you could cover it with a power of attorney for property, allowing someone else to sell it on your behalf under specified circumstances.

Since many people amass large, multi-faceted estates, they need more planning and more instruments to manage their assets and affairs under a variety of circumstances, including death. People who own one or more pet animals need to exercise extra diligence to ensure their pets' survival if they are not able to look after them.

Preparing a comprehensive estate plan that includes the relevant documents requires the services of an attorney and possibly a certified public or chartered accountant. While there are many such professionals who specialize in trust and estate issues, it may be difficult to find people experienced at providing for pets. Ask your local animal shelter or humane society for a list of pet-friendly attorneys and accountants. These organizations use such services on a regular basis and may be able to help with some referrals.

"If you get to thinkin' you're a person of some influence, try orderin' somebody else's dog around."
– COWBOY WISDOM

"A boy can learn a lot from a dog: obedience, loyalty, and the importance of turning around three times before lying down." – **ROBERT BENCHLEY**
(1889-1945), AMERICAN ACTOR, AUTHOR & HUMORIST

Something else to remember: If possible, find an attorney and accountant who have worked together before.

For your first meeting with your estate planning team, bring along a list of all your assets – stocks, bonds, bank accounts, real estate, automobiles, life insurance policies, title documents for real estate and any specialty items, such as art or coin collections. You will also need a list of liabilities – mortgages, credit card debt, loans. Bring any previous estate planning documents, such as wills and powers of attorney. If you already know who will be taking care of your pets and the amount of money that will be required to look after them, bring this information too, but remember, you can start the estate planning process without having all the details worked out.

It's the job of your estate planning team to inventory your assets, determine which ones will grow or shrink, and to figure out the best way to shift your wealth in accordance with your wishes – to children, grandchildren, a charity, an institution or a pet – and, finally, to determine how long your money will last and the tax implications of any instruments proposed to deal with your estate.

It is important in developing your estate plan to make sure it suits your special needs. You should not predicate an estate plan on saving taxes or expanding your wealth – you should predicate it on dealing with your needs and those of your human and non-human dependents when you die or become incapacitated. Saving taxes and expanding wealth should be secondary.

If you own a pet, you can use at least three estate plan documents to help provide for its care:

Durable powers of attorney (called enduring powers of attorney in some countries). You should have one for financial affairs and one for health matters. You can include provisions for your pet's care should you fall ill or become incapacitated. The person to whom you have given power of attorney can carry out these provisions on your behalf. (See *Appendix C* for sample wording.)

Trusts. Several types of trusts (See *Chapter 10*) can be used to provide for your pet on an ongoing basis while you are alive (and/or incapacitated) or after you have died.

Last will and testament. In your last will and testament, you can specify your desires for your pet's future: who you want to be its caregiver, how you want it to be treated under a variety of circumstances, what is to happen to it after it dies, and so on. You can also leave your named caregiver funds for its upkeep.

One further note on estate plans: You must review them regularly. This is especially true when you are including a pet in your estate plan, because nothing is permanent. You may leave *Fido* to Aunt Mary (with her consent) this year, but, in 12 months, Aunt Mary may be:

- confined to a wheelchair after an auto accident;
- living in Turkey with her new husband;
- out of a job and on social assistance; or
- dead.

And it's not only Aunt Mary's circumstances that may change. *Fido* may be a perfectly healthy, well-adjusted and friendly Springer spaniel today, but by the time you become ill or die, he may be:

- diabetic and require daily shots of insulin;
- in need of weekly or monthly medical treatment for some other chronic ailment;
- ill-tempered because of physical discomfort or pain; or
- dead.

Finally, your own circumstances may change drastically over even a short time. Between now and next year, you may:

- suffer a drastic decline in income through the loss of your job or a stock market debacle;
- see your pension fund lose much of its value;
- get divorced or married;
- have more or fewer children or grandchildren; or
- become disinherited by Uncle George.

Despite the need for regular review, studies show that most people revisit their estate plans only about once every two decades, rather than every two or three years. Don't be one of them, especially if you have a pet.

"One dog barks at something, the rest bark at him."

– CHINESE PROVERB

CHAPTER 3

The law and your pet

- Under the law, any animal is property. When you die, it becomes part of your estate.
- You need a plan for the long-term care of your pet in case you become disabled and for when you die.
- If you do not have a long-term care plan, start putting one together. In the meantime, there are interim measures you can take to protect your pet in case you die or suffer a debilitating illness next week.
- There are at least five key occasions when your pet is in danger:

  1. when you are incapacitated and are unable to care for your pet;
  2. immediately after you die and your pets are at home alone, perhaps for days;
  3. during the time between your death and when your will is read;
  4. during the time between when your will is read and when it is probated;
  5. the ongoing period after your will is probated.

- Once your interim measures are in place, which are covered in Chapter 4, you can set out a more permanent plan for your pet, using the legal system to help ensure that your wishes are carried out.

How the law views your pets

Something to remember when planning for your pet's future is that your animal friend is an *it*, not a *who*. While you may see *Fido* or *Felix* as one of the family, the legal system does not. Whether you live in Toledo or Toronto, Christ Church or Corpus Christi, Perth, Australia, or Perth, Scotland, in the eyes of the law, an animal is considered property, like the money in a bank account or a stamp collection. And the more valuable the animal, the more adamant the courts will be in treating it as property.

For example, if you die without having made provision for your animals, the law will be wary of anyone who volunteers to take responsibility for your three-year-old thoroughbred racehorse without clear instructions from you. Even if the animal is simply a rider, rather than a racer, the court will consider the horse a valuable asset of your estate and would likely permit an applicant (who may not be someone you would have chosen) to take steps to ensure its security and care until legal ownership can be established.

On the other hand, the same court is unlikely to be as fastidious about the future of *Porky*, your old and overweight guinea pig. Both are pet animals, but there's an obvious difference: it's called market value.

"Every animal knows more than you do."
– NATIVE AMERICAN PROVERB

Because the law views animals as property, media articles and movies about wealthy people leaving money *to* a cat or dog are stretching a point.

In the United States and in other jurisdictions, courts have largely ignored the wishes of deceased pet owners who have left property directly to pets for their ongoing care for one or more of the following reasons:

1. **Animals cannot hold title to property.**
   An animal is property and one piece of property cannot hold title to another. You can't leave a set of dishes to a table and you can't leave cash to a cat. If you try to give money, or anything else, to your pet in your will, the courts will disallow it.

   Furthermore, in most jurisdictions, you can't make an animal a beneficiary of a traditional trust because a beneficiary has to be able to enforce the trustee's duties, something an animal cannot do. (More about this later.)

2. **A gift to your pets is not a charitable donation.**
   Some people may try to leave money for their pets and call it a charitable contribution. The courts usually find that a gift which benefits an indefinite number of animals (in an animal shelter, for example) may be regarded and enforced as a charitable gift. But a gift for the care of specific animals (such as your pet cats) does not benefit the entire community and is normally considered non-charitable.

3. **A gift to an animal violates the Rule Against Perpetuities (or a related rule).**
   One reason for refusing to allow a trust with a pet animal as the beneficiary is that it violates the Rule Against Perpetuities (or some similar rule).

Under this complex legal restriction, the maximum length of time a trust may last must be based on the life a human, not an animal. Note that some states in the United States have repealed the Rule Against Perpetuities, permitting a trust to continue until the animal dies.

4. **The value of a gift is excessive.**
   In some cases, courts have ruled that while a pet owner used proper legal instruments to provide for a pet, the amount of money or property involved was excessive. Under judicial decisions or statutes, a court may have the power to reduce the value of a gift for the benefit of a pet to an amount it considers more reasonable. This may not represent an outright failure of a gift, but it does thwart the last wishes of the pet owner.

5. **Other grounds for disapproval of a gift to a pet**
   Pet owners may not get proper legal advice and therefore fail to use the correct legal instruments to transfer funds for the benefit of their pet or the caregiver. Their wishes may also be frustrated because, often, there is no legal mechanism for enforcing such wishes and no one voluntarily makes the effort to carry them out.

What would happen to your pet if the courts ruled that your wishes were invalid for one or more of the reasons given above? Normally, the judge would award the pet and any property you wanted to be used for your pet's benefit to your residual beneficiary (the person you named in your will to receive any property not specifically awarded to anyone else named by you).

Any money or other property you intended for the care of little *Felix* would not necessarily accompany him when he is given to the residual beneficiary. Furthermore, *Felix's* new owner would be under no legal obligation to keep him or to use any accompanying property (if there were any) for his benefit.

To avoid such problems, ask your lawyer to draft any provisions you want to make for your pet using the appropriate legal instrument and in proper legal language (See *Appendix F.*)

Changing attitudes

While the hard-line legal view of pets as property still prevails, attitudes are beginning to change. Many law schools in the United States, including those at Harvard and Yale, are offering animal law classes with sections on

- **He's mine!** Divorce lawyers offer this advice if you live in the United States and want to be sure you get to keep your pet in a custody battle: Keep a diary showing that you are the primary caregiver.

- **Capital punishment for killing Fluffy.** Death was the penalty for killing a cat 4,000 years ago in Egypt. Cats' lives had become cheaper by the 9th century, when King Henry I of Saxony decreed that the penalty for killing a cat should be a fine of 60 bushels of corn.

- **Dingos.** The dingo arrived in Australia about 4,000-6,000 years ago, and may have been introduced by Indonesian fishermen trading with Aboriginals. Several Australian states forbid the keeping of dingos as pets; others require owners to obtain a special permit. Only two (New South Wales and Western Australia) permit dingos as pets without a license.

- **Endangered.** Seahorses may soon become an endangered species because of the international aquarium fish trade in seahorses and because their natural habitats are becoming polluted.

pet custody. Some United States cities (Boulder, Colorado; Berkeley, West Hollywood and San Francisco, California; Sherwood, Arizona; Amherst, Massachusetts; and Menomonee Falls, Wisconsin) and one state (Rhode Island) have taken the controversial step of referring to pet owners as *pet guardians*. Although all states and Canadian provinces allow a *traditional* trust to be crafted to care for your pets, at the time of writing, at least 42 states and the District of Columbia also recognize simple and economical *statutory* trusts to provide benefits to your pets.

Another way some United States courts have responded to what would normally be invalid trusts set up for the benefit of animals has been to look for ways to fulfill the wishes of the deceased. Several courts, for example, have simply allowed a questionable pet trust to stand when the other (human) will beneficiaries did not object.

In the first case in the United States pertaining to the legality of a bequest for the benefit of a pet, the Kentucky Supreme Court declared that a gift in a will for the care of a specific animal was a *humane purpose* and therefore lawful under a state statute that validates any gift that had a humane purpose.

In Canada, amendments to the Criminal Code have been proposed that would remove animals from the property section. And almost everywhere, courts acknowledge that animals, especially those in the higher orders, such as dogs, cats and horses, are sentient beings with feelings, emotions, personalities and foibles. They eat, sleep, give birth to young, play, get sick and die, just as we do. Although they are not human beings, they are substantially different from other types of property and have special characteristics and needs.

When your pet needs protection

Regardless of where you live, it is a good idea to understand when your pet can run into problems, given its legal status as property. There are five situations that can result in a bad outcome for your pet. Each of these can be handled by making arrangements now so you can control events and retain a voice in your pet's future. These are the five situations:

1. **When you are incapacitated.** If you were rushed to the hospital in an emergency situation, perhaps unconscious or unable to communicate, who would look after your pet until you recover? Would anyone even know you have a pet? Some pets, such as rabbits housed in a pen at the back of your yard, may be invisible to police and other emergency personnel who arrive to take you to hospital. What if you didn't recover your full capabilities and had to remain in long-term care?

2. **Immediately after you die and your pets are home alone.** You may die of a heart attack in a neighborhood shopping mall or in a car crash many miles from home. It might be days before anyone thinks to check (or can get authorization to enter) your home to look for, or check on, pets.

3. **Between the time you die and the time your will is read.** It may be several days, weeks, months, or even years after you die before your will is read (or even found). If you have made no provisions outside of your will, a well-meaning friend, relative or emergency service person may trundle your pets to the pound rather than leave them in the house alone. A trip to the pound can be a death sentence.

4. **Between death and the admission of your will to probate.** Many people forget that there can be a gap between the time you die and the time your will has been probated (in essence, validated by the court) in jurisdictions where probate is necessary.

   (Probate is a legal process whereby the courts determine that a will is valid and formally appoint the executor, who will administer it by distributing assets to the intended beneficiaries once debts, expenses and taxes are paid. Probate laws in every jurisdiction vary, so it is best to consult an attorney to determine if probate is necessary and what rules are to be followed.)

Note: Oregon has recognized that, when someone dies, their pet can find itself in immediate danger. Consequently, in 1999, the Oregon Legislature passed the Jansen Bill, which removes pets from the probate process so they can quickly be placed with a guardian. It permits, but does not require, any of the deceased's friends or family (or any animal shelter) to take custody of a pet. Anyone who does take custody is then entitled to reimbursement from the estate of the deceased pet owner for the cost of taking care of the animal. So a friend, family member or shelter may intercede to protect a pet, even if the pet owner failed to make provisions.

5. **The ongoing period after your death.** Your pet will need some type of permanent long-term care after you die.

There is a sixth period when your pets may be in danger and require protection – during times of natural disasters, such as floods, earthquakes, tornados, hurricanes and forest fires, or during man-made disasters, such as the terrorist attacks of 9/11 in New York City. You may not be able to get home at such times, but many of the steps you put in place to protect your pets in the event you become incapacitated and when you die will also help, should they need to be rescued by emergency workers during disasters.

"Animals are a gift to the human race – a gift that humans seldom fully appreciate." – ALLEN M. SCHOEN, DVM, PRACTICING VETERINARIAN & AUTHOR OF THE BOOK **KINDRED SPIRITS**

"It is not just that animals make the world more scenic or picturesque. The lives of animals are woven into our very being – closer than our own breathing – and our souls will suffer when they are gone." – GARY KOWALSKI, AMERICAN AUTHOR OF BOOKS THAT EXPLORE OUR CONNECTION WITH OTHER LIVING CREATURES

CHAPTER 4

Start protecting your pets now with an interim plan

OVERVIEW

- A thorough, well-thought-out, permanent care plan can take some time to assemble, especially if you have a number of pets, or exotic animals that need a special type of caregiver and special care requirements.
- Given that you could suffer an accident or serious illness, such as a stroke, tomorrow, you should put in place some quick-to-institute interim measures to ensure the safety of your pet.
- Pet cards for your wallet and automobile, signage for your home and letters authorizing someone to look after your pets temporarily are quick and easy to put together and can help protect your pet until you get a permanent plan in place.
- You should also plan for certain types of disasters and emergencies, such as hurricanes, tornados, floods, fires, terrorist attacks and times when services such as electricity and water may be shut down.
- The interim steps – signs, cards and documents – will help in many situations, but disaster planning specialists suggest you also assemble a pet disaster kit.

Getting started

The main focus here is to help you create a plan for the long-term protection of your pet if you were to die or become permanently disabled. While it is not difficult to put such a plan together, it can take a little time, perhaps several months, before all the pieces are in place.

But what would happen to your pets if tonight, tomorrow, or next week, you were rushed to hospital? Is there someone at home right now to look after them? If not, it is essential for you to make some provisions right now. Here are some steps you can take.

- Ask a friend, relative, or neighbor to help out in an emergency. This person would take your pet into his or her home and look after it for the short term. Both of you would understand that this would be a temporary situation covering the time required for you to recuperate or, if you die, until your will is read and probate is complete so that the ownership of the pet is transferred to its permanent caregiver (who may, in fact, be the same person).

- If there is a concern about the cost of this temporary care, you could insert a small amount of cash into an envelope and keep it with the pet's care document, or sign an undated check for a specific amount and give it to the person who would be looking after your pet. Allow for several months of expenses.

- Once you have selected a temporary caregiver – and preferably a backup as well – follow the instructions below regarding pet cards, signs and documents. When you finalize a permanent plan, you may or may not retain your temporary caregiver as your pet's permanent caregiver. If you do, many of these temporary documents, such as the cards, signs, letters, etc., can stay in place.

In Case Of Emergency signs, pet alert cards and interim animal documents

In Case Of Emergency signs. The first step is to post an *In Case Of Emergency* sign near the entrance to your home (and in other prominent locations, such as on the door of your refrigerator, the inside of external doors, on the walls of outbuildings and anywhere else that makes sense), stating the number and types of animals that live on the premises. This sign tells emergency workers that animals are on site. A dog may rush the door when a person arrives and escape if the person does not block the door. Rather than fleeing, other animals, especially cats, may hide from strangers.

Other animals, such as gerbils, hamsters or reptiles may live in cages away from view. Remember to update these signs as the number and types of your pets change. You wouldn't want firefighters risking their lives to save pets that are no longer in your home. Conversely, if you acquire additional animals, make certain they are listed on your signs.

In the United States, pet alert stickers are available from the Humane Society of the United States (HSUS), 2100 L Street, NW Washington,

DC 20037 (Fax: 202-778-6132) Web www.hsus.org. The society informs us that no more than two can be sent to any particular address. If someone wanted to order them in bulk, they would have to contact the Office Services Department at the HSUS.

Pet alert cards. You should also prepare and carry a pet alert card or note in your wallet or purse. This document should include basic information about your pet, such as:

- the type of animal;
- its name;
- its location (in your home, in a cage behind the house, at a boarding stable, etc.);
- instructions about any special care it requires (especially food and medicine);
- the name and contact information of the person you have authorized to have access to and look after the animal, should an emergency arise; and,
- where to find more detailed pet care instructions.

In addition, keep a wallet card in the car or cars you drive regularly – either in the glove compartment or in a pocket on the sun visor where anyone can easily spot it. (See *Appendix D* for sample wording.)

> *"Authors like cats because they are such quiet, lovable, wise creatures, and cats like authors for the same reasons."*
> – **ROBERTSON DAVIES** (1913-1995), CANADIAN NOVELIST

> *"Cats are smarter than dogs. You can't get eight cats to pull a sled through snow."* – **JEFF VALDEZ**, AMERICAN AUTHOR

The person you name as the animal's temporary or emergency caregiver may change when you put a permanent plan in place. For now, simply name someone willing to help out during an emergency – a neighbor, friend or relative. Give this person a letter authorizing him or her to access and, if necessary, remove the pet in an emergency. You can always cancel these interim plans and recover the letter, if necessary, once your permanent plans are in place.

If there is no one you can name as a temporary caregiver, at least carry a wallet card and post signage alerting emergency workers to the fact that you have a pet. They can contact the appropriate animal authorities so your pet won't die of thirst or starvation. If you do nothing else about your pet's future, at least make up pet cards and post signs.

Animal document. The third and final step in the process of setting up a temporary plan for your pet is to prepare an animal document for each pet. This is really no more than an enhanced version of the animal card. Again, you may want to change some of the details of this document later, after you have had a chance to set up a permanent plan. For now, simply provide basic information, such as your pet's name, age, the name of its vet, medical problems and medication, special diets, and other facts you consider important to your pet's well being. It should serve as a basic guide to whomever looks after your pet if you are run over by a cement truck the day after tomorrow. Place this document with your estate planning papers and give an original (signed) copy to the person you asked to be your pet's interim caregiver.

Once you have these three items in place – entrance sign, wallet card and interim animal document(s) – you can take some time drawing up more detailed preparations for the long-term protection of your pet. These preparations will likely include specific legal tools in your estate plan – powers of attorney, a will, trusts, advanced health care directives and other documents to carry out your wishes for your pet, should you become disabled or die.

For both interim and long-term pet care plans, remember to update all information on your animal regularly. Any change in its health or habits should be recorded.

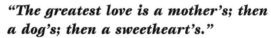

"The greatest love is a mother's; then a dog's; then a sweetheart's."
– POLISH PROVERB

Dealing with disasters and emergencies

As a side issue, but within the context of protecting your pet during times when you are unable to look after it as you normally would, you should plan for certain types of disasters and emergencies, such as hurricanes, tornados, floods and fires, terrorist attacks, and times when services such as electricity and water may be down.

In Australia in 2003 and 2009, for example, extensive brush fires, which destroyed hundreds of homes, also created considerable confusion and consternation regarding pets. Many were saved, but there were mix-ups about who had saved them and, more importantly, where they were. Similar fires in California have moved animal welfare groups to urge people in high-risk areas to plan ahead for their pets' safety.

The interim steps – signs and cards – will help in many situations, but disaster planning specialists suggest you also assemble a pet disaster kit that can be used by you or a neighbor to help your pet in times of crisis. Check the United Animal Nations' Emergency Rescue Service website (www.uan.org) for more ideas. Here are some of the UAN's tips for keeping your pets safe during disasters:

Collar and tag. Always keep a collar and tag on animals that should normally wear collars, including cats that never go outside. A tag is your pet's quickest ticket back home. Make sure it includes your name, phone number and address. If your pet has only an identifying tattoo or an embedded electronic chip, its return could be much slower because a finder may not easily spot them.

Medication. Keep a week's supply of medication and copies of medical records (including vaccination records) on hand for each of your pets. Vaccination records will be required by kennels or airlines if you have to transport or board your pet during an emergency.

List of safe locations. Identify boarding kennels, pet clinics, veterinarians, cat clubs, relatives' homes, etc., outside your immediate area where you could leave your pet if there were an emergency at home. You should have a list of pet-friendly motels and hotels in case you have to evacuate your area. Most shelters, including those set up by the American Red Cross, do not allow pets. This may change to some degree after the public outrage following the prohibition of pets in shelters during the hurricane Katrina disaster.

Buddy system. Start a buddy system with a neighbor. The neighbor will check on your pets in an emergency if you are not home. You will do the same for him or her.

Emergency food and water supply. In addition to your pet's normal food supply, have at least a week's emergency rations on hand – preferably the food your pet normally eats. Also, store enough water to last each of your pets for a week. Do not let your animals drink flood water or any water, including tap water, that has been declared unsafe for humans. If you have to leave an animal for any length of time, you can purchase special dispensers that will hold several day's worth of food and water.

Cat carrier. Have a cat carrier for each cat. An Evacsak can be used as an alternative. It's much like a pillowcase and you can transport any small animal in one. It takes up less room than a standard carrier or cage. In the United States, you can purchase them by contacting Animal Care Equipment and Services at 1-800-338-ACES.

Dog stakeout. Have a stakeout chain for your dog. Falling walls and fences may make it necessary to keep your dog confined on a chain leash until repairs can be made. The dog should be able to move around and reach shelter. When there is a danger of flooding, however, animals confined by chains or cages are in danger of drowning. Use common sense.

Taking responsibility for your pet's safety

Most people would agree that, when you acquire a pet, you also acquire moral responsibilities. One of them is to feed, water, and shelter your animal and protect it from pain and suffering. The law in civilized jurisdictions forbids cruelty and neglect.

Yet there are no laws that require you to make arrangements for your pet should you fail to return home due to an automobile accident or heart attack. If your pet starves at home while you are unconscious in hospital, you will not be held accountable if you survive. It is, however, your moral responsibility to see that such a terrible fate does not befall your pet. Take the first preventative steps now.

Of course, some disasters are so severe and so overwhelming that even the best-laid plans and precautions will not guarantee protection for pet animals. Hurricane Katrina, and the resulting flooding of New Orleans in 2005, is an example of such a disaster. Only pet owners who evacuated to higher ground with their animals before the storm hit were able to guarantee the safety of their pets.

Animals belonging to people who were unable to leave the storm area, or chose not to, were vulnerable. In some cases, their owners could not get home to look after their pets. In others, owners who were eventually rescued from flood waters were forced to leave pets behind because rescuers were under strict *humans only* orders, and because shelters wouldn't accommodate pets.

About the best you can do under such circumstances is to make advanced reciprocal arrangements with neighbors to do all you can for at-risk pets.

On a more positive note, the plight of pet animals in distress is drawing increasing attention from the media, rescue organizations and emergency workers, even during natural disasters. Given the growing attachment many people have to their pets, it seems likely that emergency services will make increasing efforts to save both people and pets where possible.

"Did you ever walk into a room and forget why you walked in? I think that's how dogs spend their lives."
– **SUE MURPHY,** AMERICAN COMEDIAN

"It is just like man's vanity and impertinence to call an animal dumb because it is dumb to his dull perceptions."
– **MARK TWAIN** (1835 - 1910), U.S. HUMORIST, NOVELIST, SHORT STORY AUTHOR & WIT

"There are no ordinary cats."
– **COLETTE** (1873-1954), FRENCH NOVELIST

CHAPTER 5

Choosing a permanent caregiver

OVERVIEW

- Your first job is to choose someone who will take care of your pet if you cannot.
- Compile a list of candidates you feel would make good long-term caregivers and list the pros and cons of each candidate.
- Ask yourself these questions:

  1. Is my prospective caregiver temperamentally suited to care for my pet?
  2. Does she have any animals that might not get along with mine?
  3. Does she have experience with pets, particularly with the type I own?
  4. Is she allergic to any animals?
  5. Is she financially stable?
  6. Is she on any type of social assistance that might be withdrawn or taxed if I give her money for the care of my pet?

- Once you have determined your top candidates, discuss your plans with each. Try to figure out who seems to really want to look after your pet.
- Select at least one or more backup caregivers, in case your first choice cannot fulfill the role when the time comes. If you rank the candidates on your list, perhaps the second and third choices can become backups. If you have several pets, you may need to choose more than one primary caregiver plus backups.
- If you cannot find a caregiver, consider appointing an animal shelter, humane society, veterinarian college or other establishment to look after your pet, either permanently, or until a new home for it can be found.

Don't wait!

The biggest mistake people make in providing for their pet's long-term future is waiting too long to do anything.

One estate-planning client – a lady with two golden retrievers – called her lawyer one Friday afternoon to say she wanted to revise her will to leave instructions for the care of her pets. Her lawyer offered to meet with her the following day. She couldn't make it. They made an appointment for the following Monday. Guess what happened? She suffered a heart attack and died on the weekend. Her two faithful pets were orphaned.

In this case, the story ended happily for the pets when her nephew volunteered to take the dogs, even though his aunt had not left him any money in her will to provide for them.

The incident could have ended differently. There are some things you should do right away. Making a will, naming agents in a power of attorney, and providing for your pet upon your death or illness should be high on your priority list.

> *"If you have men who will exclude any of God's creatures from the shelter of compassion and pity, you will have men who will deal likewise with their fellow man."*
> – ST. FRANCIS OF ASSISI
> (1181/82–1226), PATRON SAINT OF ANIMALS AND THE ENVIRONMENT

> *"He who is cruel to animals becomes hard also in his dealings with men. We can judge the heart of a man by his treatment of animals."* – IMMANUEL KANT
> (1724-1804), GERMAN PHILOSOPHER

Even if you are young and healthy, there are always forces of nature, unexpected diseases and accidents to knock your life off track. Who, for example, could have predicted the events in New York City on September 11, 2001? Some pets were stranded during those days when their young and healthy owners failed to return home because they were dead or injured.

While there are still people, lawyers included, who think that providing for a pet in a will is eccentric, the fact is, more people are doing just that. Documented studies show that up to 27% of pet owners in the United States who have wills provide for their pets in their wills in some fashion, although in most cases, not in a comprehensive manner. Many more make informal arrangements for pets outside their wills.

Getting started

To protect your pet in the event you cannot look after it, the first step is to recognize the need for a plan of some type. Step two is to decide the type of plan that would best fill your needs and those of your pet – a handshake agreement with a trusted friend or relative; a provision in your will; an honorary trust that is administered by friend or relative; a comprehensive traditional pet trust, or, if you live in one of the jurisdictions that permits it, a simple but legally enforceable statutory pet trust.

We will cover these different types of arrangements in more detail later in the book. Your first task is to choose a caregiver and at least one backup.

No matter what type of arrangement you make, you are going to have to find a caregiver – either an individual (friend or relative) or an organization (a no-kill animal shelter, veterinary school, or other type of establishment).

This is a critical step. We suggest you take pen and paper right now and draw up a list of candidates you feel would make good long-term caregivers for your pet, and list the pros and cons of each.

Some points to consider:

Is your prospective caregiver temperamentally suited to look after your pet?

There is no point in naming your niece as caregiver of *Plato*, your pet python, if she is afraid of snakes or thinks white rats are cute (or both). *Plato* will starve to death, find himself in a home for orphaned pythons, or may wind up as part of an exotic dancer's act.

You should also rule out people who cherish the freedom to take off whenever their feet get itchy. These free spirits will not appreciate being tied to *Fido's* schedule or having to make pet-sitting arrangements every time they get the urge to roam.

Furthermore, consider your pet's emotional requirements. If your canine buddy requires a great deal of attention, kindness and affection, neither your narcissistic brother-in-law nor your *I've-got-a-business-to-run* sister will be able to satisfy its needs.

Give serious consideration only to people who are even tempered, patient, emotionally stable, reasonably intelligent and physically able to handle your animal.

Does your prospect have any animals that might not get along with your pet?

We know of a man who became the caregiver of a Lab-basset cross named *Austin*. *Austin* had the head of a Lab, the body of a Basset, and a deep hatred of cats. The man already owned a black cat named (you guessed it)

Blackie. Whenever *Blackie* tried to enter his own house, *Austin* charged to the door and threatened to transform the feline's innards into violin strings. *Austin* could not be reformed and was shortly packed off to the pound, much to *Blackie's* relief.

Does this person have experience with pets, and particularly with the type of pet you own?

It would be helpful if the person you select as the caregiver for your parrot had, at some time or other, owned such a bird. If not, would this person be conscientious enough to do some basic research on parrots to learn something about their likes and dislikes, medical problems and special needs?

Do you know whether your candidate has any allergies to animals?

If you don't know, better ask. Many people are strongly allergic to cats and some are allergic to dogs. There are also people who are allergic to feathers.

Could the caregiver's age be an issue?

Parrots can live for decades. Avoid leaving yours to an elderly uncle, who will in turn have to figure out what to do with it when he dies. In a worst case scenario, your uncle could die before he gets around to implementing a succession plan, and your bird could be orphaned. While anyone, regardless of age, can die or become incapacitated at any time, the younger your caregiver is (within reason), the better chance your pet will have for long-term survival.

Does the caregiver live in a pet-friendly environment?

A great many people now live in housing (apartments, condos, rented houses) where pets are unwelcome, unless they happen to be fish. Your Great Dane would be rather easy to spot in such surroundings. You need to inquire about your intended caregiver's future plans in this regard, just in case a move to such accommodations is being contemplated.

Keep in mind that even pet-tolerant landlords can have a change of heart depending on circumstances. If your Great Dane frightens neighbors in an apartment building, they may complain that the dog is interfering with the reasonable enjoyment of their apartments.

A pet-friendly environment can also mean something else altogether. Is your intended caregiver a heavy smoker? Is your pet a sensitive bird? In 2004, a British couple entered a clinic to stop smoking after their veterinarian told them they were making their beloved parrot extremely ill with their 50-cigarette-a-day habit. Air quality is critical to parrot health.

Is the caregiver financially stable?

There are numerous instances where someone has received money to take care of a pet and used it to pay off debts, take a vacation or meet day-to-day living expenses. Exit pet to the local animal shelter. If you have several pets, or large pets, such as horses, which must be fed, stabled, groomed, exercised, and attended to by a veterinarian, the sums of money left to a caregiver can be substantial. Make sure your caregiver is not the type to use pet-care funds to pay off a mortgage or take a holiday.

Is your prospective caregiver on any type of social assistance?

If you leave your pet and several thousand dollars in a lump sum for its care to someone who is on some form of public assistance, that person's public assistance could be reduced or cut off, depending on the regulations associated with the assistance.

> *"The great pleasure of a dog is that you may make a fool of yourself with him and not only will he not scold you, but he will make a fool of himself too."*
> – **SAMUEL BUTLER** (1835 – 1902) ENGLISH COMPOSER, NOVELIST & SATIRIC AUTHOR

> *"In order to really enjoy a dog, one doesn't merely try to train him to be semi-human. The point of it is to open oneself to the possibility of becoming partly a dog."* – **EDWARD HOAGLAND**, AMERICAN WRITER & TEACHER

Down to the short strokes

Once you have narrowed your list to a few candidates, discuss your plans with each of them. Try to determine which one seems the most enthusiastic and appears to really want to look after your pet.

It may sound odd, but occasionally a caregiver for a pet is selected without ever having been consulted. A few years back, a Toronto woman was selected to take care of her father's Jack Russell, a small breed of dog with a reputation for needing a lot of attention. Had he sought her consent, she would have told him that she did not have enough free time to spend with the dog. She tried to fulfill her father's wishes but, in the end, had to give his pet to someone with more time to devote to its care.

Backups

It is essential to select at least one backup caregiver for each primary caregiver, in case your first choice cannot fulfill the role when the time comes. If you rank the candidates on your list, perhaps the second and third choices can become your backups. If you have several pets, you may want to (or have to) choose more than one primary caregiver and backups for each. Uncle Bob may be willing to take your budgie, but not your Russian blue kitty and the two white rats.

You might also direct the executor of your estate to choose between two potential caregivers you have named. The advantage of making this type of arrangement is the executor can take a reading of the situation at the time of your death and accurately determine which of the caregivers is in the best position to care for your pet.

What if you cannot find a caregiver? Consider appointing an animal shelter, humane society, veterinary college or other establishment to look after your pet. You might direct the organization to care for *Fido* for the remainder of his natural life, or you might ask that it keep him until it can find him a suitable home. Many organizations have specific facilities to house pets they have accepted for long-term care without resorting to continuous caging.

 **FACTOIDS**

- **Banned.** In the U.S.A. some states allow ferrets as pets, while certain cities within those states disallow them. In Australia, ferrets are banned as pets in Queensland and the Northern Territory, while a license is required to keep them in the ACT and Victoria.

- **Oh, no!** Sir Isaac Newton's favorite dog, *Diamond*, upset a candle which in turn set fire to notes on the scientist's experiments conducted over a course of 20 years. In one account, Newton is said to have exclaimed: "O Diamond, Diamond, thou little knowest the damage thou hast done" (or alternatively "O Diamond, Diamond, how little knowest thou the mischief thou hast done.").

- **Leave a message after the tone.** Recent polls show that up to one third of dog owners in the U.S. admit to having talked to their dogs on the phone or having left messages for their dogs on an answering machine.

- **Who cares about arch ability?** A cat's body comprises 230 bones. A human only has 206 bones. A cat can arch its back extremely high (usually when it feels threatened) because its spine contains nearly 60 loose-fitting vertebrae. Humans possess 34 vertebrae with comparatively minimal *arch ability*.

Read over any information these organizations provide and discuss your pet with their representatives to be sure they will be suitable. Be prepared to leave the organization a larger sum of money than would normally be required for the care of your pet. They use such funds to help support the organization.

In 2005, an elderly Ottawa man, David Harper, found his own solution to not being able to find an individual caregiver for his pet. He died and left an estate of CDN$1.3 million to the United Church of Canada, stipulating in his will that the church was to arrange to look after his three-year-old tabby cat, *Red*, for the rest of its life. Harper was a bachelor who died at age 79 after a lifetime of work in the public service sector as a gardener. He lived simply, which is how he accumulated a small fortune, including his 100-year-old house.

"I care not for a man's religion whose dog and cat are not the better for it." – ABRAHAM LINCOLN (1809-1865), 16TH PRESIDENT OF THE UNITED STATES OF AMERICA

"The greatness of a nation and its moral progress can be judged by the way its animals are treated."
– **MAHATMA GANDHI** (1869-1948), INDIAN PHILOSOPHER, LAWYER, TEACHER & NON-VIOLENCE ADVOCATE

CHAPTER 6

Allocating money or other property to care for your pet

OVERVIEW

- All pets have some expenses for food, housing, and medical care, so making a gift of money or other property to your pet's caregiver makes sense, even if this person is a family member or close friend.
- Estimate how much your caregiver will spend on your pet, based on its annual needs and the number of years you think it has left to live.
- Discuss the estimate with the caregiver to ensure you are both comfortable with the amount.
- Whether you are dealing with the care of your pet by means of informal agreements with a family member or friend, or by formal arrangements through your will or in a trust, consider setting up separate arrangements for veterinary care.
- Remember, when you leave someone an unconditional or outright gift in your will, you cannot dictate how it is to be spent, so choose your pet's caregiver carefully; otherwise, your pet could be short changed.

All pets incur some expenses

Many people make informal reciprocal agreements with family members or close friends for the care of their pets (usually cats and dogs). In other words, two pet owners agree that, should one of them no longer be able to look after his or her pet, or pets, the other will step in to help. Money does not enter the equation.

But in cases where there is no reciprocal agreement and a pet owner is simply entrusting the care of a pet to a relative or friend, an accompanying gift of money often makes sense, because all pets accrue expenses. For example, vet costs alone can add up to a considerable sum over a period of years. According to the American Veterinary Medical Association, the average annual veterinary expenditure per household in the United States is $186 for dogs, $147 for cats, $11 for birds and $226 for horses.

While there is no magic formula for establishing exactly how much your pet will need over the remainder of its life, here are some things to consider:

- the number of years you estimate your pet will live;
- the cost of food per year;
- the cost of routine vet bills per year for checkups and shots;
- the cost of special medical attention your pet needs on a regular basis (for example, a friend's dog requires antihistamines, steroids and liver oils for about six weeks every summer to counter a pollen allergy);
- the cost of special needs, such as boarding, grooming and exercise for a horse;
- the cost of boarding your pet if the caregiver has to go out of town on business trips or vacation, and the cost of providing for an animal sitter if your caregiver has to work long hours away from home;
- the maximum amount of money you are willing to devote to the pet's future care;
- any compensation you consider appropriate for the caregiver's time;
- how the amount you leave for your pet's care will affect your family members and what they may do if they think it is excessive;
- any unforeseen catastrophic events that might affect your pet, such as the need for an expensive operation; and
- the possible effects of inflation, if your pet lives for more than a few years.

Write down all of the expenses associated with your pet for a year and calculate how much money would be required, based on the number of years you expect it to live. *Appendix E* lists the average lifespan of many types of animals kept as pets.

"The clever cat eats cheese and breathes down rat holes with baited breath." – W.C. FIELDS
(1880-1946), AMERICAN COMIC & FILM STAR

"The cat is a dilettante in fur."
– THEOPHILE GAUTIER (1811-1872), FRENCH POET

Once you have determined the amount of money you would like to leave, based on your pet's needs and your ability to pay, discuss the matter with your caregiver to ensure you are both satisfied that it will be enough to care for your pet without burdening the caregiver.

Remember, however, any informal arrangement offers no legal protection for your pet. When you leave someone an unconditional or outright gift of money in your will, you cannot dictate how it is to be spent. Any verbal agreement you make with the beneficiary regarding the care of your pet cannot be enforced by the legal system. In other words, your caregiver can send your pet to the pound and use the money to buy a home theatre system. Choose your pet's caregiver carefully. If you have any doubts, there are more formal legal arrangements you can put in place.

One more point to consider. You can qualify the amount of money you want to leave to the caregiver based on the number of years left on your pet's estimated lifespan when you die. Or, from time to time, you can adjust the amount given in your will.

Let's say your dog is five years old and, given its size and breed, you believe it could live for another 10 years. You estimate that it costs $500 a year to maintain your dog. You could state in your will that, should you die in the year you made your will, you bequeath $5,000 for the care of your pet, given that it could live another decade at $500 a year. Should you die a year later, the caregiver would receive only $4,500 because your pet could expect only another nine years of life. Should you die in year nine, the amount the caregiver would receive would be $500 to cover the last expected year of your pet's life.

You should also take into consideration that, as your dog ages, its medical bills may increase, just as they generally do for humans, so the $500 a year maintenance may be more like $700 in the last years of life. You might also make any necessary adjustments for the effects of inflation over the number of years you expect the pet to live. (The amounts given are examples, not suggestions.)

Whether you are dealing with the care of your pet by means of informal agreements with a family member or friend, or by formal arrangements through your will or in a trust, consider setting up separate arrangements for veterinary care. You may want to purchase veterinary health insurance for each of your pets to take care of routine and emergency medical situations. You can leave money to your caregiver, estate executor, or other designated person to pay the premiums. Alternatively, you could leave money to one of these representatives to pay for veterinary care on a visit-by-visit basis.

Another issue to consider: what will happen to your pet's remains after it dies? Do you want to leave these decisions to your pet's caregiver or your executor? Or do you want to have a say in the arrangements? Whatever you decide, there will be costs involved, and you need to allow for such expenses in calculating the sum of money to leave your caregiver. (See *Chapter 12: Planning for your pet's death.*)

Tax issues

Be aware that if you leave funds to someone with the informal understanding they be used for the care of your pet, some jurisdictions may levy some type of tax on either the beneficiary or on the estate itself. In fact, a tax could be applied not only on the monetary gift, but also on the value of the animal or animals. This could be an expensive proposition for your beneficiary, if you left him or her several valuable thoroughbred horses plus the funds for their care – and if a tax applied to both the value of the animals and the funds.

In jurisdictions where there is no tax applied to a pet and/or a sum of money to be used for the care of the pet, any funds that earn interest or dividends within a trust may (and likely will) be subject to income tax.

Be smart – ask your lawyer or accountant about the tax implications of such a gift in your jurisdiction. You may need to devise alternative strategies to reduce the impact of the tax collector.

"Recollect that the Almighty, who gave the dog to be companion of our pleasures and our toils, hath invested him with a nature noble and incapable of deceit." – FROM **THE TALISMAN**
BY **SIR WALTER SCOTT** (1771-1832)

"A dog is the only thing on earth that loves you more than he loves himself." – JOSH BILLINGS
(1818-1885), AMERICAN HUMORIST

"A dog doesn't care if you're rich or poor, big or small, young or old. He doesn't care if you're not smart, not popular, not a good joke-teller, not the best athlete, nor the best-looking person. To your dog, you are the greatest, the smartest, the nicest human being who was ever born. You are his friend and protector." – LOUIS SABIN,
AUTHOR OF NUMEROUS BOOKS FOR YOUNG PEOPLE

CHAPTER 7

Making sure your pet receives the quality of care it deserves

OVERVIEW

- Consider how you normally treat your pet. Start by writing down its daily and weekly routines and any idiosyncrasies.
- Note any special requirements or preferences your pet may have, such as scented kitty litter, a favorite dog bed or a food preference.
- Discuss with your chosen caregiver how you would like your pet treated in general terms.
- Let your caregiver take care of your pet for a week as a dry run.
- Provide instructions for your caregiver as to how far you want him or her to go to save the life of your pet, should it become ill or injured. Vet bills can add up quickly if there are serious problems and your pet may have a poor quality of life afterwards.
- Take steps to establish and document your pet's identity so that no other animal can be mistaken for it – accidentally or deliberately.

Consider how you treat your pet

Many pet owners want their pet to receive the kind of care to which it has grown accustomed. Obviously, some types of pets require more in the way of affection, companionship and routine than others. Dogs, for example, have considerable needs in these respects. At the other end of the scale, snakes, lizards and fish have few. But there can be differences even among dogs and cats. Some need more human attention than others. Discuss your pet's special needs with the person you have chosen to be its caregiver if you die or get sick.

Consider how you normally treat your pet. Do you bundle up little *Snuffles* in a doggie coat for his walks in the winter? Do you have scented litter for *Fang*, your Persian kitty? Does *Letterman*, your gabby parrot, prefer a specific brand of food? What about his crackers?

Like humans, many pets, especially dogs, are most comfortable when they follow a daily routine. Do you always feed *Snuffles* at noon, with an evening treat of biscuits? Does a walk always follow his meals? Do you go to a leash-free park on Saturday mornings?

Write down your pet's daily and weekly routines.

Pets also have personalities and, with them, idiosyncrasies. Another list! Will your dog only drink water from a special dish? Does your cat prefer to be left alone after it has eaten its supper? Will your parrot settle down for the night only after your have covered its cage with a black cloth?

It is a good idea to let the person you have chosen as caregiver keep your pet for a few days, or even a week, as a dry run – with you sitting by the telephone to answer questions. This will help guarantee that all will go smoothly should an emergency arise. Your caregiver can ask any questions pertaining to your pet's care and determine whether he or she is truly comfortable with it. It will also help ensure that your pet will not have to tolerate a fumbling new human caregiver some day.

What do you want done if your pet is badly injured or really sick?

As part of your overall instruction package, provide guidance for your caregiver as to how far you want him or her to go to save the life of your pet, should it become ill or injured. Vet bills can add up quickly if there are serious problems, and your pet may have a poor quality of life afterwards.

Also, you cannot expect your pet's caregiver to go to unreasonable lengths to look after your pet. For example, it may be asking too much to expect a caregiver to give your cat a daily shot of insulin, should it develop diabetes at some point in its life. The requirement to give such shots every day without exception may simply be too demanding.

If you establish a trust for the care of your pet, you may want to include a provision that any major decisions, such as euthanizing the animal, must be made by a panel of people, including a veterinarian.

Identify your pet in detail

When you go to the trouble of arranging high-quality care for a pet, especially under the terms of a trust or other legal instrument that pays out funds to a caregiver over the pet's lifetime, you need to be certain that the animal receiving the care is indeed your pet. There are reports of caregivers replacing a dead or missing pet with a double to keep trust benefits coming. This might be particularly tempting if, in your trust, you provide the caregiver with a home in which to look after your pet. Who would want to move out of comfortable lodgings simply because *Felix* dies or wanders off?

That means you should go to some lengths to properly identify *Rover* or *Whiskers*. Indeed, all pets should be identified in some way. Sadly, research indicates that, in the United States, only about 25% of pets are properly identified.

There are a number of ways to identify your pet, from unreliable to foolproof. Use the one best suited to your circumstances. Take into consideration the value of the assets involved and the amount of trust you have in your caregiver and others who might be involved in your pet's ongoing care.

These are the most common forms of identification:

Detailed written description. Individual animals of many breeds look remarkably alike. To an untrained eye, one black Labrador dog, Russian blue cat, or blue-fronted Amazon parrot looks much like another. So in your documentation, describe the physical characteristics of your pet, noting any unique features, especially coloration, scars or disabilities. Accompany your description with photos or a video recording and veterinarian records, if possible. You may even want to ask your vet to help with the description.

Tattoo. Tattooing animals with an alphanumeric (letters and numbers) identifier has been common for many years, and some animal breeders tattoo members of litters before they sell them, so check to see whether your pet has already been tattooed and registered. If not, your veterinarian will advise you as to where you can have the tattooing applied.

The tattoo process is safe, painless, and cosmetically acceptable when done in the groin. It generally takes about five minutes and requires no anesthesia except in very special circumstances. The tattoo is permanent. Furthermore, most properly applied tattoos can be read by anyone anywhere.

Once the tattoo has been applied the animal can be registered. Check with your veterinarian or animal tattooist to identify registries used in your area of the world. While it is a continuing challenge to educate the general population about tattooing, most shelters, police departments, and others who need to be aware of lost or stolen animals are knowledgeable about the process.

Tattoo and registry prices vary, but are generally quite reasonable. In the United States, you should be able to find a service that will provide a tattoo and registration for one animal for about $50-$60. If you have several animals tattooed at the same time, you will likely pay less per animal. And in some jurisdictions, the local animal control agency (or other municipal animal welfare organizations) will provide free tattooing services for dogs and cats and register them locally in the municipal database. Tattooing services are available in most countries. Check with your veterinarian about availability and prices in your area.

Some people believe tattoos have several advantages over microchips (see the next section), because a microchip requires a special reader and the chip sometimes migrates under an animal's skin and can be difficult to locate. On the other hand, tattoos may also be difficult to spot. Sometimes they become overgrown by fur, or a lost, frightened animal may struggle so much that no one can locate the tattoo. Furthermore, if a tattoo is applied when an animal is too young, it can become distorted through normal growth.

Also, if an animal is valuable as a breeder, a thief may alter the tattoo (for example, by changing a *1* to either a *9* or a *7*) or remove it through mutilation.

 **FACTOIDS**

- **They're off!** The forerunner of the modern greyhound was developed in Egypt about 5,000 years ago.

- **Happy cats.** A cat purrs by moving air in spasms through contractions of the diaphragm. First purring occurs when kittens suckle milk from their mother, and after that, cats purr whenever they are happy and contented.

- **Say meeeooow**. According to informal surveys, some 95% of cat owners say they talk to their cats.

- **Licorice tongue!** The chow is the only dog with a black tongue.

- **Caterwauling.** Cats seldom meow at each other, reserving that sound for humans. They actually have about 100 different vocalization sounds, compared with about 10 for dogs.

- **Stormy weather**. During severe rain storms in 17th Century England, many cats and dogs drowned and their bodies washed down the streets in torrents of water, giving the appearance that it had literally *rained cats and dogs.*

Microchip. This is a relatively simple technique in which a unique microchip, roughly the size of a small rice grain, is injected in the shoulder area of an animal. It can usually be done in the veterinarian's office. The chip carries a unique numerical code that anyone can read by passing a scanner over the area where the microchip is lodged. This code number can be held in a database that includes your name, address and phone number.

- **Poodle cut.** Europeans originally used poodles for hunting, but their thick coats hindered them in water and thickets, so the hunters sheared their hindquarters, leaving cuffs around the ankles and hips to protect against rheumatism. Each hunter identified his dogs by attaching a ribbon of his own color to their heads.

- **Pretty kitties.** Cats with calico or tortoiseshell coloring are nearly always female and are believed to bring good luck in the folklore of many cultures.

- **Help for epilepsy sufferers.** It is said that "seizure alert" dogs can alert their owners up to an hour before the onset of an epileptic seizure.

Microchips are inserted into an animal like any other injection or vaccination. Although the microchip needle is slightly larger than a typical needle used for vaccinations, anesthesia is not usually required. Animals react to the needle about the same as any other type of injection. There is no scarring or loss of physical performance. The chip cannot burn or irritate the animal because the chip is biocompatible with the animal.

While microchip pet identification is a simple concept, the technology is still evolving and changes are inevitable. For example, there is a growing trend toward standardization to make chips and scanners truly universal. So, for example, if you took *Rover* on a trip to France and he became lost, a French shelter worker could scan him, read the information on his implanted chip and, hopefully, get in touch with you. Many countries already comply with guidelines set by the International Organization for Standardization (ISO) for these microchip systems.

A 2002 member survey conducted by the World Small Animal Veterinary Association found that adoption and use of ISO-standard readers and microchips for small animals was "well advanced... in Western Europe and Australia/New Zealand, achieving market dominance in eastern Europe, the Middle East and Asia, in its infancy in Canada and South America, and non-existent in the United States and Africa."

With regard to the United States, the use of ISO-standard readers and microchips remained relatively non-existent in 2009. Most chips and readers used in the United States are still incompatible with those that adhere to ISO standards in other countries. Indeed, there isn't even universality among U.S. manufactured chips and scanners.

Check with your vet or local animal shelter for an update and advice if you are serious about using this technology.

While microchip identification is largely used to help return lost animals to their owners, for our purposes, it also serves to identify a specific animal. If your pet has an implanted microchip, it can be scanned by anyone who is suspicious that a caregiver has substituted animals to retain ongoing trust benefits. On the other hand, an unscrupulous person could remove a chip from a dead animal and have it implanted into a substitute.

DNA. The most foolproof (and expensive) option is to take a sample of a pet's DNA so that the trustee can check it against the DNA of the animal under care at a later date. If a switch has been pulled, it will show up.

If you are interested in the DNA approach, the easiest route would be to ask your veterinarian to make the necessary arrangements to obtain a genetic profile of your pet. You could contact a commercial lab yourself, but finding a suitable lab may be a challenge. If you have access to the Internet, a search will turn up a number of labs, most of which are geared to testing human DNA. Some will work with animals as well, but you may have to inquire.

One such North American lab is Veterinary Diagnostics Centre (www.vetdnacenter.com) of Fairfield, Ohio. This organization will provide DNA profiling identification for dogs, cats, horses and birds worldwide. Contact them at 1-800-625-0874 to receive an information package and a mail-in kit for collecting DNA samples. Instructions are included. Veterinary Diagnostics Centre says it has customers in all 50 U.S. states and in more than 70 other countries.

In the Asia-Pacific region, including Australia and New Zealand, contact Genetic Technologies Limited (www.gtg.com.au) for DNA testing on animals, including pets. For other areas, consult your veterinarian.

Banding. Bird owners often use leg bands to identify their pets and to record relevant information. Males are banded on the right leg and females on the left. The materials used are aluminum and steel. Aluminum is light and easy to work with, but it is also easier to remove and may be mangled by large parrots and similar birds. Also, the information tends to wear down over time. Steel is difficult to remove and can cause serious injury to the bird if not removed properly. You must also ensure when using aluminum or steel that you have the correct size and that the band is neither too tight nor too heavy.

Although some of the measures to uniquely identify your pet may seem extreme, you can't be too careful in situations where humans, money and defenseless animals are involved. You have to take human greed into account if your pet is a valuable sire in the horse world, or a prize-winning bitch in the canine community, or if you have treated your caregiver very generously (providing ongoing trust funds or accommodations) for as long as a pet lives.

"I've never understood why women love cats. Cats are independent, they don't listen, they don't come in when you call, they like to stay out all night, and when they're home they like to be left alone and sleep. In other words, every quality that women hate in a man, they love in a cat."
– JAY LENO, AMERICAN COMEDIAN

"Women and cats will do as they please, and men and dogs should relax and get used to the idea."
– ROBERT A. HEINLEIN, SCIENCE FICTION WRITER

CHAPTER 8

Setting up an informal long-term care plan for your pet

O V E R V I E W

- The simplest plan you can make for your pet is to ask a friend or relative to assume ownership and take care of it, should you become disabled or die.
- Provide him or her with written information, such as:

  1. Any medical problems your pet has that require ongoing attention.
  2. The name, address and telephone number of your vet.
  3 Types of food your pet likes and dislikes.
  4. The kinds of activities your pet enjoys, such as playing fetch with a ball.

- Remember, this type of informal arrangement is neither legally binding nor enforceable.
- If you make an informal agreement with a friend or relative, put everything down in writing and have it notarized, which confirms that you are the person who prepared and signed the document. Provide copies of the documents to everyone concerned – and keep your copies with other important papers, such as your will and powers of attorney.
- Remember, however, notarization does not make your agreement legally binding, it simply formally attests to what you would *like* to happen.

The simplest plan

There are several types of informal arrangements you can make for the care of your pet, should you become ill or die. We define informal as meaning these plans are not legally enforceable, but they are better than doing nothing at all.

The simplest plan you can make for your pet is to ask a friend or family member to care for it and then make an outright gift of the pet to this person in your will. This person would then become your pet's owner and its caregiver. You should give your pet's caregiver-in-waiting detailed written information and instructions concerning your pet: medical information, the type of care you would like it to have, its likes and dislikes, and contact information, such as the name and telephone number of your pet's vet.

If you have more than one pet, prepare one or two pages of written information on each of them.

Here is how such an informal plan could work.

Imagine you have a 5-year-old schnauzer named *Bunkie*. You enter an informal arrangement with your cousin, Jane, who will look after *Bunkie* if you die or become disabled.

Deed of gift

Revocable version: The donor (you) keep the legal document until you decide to give the document (and thus *Bunkie*) to the recipient (Jane). You can, at any time, revoke the gift deed document, because the deed and *Bunkie* have not yet been delivered to Jane, and you are not legally obligated to make the gift.

Irrevocable version: The person who has received the gift (Jane) becomes *Bunkie's* legal owner as soon as you physically deliver the gift deed document and *Bunkie* to the recipient, and the donee accepts the gift. The gift cannot ever be revoked.

In both cases, the right to obtain physical possession of *Bunkie* may be postponed until the gift deed is actually delivered, or you become mentally incapacitated, or die.

To make sure there's no delay or confusion, you give your lawyer or other trusted person a key to your condo and written instructions to deliver the key to Jane if you suffer a medical emergency, become incapacitated, or die. The letter also authorizes Jane to enter your home and remove *Bunkie* immediately. You have already established your intent for Jane to be *Bunkie*'s permanent owner. Your wallet pet card also names Jane as the person to call in an emergency and provides her contact information.

To make sure the transition goes smoothly and to ensure that Jane is clear about your wishes for *Bunkie*, you can also write a letter for her, outlining some basic information about *Bunkie*.

Under the heading **Vital Information** your letter includes a brief note on *Bunkie*'s medical history and the name, address and telephone number of his vet, plus a line or two about any medical problems. It also notes the month when *Bunkie*'s routine shots come due.

Under the heading **Important Information** you list the kinds of food *Bunkie* likes, the foods that don't agree with him, his bathroom habits (once in the morning, once before supper, and again before bedtime) and a few of his foibles, such as his dislike for anyone wearing a hat or carrying anything that looks like a stick (cane, shovel, etc.). Perhaps *Bunkie* also hates mail carriers and delivery people.

Finally, under the heading **What *Bunkie* Likes** you summarize some of the activities you and *Bunkie* enjoy together: playing fetch with a tennis ball, walks in parks where there are plenty of bushes, and going for rides in the car. You also note that, despite all the warnings in dog training books and from vets, you usually save *Bunkie* a tiny piece of crust from your toast or sandwich – a lapse in discipline the dog seems to enjoy with a satisfaction that goes far beyond the actual morsel of food. To *Bunkie*, it seems to mean his human companion is always thinking about him.

You note in your letter that you understand that Jane's time and energy may be limited because of her other commitments but, should she be able to break free occasionally to indulge in some of these activities, both you and *Bunkie* would be grateful.

In this instance, no money changes hands. Your cousin has made it known that she likes *Bunkie* and wants nothing more than to help in a time of need, if that time ever comes. Because you and your cousin are so close, the arrangement is not included in the will, but you hope that the letter provides all the authorization Jane needs to gain possession of *Bunkie* in an emergency.

Keep in mind, however, that while this technique will work in Canada and some other jurisdictions, it is not recommended in the United States, because the personal representative of the estate would be duty-bound to get *Bunkie* back from Jane and dispose of him under the will or via intestacy. This is too risky for *Bunkie*.

Also, in some jurisdictions, such a letter might be regarded by the courts as a type of power of attorney, and its authority would end when you die. Also remember that, if another family member wants *Bunkie*, they might be able to make a successful claim because there is nothing in the will giving Jane clear, unassailable ownership.

Caution!

The person you select as caregiver is not bound to keep your pet, no matter what agreement you have made. He or she can ship the animal to the pound the day after you die and go on vacation with any money you leave for its care.

While such callous behavior is unusual, you should be aware that your wishes under this type of arrangement are irrelevant. If you go this route, you need to be absolutely certain you have chosen the right person as your pet's caregiver and that other family members know about, and agree with, your decision.

Also, if you make an informal agreement such as this with a friend or relative, put everything down in writing and have it properly notarized. Provide copies of the documents to everyone concerned – your lawyer, veterinarian, caregiver and family members – and keep your copies with other important papers, such as your will and powers of attorney.

This will ensure that everyone to whom you have provided documents knows the exact terms of the informal agreement and may be able to informally intervene to save the animal if the caregiver does not fulfill his or her responsibilities, for whatever reason.

"Lassie looked brilliant, in part because the farm family she lived with was made up of idiots.

Remember? One of them was always getting pinned under the tractor, and Lassie was always rushing back to the farmhouse to alert the other ones. She'd whimper and tug at their sleeves, and they'd always waste precious minutes saying things like: 'Do you think something's wrong? Do you think she wants us to follow her? What is it, girl?' etc., as if this had never happened before, instead of every week. What with all the time these people spent pinned under the tractor, I don't see how they managed to grow any crops whatsoever. They probably got by on federal crop supports, which Lassie filed the applications for."

– **DAVE BARRY,** AMERICAN COLUMNIST & HUMORIST

CHAPTER 9

Making a handshake arrangement more formal

OVERVIEW

- If you are uneasy about hanging your pet's future on a simple handshake agreement, you can create a slightly more formal arrangement through your will.
- Despite the appearance of formality, the arrangement described in this chapter is legally no more enforceable than the casual agreement discussed earlier, but it will:

  1. Put pressure on the caregiver to stick to the agreement (because everyone will know about it).
  2. Allow you to create a more formal structure with a trustee and a protector to help ensure your pet is being treated as you have requested.
  3. Allow you to set out what you want to happen under specific circumstances; for instance if your pet becomes seriously ill.

- This arrangement involves leaving your pet – and often a sum of money (or other type of asset) – to a caregiver (friend, relative or institution). The caregiver accepts the funds with the clear understanding they are to be used to offset costs involved in caring for the pet.
- The first step in setting up an agreement of this type is to make a will, or have your lawyer modify your existing will to include the following provisions for your pet:

  1. Name a caregiver and alternatives.
  2. Name a trustee and/or protector (and alternatives) and set out their duties, making the provisions enforceable.
  3. Outline the kind of care you want for your pet.
  4. Consider assigning a sum of money for the care of your pet and set out how it is to be distributed.

Step up to a more formal arrangement

With a handshake agreement, such as the one we discussed in the previous chapter, you are betting that the person you have chosen as your pet's caregiver will remain healthy, dependable, responsible, committed, and financially and emotionally secure. Since change is a part of life, think carefully before relying on this type of agreement for the care of your pet. If you are not completely comfortable with your caregiver, or you simply want added protection for your pet, consider stepping up to a more formal arrangement by providing for your pet in your will. (Remember, however, that an animal cannot be a direct will beneficiary.)

At last estimate, about 27% of pet owners in the United States who have wills now include provisions for their pets. Often, these will provisions are ill-conceived or inadequate, comprising a paragraph of the *I-leave-my-dog-Max-to-my-Uncle-Harry* type, with no provisions for interim care, no gift of money to cover the cost of keeping *Max* fed and healthy, and no backup in the event Uncle Harry dies, becomes ill, moves to Mexico, or marries a woman who is allergic to dogs.

Obviously, it is preferable to increase your pet's chances of living a reasonably happy life by devising an arrangement in your will that involves leaving both your pet and a sum of money (or other type of liquid asset) for its care to a friend, relative, or institution. The caregiver would accept the money, or other asset, with the clear understanding it be used to offset costs involved in caring for the pet.

The first step in setting up this type of arrangement is to make a will, or have your lawyer modify your existing will. Here are major steps you should take on behalf of your pet:

- name a caregiver plus alternates;
- outline the kind of care you want for your pet;
- assign assets for the care of your pet (if necessary);
- name a trustee and/or protector (plus alternates) if you assign assets;
- inform your family about what you are doing and why.

Remember, by naming a trustee and/or protector if you assign assets, you are making the arrangement enforceable (as opposed to simply leaving a pet and some money to a beneficiary with the hope he or she will take care of it).

"All knowledge, the totality of all questions and all answers is contained in the dog." – FRANZ KAFKA (1883-1924), CZECH-BORN, GERMAN-SPEAKING WRITER

"I agree with Agassiz that dogs possess something very like a conscience." – **CHARLES DARWIN** (1809-1882), BRITISH NATURALIST

"Dogs feel very strongly that they should always go with you in the car, in case the need should arise for them to bark violently at nothing right in your ear."
– **DAVE BARRY**, U.S. COLUMNIST & HUMORIST

Take care when choosing the executor of your will

Whether you are making a will for the first time, or modifying an existing will, be careful about whom you choose to be executor (both primary and alternates). The executor will carry out the instructions in your will. This person is your representative and has considerable responsibility, some flexibility, and the power to affect your pet's future. Be certain the person you choose will have your pet's best interest at heart. Also, avoid making the executor of your will and the caregiver of your pet one and the same person – unless this person is someone you trust implicitly, such as your spouse or other close relative.

Look for someone to serve as executor who moves quickly and has a reasonable sense of business and financial matters. Also, check with your lawyer to find out whether the person you are considering meets the legal requirements for an executor in your area. For example, in most jurisdictions, an executor needs to have reached the age of majority. In some places, a will-maker and his or her executor must reside in the same state or province, or at least in the same country. (Most jurisdictions, however, permit non-residents to serve as executors, although they may have to post a bond, apply to court to dispense with the bond, appoint a resident agent to accept service of process, or follow some other legal procedure.)

Some people choose two or more individuals to act as executors. We suggest you also choose alternates who would serve if any of the first choices were unwilling or unable to.

Remember, none of the parties you chose to administer your estate should be your pet's protector. The two functions are completely different and could represent a conflict of interest. We suggest you keep them separate.

Inform your family

An important final step in using your will as an instrument for providing for your pet is to inform your family about what you are doing and why. If the family learns for the first time at the reading of your will that you are leaving your dog and $10,000 for its care to your friend Ralph down the street, there may well be a challenge and a court case.

And, if a lawyer can convince a judge that you left a disproportionate amount of money for your dog at the expense of family members, or even that you were incompetent when you made your will, your dog may end up with nothing. Remember too, there may be a cost to your estate regarding any lawsuit.

If there are going to be objections to your arrangement for your pet, better to find out about them while you are still alive and can take countermeasures. You may need to go back to your lawyer for suggestions on how to proceed.

If your will is challenged as invalid by a disgruntled family member, what would happen to your pet during the weeks, months or years it would take the courts to sort things out? Would your pet still be delivered to the person you named as its caregiver in your will?

In the United States, during the duration of the contest, some type of personal representative may be serving – either the one named in your will, if the challenge was filed after probate, or a temporary personal representative, if the contest was filed before probate. The personal representative is in charge of managing the property in a reasonably prudent manner. Thus, it may be possible for the personal representative to deliver the pet to the designated party, at least until the contest is resolved. If the administration was independent (not under court control), this could probably be done without court order. If the administration was dependent (under court control), a court order would likely be necessary.

If you want to make sure that your pet will end up with the caregiver of your choice, regardless of any challenges to your will, there are two mechanisms you may consider, where the law in your jurisdiction permits:

1. Create an *inter vivos* (or living) trust (See *Chapter 10.*) You retain ownership and control of your pet while you are alive. On your death, your executor is directed to deliver your pet to the trustees under the *inter vivos* trust for the benefit of the beneficiary of your

trust. Your lawyer will be able to advise you on the wisdom of such a move in your part of the world.

2.   Put a strongly worded dispute mechanism in your will, setting out what you want done with your pet and state that anyone who challenges your wishes will lose his or her own bequest.

Alternatively, if you have a large estate, we suggest you leave a small percent of it for the care of your animals. If you leave 5% of your assets for animal care, and 95% to human beneficiaries, it would be tough for anyone to make a case that you were being unreasonably generous to your animals at the expense of your human beneficiaries, unless you are fabulously wealthy. If Microsoft's Bill Gates left even 5% of his estate for the care of a cat, the cat would be a multi-billionaire, at least until the courts decided otherwise.

In an article in the July 2001 Journal of Accountancy entitled *When The Client Wants to Leave It To The Cat*, author Michael Hayes quotes Kenneth Brier, a Boston CPA and lawyer, who had an 85-year-old client with no family who asked that her estate plan include several pets. Mr. Brier said:

"We carved out a piece of the estate – about $100,000 – so the income from it would take care of them. The balance went to charity. Leaving too much to pets creates a litigation target for family members as well as a perception that the donor is mentally unbalanced."

Whether or not $100,000 is too much can perhaps be debated, depending upon the actual number of pets involved and the overall size of the estate. There were no human beneficiaries for whom the pet gift would represent a hardship.

Also remember that it will likely be important (depending on where you live) for you to state clearly in your will who is to be the remainder, or alternate, beneficiary of any assets remaining after your pet dies. The alternate beneficiary may be the pet's caregiver but, in our opinion, this is a bad idea because it provides motive for the caregiver to terminate the animal. It would be better, perhaps, to name an animal welfare agency, or one of your relatives.

It is also advisable to set up your will so that, no matter who the remainder beneficiary is, his or her inheritance is not dependent on the death of your pet; otherwise, this could put your pet in mortal danger.

Despite its appearance of formality, when you employ this type of arrangement, where the asset(s) is an outright or unconditional gift to an individual, it remains legally unenforceable. Once you are gone, the person you named as caregiver can still refuse to take the pet, or can take it and dispose of it and then freely spend any money you left for its care.

And if, for any reason, the courts decide not to honor your wishes, the funds you set aside for the care of your pet will return to the estate to be distributed as part of the residual property; that is, the property that is not specifically listed in the will.

> *"The world was conquered through the understanding of dogs; the world exists through the understanding of dogs."*
> – **FREDRICH NIETZCHE** (1844-1900), GERMAN PHILOSOPHER

> *"Outside of a dog, a book is a man's best friend. Inside of a dog, it's too dark to read."* – **GROUCHO MARX** (1890-1977), AMERICAN FILM STAR, COMEDIAN & RADIO/TV PERSONALITY

Why bother to set up such an arrangement in your will if it is difficult to enforce?

There are several reasons.

For one thing, you broadcast your wishes to all of your survivors. Everyone will know that the person named in the will informally agreed to care for your pet, creating social pressure for this person to actually fulfill the agreement. Conversely, if the caregiver breaks the agreement without good reason, he or she runs the risk of ostracism by your relatives and friends. At the very least, such a person would be viewed as untrustworthy.

Another advantage? You can structure the agreement a little more elaborately. You might, for example, name someone other than the caregiver to act as a trustee of the funds and/or a protector. A protector, as the name implies, ensures the animal is being cared for according to your instructions. Perhaps you would want to name both a trustee and protector, setting out their roles in your will.

You can formally record what you want to happen under a variety of circumstances. For example, you can outline what you want done, should your pet become seriously ill. You can set out any after-death arrangements for your pet. And you can leave instructions for the disposal of any funds left over after your pet dies.

You might also put the executor of your estate in control of any funds you leave for the care of your pet, with the provision that he or she remunerate the caregiver periodically with verification that the pet is still alive and being cared for properly. If your chosen caregiver happens to be on some form of public assistance (or whose financial situation is so shaky that public assistance is a possibility in the near future), you may want to leave any money for your pet's care in a manner that precludes it from having a negative effect on your caregiver. In some jurisdictions, a person's public assistance funds may be cut off, or reduced, if they receive a significant lump sum of money. If you have any concerns regarding your prospective caregiver's situation, consult your lawyer.

Also, in some jurisdictions, the person to whom you bequeath a pet and a sum of money for its care may have to pay inheritance tax on all or part of the gift (including the value of the animal itself).

> *"The problem with cats is that they get the same exact look whether they see a moth or an axe murderer."*
> – **PAULA POUNDSTONE,** AMERICAN STAND-UP COMIC

Why involve a larger number of people in your pet's ongoing care?

Would involving a trustee and protector suggest you don't trust the person you named as caregiver?

Not necessarily. In fact, your caregiver might be grateful. Let's say you need to find a caregiver for your Great Dane, *Lummox*. Your uncle Joe knows a lot about dogs and has shared his life with several of this breed, but he's now living in a condo that bans pets. Harry, your best friend, is an accountant, but he has no interest in living with a dog. In fact, the only person you know who really wants *Lummox* is your nephew, Gene.

Gene is young, lives in a rented house in the suburbs, loves *Lummox* and is eager to take him should anything happen to you – but he knows little about dogs of any type.

So, you name Gene as caregiver, Harry as special trustee, and Joe as protector. Joe and Harry not only keep an eye on how Gene is looking after *Lummox* and how your money is being spent, but they become resource people for Gene. Joe helps with dog-related issues; Harry watches over how the funds are handled – perhaps how the unused portion is invested, if investment is appropriate. You might even leave the money to Harry, who would then control the flow of funds to Gene.

Alternatively, you might name more than one person as either protector or trustee. After you have found your caregiver, look at your other friends and relatives to determine who might be able to help out the caregiver because of any special knowledge or skills they have.

On the other hand, perhaps the only person you can find to become your pet's caregiver is someone in whom you don't have full confidence – perhaps a young relative prone to debt or fickleness. In this case, you might want to name a protector and, or, trustee to provide a degree of social and legal pressure to ensure that the provisions in the will are carried out.

You could also leave instructions in your will requesting that your estate executor make periodic checks on your pet to ensure the caregiver is caring for it according to your instructions. In addition, or alternatively, you could instruct your pet's veterinarian to submit regular reports to your caregiver and trustee as to the pet's general condition. You can make the receipt of such reports a *condition subsequent* (see the next section) to the caregiver receiving funds for the care of your pet. If you leave the money in trust to a trustee, rather than the caregiver, that person can then withhold funds if the pet is not being cared for in the manner you outlined in your will.

(This assumes that such arrangements in your will are legally sanctioned and can be made enforceable in your jurisdiction.)

You might also want to give your trustee the authority to appoint another vet in case the one you name moves or dies, or because your caregiver finds it more convenient to use someone different.

Of course, under this type of arrangement, there is always the possibility of collusion between the humans involved, which could result in the early demise of the pet and a sharing between them of any money you left for its care. But generally speaking, the more people you involve in your pet's care, the less opportunity there will be for such collusion.

> *"You call to a dog and a dog will break its neck to get to you. Dogs just want to please. Call to a cat and its attitude is, 'What's in it for me?' "*
> – LEWIS GRIZZARD (1947-1994), AMERICAN WRITER

"If a dog jumps up into your lap, it is because he is fond of you; but if a cat does the same thing, it is because your lap is warmer."

– **ALFRED WHITEHEAD** (1861-1947), BRITISH MATHEMATICIAN
& PHILOSOPHER, FROM **DIALOGUES OF ALFRED NORTH WHITEHEAD**

Putting more teeth into the arrangement

If you use your will to safeguard your pet's future, you can put some teeth into the arrangement by gifting the animal and a sum of money to a caregiver/beneficiary, but with strings attached. The strings, or conditions, can be set by you and can include whatever you want them to include. Discuss with your lawyer whether these conditions should be *conditions precedent* or *conditions subsequent.*

Condition precedent. A true *condition precedent* relies on an action or decision by a third party, who could be anyone you name. For example, you might gift $10,000 and your cat to your nephew, on condition that your estate executor (or someone else you name) approves the gift once you have died and your estate is being settled.

Why would you include a *condition precedent* such as this one?

Perhaps you don't see much of your nephew because he lives in another city or state. You might have no way of checking on whether or not he has become an alcoholic, fallen into financial ruin, gotten in trouble with the law, or married a woman with cat-hating kids. So, basically, you leave it up to someone else to make a determination when the time comes.

To sum up, under a condition precedent, the gift (your cat and the $10,000) does not go to the beneficiary (your nephew) until the condition (the approval of your executor) is met. If your executor approves, your nephew gets the money and the cat; if your executor doesn't approve, your nephew gets nothing. (Remember, however, this could lead to litigation.)

You also need to put a provision in your will as to where the cat and the money go, should the *condition precedent* not be met.

A *condition subsequent*. Let's apply a *condition subsequent* to the same situation. You are giving your cat and $10,000 to your nephew. With a *condition subsequent* in place, your nephew automatically receives the cat and the $10,000 when you die. No third party approval required.

But your *condition subsequent* might be that the cat has to be examined by a vet twice a year, receive high-quality food, and be given the run of your nephew's home. Your executor, a trustee or someone else you appoint could check to make sure the conditions were being fulfilled. Failure to meet any or all of these conditions would mean your nephew would lose the cat and the remainder of the $10,000.

A common *condition subsequent* is that the animal must be alive. Let's say you make this a *condition subsequent*. Your nephew receives your cat and a check for $1,000 every year (for up to 10 years) for its care. At the end of the second year, the cat dies. Under the *condition subsequent* (the cat must be alive), your nephew would not automatically receive the $8,000 remaining in the account for the cat's care. Naturally, in your will, you must state what is to happen to any money remaining in the cat account, unless you want it to go to whoever you named to receive the remainder of your estate.

You could also put a *condition precedent* and a *condition subsequent* on the same gift. For example, you could name your nephew as your cat's caregiver and leave the cat and $10,000 to him upon your death. As per the instructions in your will, he would receive a $1,000 check every year for 10 years for the cat's care.

The *condition precedent*? The money vests with your nephew only if the executor/trustee of your will approves the gift at the time of your death. The *condition subsequent*? If the cat dies in less than 10 years, the nephew/caregiver does not automatically receive the money remaining in the cat care account: it goes to whomever you named in your will.

Remember too, any provisions for your pet that are contained solely in your will, and nowhere else, will not cover any interim or temporary situations – when you are injured or ill, before your will is read and before your will is probated.

So, unless you have authorized uncle Harry to care for your pet in documents other than your will – a wallet card, signs in your house, power of attorney, notarized letter – he may not be allowed to take the animal in these situations.

> **"If a fish is the movement of water embodied, given shape, then a cat is a diagram and pattern of subtle air."**
> – FROM **PARTICULARLY CATS** BY **DORIS LESSING**, NOVELIST,
> BORN IN IRAN OF BRITISH PARENTS AND EDUCATED IN AFRICA

"Animals are such agreeable friends; they ask no questions, they pass no criticisms." – GEORGE ELIOT
(1819-1880), ENGLISH NOVELIST

Review your plans frequently

Regardless of the type of arrangement you make for your pet's future – a handshake agreement, a paragraph in your will, or one of the trust instruments – you need to review your plans frequently. (You should review your overall estate plan with your lawyer every couple of years anyway, or whenever you have a major change in your life, such as a divorce, death, financial windfall or disaster, etc.)

A review of your pet-care plans need not be expensive, time-consuming or difficult: simply go over your plans and note whether any changes that have taken place during the year will affect your animals should you die or become incapacitated. Has a back-up caregiver died or moved away? Have you acquired a new pet?

If you need to make a few minor changes to your will, you may be able to do it inexpensively with your lawyer through a codicil, which is a supplementary document with clauses that add to, or revoke, parts of your original will. If the changes are more extensive, you may need to prepare a new will. Your lawyer will advise you on the best course of action. We suggest that, except in very rare cases, codicils should be avoided to reduce a variety of issues.

In most cases, it's a bad idea to make your own handwritten changes on the pages of your will. This could, in certain circumstances, invalidate the entire document.

Also, remind your lawyer to review any additional requirements in your locality for validating your will and making certain there are no restrictions on transferring property from estate to beneficiaries. In most U.S. states, for example, divorce automatically revokes provisions in a will with regard to the ex-spouse – but not in all. Divorce decrees in a few states do not necessarily include a specific clause that revokes your ex-spouse's claim to part of your estate.

This means your ex could walk away with a chunk of your estate, including any pets. How do you deal with the situation? If you feel strongly that your ex would not make a good caregiver for your pet, you will need to include a provision in your will and divorce decree specifically forbidding him or her from receiving any animals you may have at the time of your death.

Euthanasia

Some pet owners have included clauses in their wills directing that their pets be destroyed upon their death. Their motivations vary. Some feel their pet would be so distraught without them that it would be kinder to end its life. Others think that no one would adopt their pet and that it would end up in a shelter and be euthanized anyway. Others worry that their pet might be adopted by someone who would treat it badly – or that it could land in some scientific research program.

Courts are notoriously unsympathetic to people who request healthy animals be euthanized, however. For example, on May 31, 1991, Mr. Clive Wishart of Tabusintac, New Brunswick, died. He had made a will 14 months earlier, which provided:

"I DIRECT AND DECLARE that my Executors have my horses shot by the Royal Canadian Mounted Police and then buried."

The Royal Canadian Mounted Police were less than enthusiastic and refused to shoot Mr. Wishart's four horses, *Barney*, *Bill*, *Jack* and *King*, unless the court ordered them to.

Mr. Wishart's executors, whose responsibility it was to carry out the directions in the will, were also unhappy with the provision. After all, the horses were in good health and less than four years of age.

They took the matter to court. That's about the time the media uncovered the story and carried it coast to coast in Canada. Naturally, the public was outraged.

No matter what anyone thought, Wishart wasn't a cruel person. He was simply terrified that his beloved horses would be abused by a subsequent owner. Better they die quickly.

Regardless of his wishes, however, the judge spared the animals, ruling that killing the animals would be against *public policy*, meaning the execution shouldn't be carried out because it offended community standards.

In his ruling, the judge said a letter from a 9-year-old helped convince him to set aside the direction to destroy the horses.

The fact is that when someone includes in their will a direction that an animal, usually a pet, be destroyed following his or her death, almost invariably the will ends up in court.

And in the United States and Canada, courts generally rule against directives that involve the willful destruction of property, especially if someone volunteers to become a pet's caregiver. A court might entertain a request to destroy an animal if it were very old, very ill and without a human champion to take over its care. Such a pet, most courts would agree, would be an unlikely candidate for adoption and would suffer unnecessarily in the cages of an animal shelter.

If you wish to keep euthanasia as an option, state in your will that you authorize your executor to care for your pet for a specific length of time while trying to find a good home for it. If such a home cannot be found, than you want the pet to be euthanized by a qualified vet. A judge may choose not to revoke such a request.

Alternatively, you could leave your pet to a friend with the understanding that the friend will have the animal put down. Such a recipient of your gift has every right to have his or her pet euthanized.

That blade cuts both ways, however. Should you gift your pet to a relative or friend with the understanding that the recipient is to become its caregiver until it dies, this person has the legal right to have his or her pet destroyed, regardless of any understanding. It is unlikely the person would do so, especially if you have chosen carefully.

A note about wills

In most jurisdictions, certain legal requirements are associated with will-making. Generally, wills are printed and need to be witnessed, signed, and possibly notarized, although there are exceptions. In some places, handwritten (holographic) wills are valid; in others they are not. Your best course of action is to ask a lawyer to prepare your will.

- **Frogs.** Frogs evolved about 200 million years ago. They make great little pets and are relatively low maintenance once they are in a proper environment.

- **Donkeys are smart.** Related to horses, ponies and zebras, donkeys are thought to be stubborn and stupid. Just the opposite is true. They demonstrate their intelligence by refusing to be commanded into dangerous situations.

- **No need for shoes.** Donkeys have tough hooves that eliminate the need for shoes. They also have loud braying voices that can carry up to three kilometres, perhaps because in the wild, donkeys live further apart from each other than horses. Their large ears help hear each other a long distances, too.

If the language in your will is ambiguous, a court may put its own interpretation in place of your intended meaning.

For example, in 1936, a State of Washington court was left to interpret the meaning behind the will of a Ms. Anna Bradley, who left her estate, including her cats, to her housekeeper, Ms. Peterson, although Ms. Bradley had known the Peterson woman for only three months before she died. The court had to decide whether the language of Ms. Bradley's will created a trust for the benefit of her cats, with Ms. Peterson as trustee.

The court found that the wording of the will was not a command and therefore created no obligation in the housekeeper to care for the cats.

In a more recent case (1968), before California permitted pet trusts, one of its courts was asked to review the holographic (handwritten) will of a certain Ms. Russell. In her will, she had left everything she owned to her friend, Mr. Quinn, and to her dog, *Roxy*. Because the dog could not inherit, the issue of Ms. Russell's intent arose. The court had to decide whether the will could be construed as giving half her property to Mr. Quinn and creating a trust for *Roxy's* benefit with the other half. The court ruled that:

- Mr. Quinn should receive his half of the property; and,
- The gift to *Roxy* was void and was distributed to Ms. Russell's human heirs.

Another reason to be crystal clear about your intentions? While it may seem obvious if you leave a sum of money to someone for the care of a pet, you must state that the money is to be given only if the animal is still alive. If it has died and if you have neglected to update your will, then the court is likely to award the money to the caregiver anyway, even if there is no pet on which to spend it. (See page 61 on *condition subsequent*.)

And a note about probate laws

In the United States: Laws regarding probate differ from state to state, but there are general guidelines in all 50 states. By the summer of 2009, at least 42 states and the District of Columbia allowed pet owners to set money aside for the care of animals in the event of an owner's disability or death, using a simple procedure called a statutory pet trust. All states permit pet owners to provide for their pets using a traditional pet trust.

If the state in which you live has not passed a pet trust law, you may still use a traditional pet trust or one of the other tools described in this book. If you have some time, you might research recent challenges to pet trusts in your state.

In Canada: Probate laws differ from province to province. Each province has its own determinations relating to different types of property which require probate.

Residents of Australia, New Zealand, the U.K. and other countries should consult a local lawyer regarding probate laws in their specific jurisdictions.

"Politics are not my concern . . . they impressed me as a dog's life without a dog's decencies."
– **RUDYARD KIPLING** (1865-1936), ENGLISH WRITER

"I love a dog. He does nothing for political reasons."
– **WILL ROGERS** (1879-1935), AMERICAN HUMORIST

CHAPTER 10

Making a conditional gift to a human in trust

O V E R V I E W

- Many people make a *conditional* gift to a human in trust. The condition is that the gift (money, real estate or other property) be used to care for their pet. This type of arrangement is established within a legal framework and can be made enforceable.
- You can establish an *inter vivos* trust, which takes effect while you are still alive, or a testamentary trust set out in your will, to be established after you die.
- *Inter vivos* trusts are easy to set up, may be made revocable, and provide funds for your pet from the moment you die, but you must part with some money or property before you die to fund them.
- Depending on the jurisdiction in which you live, testamentary trusts may provide better tax treatment than *inter vivos* trusts. They are not funded until after your will has been probated. There are frequently more technical requirements to make changes to a testamentary trust than an *inter vivos* trust.
- In either case, you will need to name a caregiver for your pet and a trustee to manage the property – they shouldn't be the same person. Appoint backups for both. Make sure each of them understands how a trust works.
- A family member may successfully challenge a will that leaves an excessive amount of money in a valid trust for the care of a pet, so keep the amount sensible.
- Establish the length of time the trust should run, the rules and method for distributing funds to the caregiver, and how to dispose of assets left in the trust after it has run its course and the pet has died.

Sidestepping the ban on pets as beneficiaries

Except in those U.S. states that have revised their rules (at least 42 states and the District of Columbia, as of August 2009), and in all other countries, courts disallow trusts that have pets as beneficiaries without the intervention of a human caregiver or other protector. They cite a number of reasons for this position, including the facts that an animal cannot own property and cannot enforce a trust in court.

If you live in an area that does not recognize statutory pet trusts, you might consider making a conditional bequest to a human in trust to sidestep the prohibition. Even if your jurisdiction permits statutory pet trusts, it may be a better idea to use this traditional pet trust technique to have greater control over the care your pet receives.

It is also interesting to note that some U.S. courts have interpreted trusts that have been drafted with pets as beneficiaries as conditional bequests to humans in an attempt to carry out the pet owner's intent. In such cases, a human would receive a bequest with a *condition subsequent* that the gift be used for the benefit of the deceased person's pet. The legacy would immediately belong to the beneficiary, but be taken away if that person failed to care for the pet.

But why leave it up to the courts to make this decision? Ask your lawyer to put together a definitive arrangement to provide for your pet.

The human you choose as the beneficiary of a conditional bequest in trust is typically the person you want to take care of your pet when you die. The property, however, does not go directly to the caregiver. Instead, the trustee will distribute funds to the caregiver according to rules you and your lawyer set up.

> *"One of the most striking differences between a cat and a lie is that a cat has only nine lives."* – **MARK TWAIN** (1835-1910), AMERICAN HUMORIST, NOVELIST, SHORT STORY AUTHOR & WIT

This type of arrangement is popular because it avoids the two traditional problems associated with gifts to animals. First, the beneficiary is a human, not an animal, and can enforce the trust. Second, there is a human measuring life, or life-in-being, to work within the rule against perpetuities. (See *How long should the trust run* later in this chapter.)

What is the difference between an *inter vivos* trust and the type of arrangement described in the previous chapter (whereby you leave a gift in your will to a person for the care of a pet)? A will specifies how you want to distribute your estate – everything you own – when you die. But the distribution of assets under a will takes place *only* after you die. If the will has to be probated, a significant amount of time may pass before any assets are distributed. Furthermore, family members may tie up assets for lengthy periods by challenging a will.

- **Foxes**. In some areas of Russia, foxes are as common around the house as dogs, according to BBC *Wildlife* magazine. "Over 45 years, the foxes in Novosibirsk…were bred to be friendly towards humans. Now, (they) look like domestic dogs, complete with floppy ears, multi-colored coats and curly tails. Not only do these foxes wag their tails and lick your face, occasionally they display more intelligence than chimpanzees."

- **How can you tell?** A cat can be either right-pawed or left-pawed.

- **The fat diet.** Cats need fat in their diet because they can't produce it on their own and they need five times more protein than dogs. Cats cannot live on a vegetarian diet.

So, if you use a will alone to plan for your pet's future, make sure you set up an interim plan to provide for its care during the time when your will is in probate or in the event of a challenge. Alternatively, make a conditional gift to a human in trust (an *inter vivos* trust) so that funds are available immediately after you die for the care of your pet.

Also, in the previous chapter we noted that someone who is willed an animal and a sum of money for its care may have to pay a tax on these gifts if he or she lives in a jurisdiction that levies such taxes. By establishing a trust, you may avoid or reduce the tax burden for everyone except possibly yourself, depending on what assets you use to settle the trust and the laws of jurisdiction in which you live. For example, if you sell a taxable asset to fund the trust, you may incur income tax that you will have to pay for the year in which you sell that asset.

What is a trust?

A trust is a method of holding title to property that separates the legal duties and responsibilities of property ownership from the ability to benefit from that property. The person creating the trust may be called the settlor, trustor, or grantor. The trustee is the person in charge of the trust and who will disburse the funds or property to or for the benefit of a beneficiary or beneficiaries. The property itself is known as the principal or *corpus* of the trust.

A trust is created within a legal framework and is enforceable. There are two basic types, and each may be made discretionary or non-discretionary. The major advantages and disadvantages of each type are discussed below.

Inter vivos trusts

You create and activate an *inter vivos* trust, also known as a living trust, while you are alive. You can be the trustee of your own inter *vivos trust.*

Advantages

- An *inter vivos* trust will provide funds for your pet's care from the moment you create it onwards, thus avoiding the problem of leaving your pet stranded without funding in the period (sometimes months or even years) that occurs between your death and the probate of your will.

- It can be written so that if you become disabled for an extended period of time, the trustee can use trust funds to pay someone to take care of your pet until you are able to take over again.

- It can be made revocable, which means you can amend it at any time, add or remove property, or even revoke it completely.

- It does not have to go through probate, which means the person or persons named in your trust receive your pets and can benefit from the trust property immediately upon your death, rather than weeks, months, or years later – or even before your death, if you set it up that way.

- A living trust is often completely private. No one will know what assets are included in the trust or how they are being distributed, but a trust created in a will is open to public scrutiny if and when the will is probated (depending on probate rules in your jurisdiction).

Disadvantages

- An *inter vivos* trust may cost more to set up and administer because it is a wholly separate arrangement from your will.

- You will have to part with property to fund it. This property is removed from your control and is not part of your estate. Initially, however, it could be nominally funded with a small amount of money just to get it set up. Additional funding could be tied to a non-probate asset, such as a small bank account (under $10,000) or a life insurance policy, which would provide the trust with immediate funds after the owner's death.

- There may be a tax consequence at the time of trust creation. For example, if you sell a house to raise money to fund the trust, you may have to pay a capital gains tax on any profit you earn. Or, you may need to pay a gift or other transfer tax on property you transfer to the trust. Of course, this all depends on the tax legislation in your jurisdiction. You may also have to file annual tax returns and pay tax on any income earned by an *inter vivos* trust. Consult a tax specialist in your area to discuss your options.

Testamentary trusts

A testamentary trust is contained in your will and only takes effect upon your death and the probate of your will.

Advantages

- You do not have to fund a testamentary trust while you are alive; therefore, you do not lose control of any of your property.

Disadvantages

- To change it, you must have your lawyer either draft a new will for you to sign, or add a codicil to your existing will, depending on the extent of your changes.
- It does not protect your pet until after your will has been probated.

Both testamentary and *inter vivos* trusts tend to be more expensive to draft than a simple will. (See *Appendix F* for sample pet trust wording.)

If you feel you want to provide for your pet using a trust, you and your lawyer should decide which type to create, based on your situation and needs. Because trusts are complex documents and need to adhere to specific state, provincial or other jurisdictional laws, do not attempt to draft your own trust agreement. Have your lawyer do it.

And remember, even if you live in a U.S. state that allows statutory pet trusts, a conditional gift to a human in trust may still be better for you and your pet under many circumstances. For example, if the state in which you live limits the duration of an animal trust to 21 years, your pet parrot may outlive it. Your lawyer, with careful drafting, can establish a conditional trust with a human beneficiary that far exceeds 21 years. In fact, such a trust may run throughout the caregiver's lifetime plus 21 years. It can be written to end when the pet dies – if that happens sooner.

If, for some reason, the trust ends before your pet dies, the trustee (if still alive and available) should – prior to that occurrence – try to find a good home for the animal and leave it, and some property, to the new owner. This possibility should be covered in the trust document.

"The more I see of men, the better I like my dog."
– **BLAISE PASCAL** (1623-1662), FRENCH SCIENTIST, MATHEMATICIAN, PHYSICIST, PHILOSOPHER, MORALIST & WRITER

"Dogs. They are better than human beings because they know but they do not tell." – EMILY DICKINSON (1830-1886), AMERICAN POET

"The average dog is a better person than the average person." – ANDY ROONEY, AMERICAN NEWSMAN & TELEVISION COMMENTATOR

Your lawyer can establish an *inter vivos* trust while you are alive, or set up a testamentary trust in your will to take effect when you die. Your job will be to:

- select a caregiver and trustee for your pet (and name alternates for each);
- document the type of care you want your pet to receive;
- with your lawyer, set out the rules for distribution of funds;
- provide instructions on how you want your caregiver to handle any serious illnesses your pet contracts; and,
- provide instructions on what you want done with your pet after it dies.

Finally, if you decide to go with an *inter vivos* trust, you need to put some assets into the trust and decide what happens to any money left over after your pet dies and the trust ends.

If you have several pets, you can set up a single trust to cover all of them, or establish separate trusts for each. If you set up a single trust to handle several pets (presumably, but not necessarily, with separate caregivers), you could name one or more trustees to handle the administration.

Naming the trust beneficiary/pet caregiver

Not only is an animal unable to go to court to enforce a trust set up for its care, but it cannot even tell anyone that the terms of the trust are being broken. With that in mind, it is wise to make sure that some checks and balances are part of any trust arrangement you make for your pet.

In a typical trust, the pet's caregiver becomes the beneficiary of the trust you set up. The trustee controls the funds for the pet's care.

In most jurisdictions, the caregiver may enforce the trust if the trustee fails to comply with its terms. Make sure your caregiver understands how a trust functions and that he or she can enforce it through the court, if necessary. The trustee can also uphold the trust by withholding funds or replacing the caregiver if your pet is not receiving proper care.

Avoid any arrangement that allows your trustee to appoint himself or herself as the caregiver of the animal, because that would eliminate one of the most important checks and balances separating the caregiver from the money provider.

Remember to name several alternate caregivers, in case your first choice cannot serve throughout your pet's life. You should also authorize your trustee to select a good home for your pet if none of the people you name as caregivers can, or will, take responsibility for the animal when the time comes.

Naming the trustee

You should choose your trustee with as much care as you do the caregiver. And remember to check with the person you want as trustee to make certain he or she is willing to serve. A trustee must have, or make, time to administer the trust for the benefit of your pet.

Not only must the trustee act with the best interests of your pet, but he or she must ensure that the caregiver is doing the same. The trustee will authorize funds for your pet's care and make sure your wishes are being carried out. You should give the trustee the power to replace the original caregiver (and any subsequent caregivers), if necessary.

If you want, you may provide a stipend for the trustee's services. Remember, in most jurisdictions, if you do not set out a fee (or indicate that the trustee must serve for free), the trustee can apply to the courts to receive compensation from the trust for acting as trustee, as set out in the laws of the jurisdiction. The amounts vary from place to place and are calculated on a number of factors, but the amount your trustee could receive might be more than you want to pay. It would be better to set an amount beforehand. Check with your lawyer on the best way to do this.

You will definitely want to name at least one alternate trustee in the event your first choice is unable to serve until the trust ends. Also, you may provide for the removal of the original trustee, if that person is not administering the trust for your pet's benefit.

Determine what other property (in addition to your pet) to transfer to your trust

In Chapter 6, we discussed how to estimate the amount of money you will need to set aside for the care of your pet, but take care not to leave an excessive amount. If you have always believed your property is yours to do with as you please, forget it. If the court feels you have left too much money for the care of your pet, given your financial circumstances, it can reduce it to something *it* thinks is reasonable. This will be more likely to occur if one of your relatives challenges your last wishes.

While wills are challenged far more often than trusts, you still run the risk of having a court overrule your wishes if it feels you have been overly generous to your pet at the expense of your potential human beneficiaries. Remember how the court reduced the amount of the trust Leona Helmsley left for the care of her little dog *Trouble* and awarded that money to the grandchildren she had disinherited?

Stick to the basics when determining the amount of money to care adequately for your pet: the type of animal, life expectancy, standard of care, expected and unexpected medical expenses. Forget the filet mignon twice a week, or Ritz-Carleton accommodations.

If you have a substantial estate, you could set up the trust so that the pet's day-to-day care could be handled by the income from the assets. The principal would be retained for unexpected incidents and emergencies. You would provide instructions in your trust for the disposal of the remainder of the principal, once the pet has died.

If your estate is modest, you may want to give your trustee discretionary authority to use income first and then principal, as may be needed. You may also wish to look into purchasing a modest life insurance policy, naming your trust as the beneficiary of the policy, with funds to be used to provide care for your pet.

Distributing funds from your trust

By the time you set up the trust to care for your pet, you should have already had a chat with your trustee and caregiver about how the funds will be distributed. There are really only two realistic methods, and a third that combines the two.

Method 1

The easiest method of distribution is for you to direct your trustee to pay your pet's caregiver a set sum each month, regardless of actual expenses. If your cat, *Jasper*, is being cared for by your best friend, Harry, you can direct your trustee to pay Harry $50 a month for the cat's expenses.

In months when *Jasper's* expenses are less than $50, Harry pockets the difference. When his expenses are more than $50 for the month, Harry makes up the difference.

Method 2

The second way to distribute funds from the trust is to reimburse your caregiver for expenses only. In the case of *Jasper* and Harry, Harry would retain receipts for any expenses for the cat, submitting them to your trustee periodically (monthly, bi-monthly, quarterly, annually, etc.). The trustee, after reviewing the expenses against the level of care you stipulated for *Jasper*, would reimburse Harry.

If your caregiver favors this method, remind him or her that it takes more time and effort to keep track of dozens of receipts for food, treats, toys, medication and other items. It may not be worth the effort. This method would, however, automatically include any unexpected bills for medical emergencies.

Method 3

This method is a combination of the first two. If Harry tells you he prefers to receive a monthly payment of $50, but can't or won't make up any expenses for *Jasper* beyond that, you can authorize your trustee to reimburse Harry for any expenses exceeding the normal $50 monthly distribution. Harry simply keeps and submits receipts for out-of-pocket costs, such as an expensive trip to the vet, or a new cat bed.

"I love cats because I love my home and after a while they become its visible soul." – JEAN COCTEAU
(1889-1963), FRENCH ARTIST & WRITER

"A cat pours his body on the floor like water."
– WILLIAM LYON PHELPS (1865-1943), AMERICAN EDUCATOR & JOURNALIST

"Cats regard people as warm blooded furniture."
– JACQUELYN MITCHARD, AMERICAN NOVELIST

What about supplementary payments for your caregiver?

You should discuss with your caregiver whether the addition of your pet to his or her household would create a sufficient burden to warrant supplementary payments from the trust. If your pet is a quiet, reclusive cat like *Jasper*, the answer will likely be no. If, however, your pet is a big, rambunctious oaf of a dog who may damage furniture or disrupt the family with loud barking and other obnoxious behavior, your caregiver may indeed need a little extra cash as encouragement to carry on as the (ahem) *beneficiary* of your largesse.

How long should the trust run?

In most jurisdictions whose legal system is rooted in English common law, trusts cannot tie up assets indefinitely. Known as the rule against perpetuities in most places, it limits the duration of a trust to the life of a human being (a life-in-being) plus 21 years. So, when making a conditional gift to a human in trust, you cannot link the duration of the trust to the life of your pet, or any animal; it must be linked to a human life, unless the law in your jurisdiction says otherwise (as an increasing number of jurisdictions are now doing).

You could set up the duration of your trust as 21 years beyond the life of your pet's caregiver and trustees, or some other life-in-being, with the trust ending sooner should your pet die. (See *Chapter 11* for more on this topic.)

Inspection by your trustee

You should seriously consider making it a requirement that your trustee inspects your pet periodically to check its physical and psychological condition. These inspections should be random so the caregiver cannot provide the pet with extra food and attention just because the trustee is coming. Ask that the inspection take place in the caregiver's home so the trustee can check out the environment in which the pet lives.

Inspections by a veterinarian

When you make arrangements for your pet that include an ongoing benefit to a human caregiver – money, living quarters, or some other long-term benefit – consider leaving instructions or imposing conditions that require someone you appoint (instead of, or in addition to, the trustee) to make regular periodic inspections of your pet and its living conditions. Or you could require the caregiver to provide your trustee with regular statements from the pet's veterinarian, outlining its general health and condition. You might ask that both of these be carried out.

Pet care committee

We have heard of people who have asked several of their friends, family members and/or professional acquaintances (veterinarian, accountant or lawyer) to serve on a pet care committee to provide direction and council to their caregiver on major health issues – medical treatment, euthanasia, etc.

Establishing a committee of this type would be most appropriate when there are a number of animals involved or when the animals are valuable, long-lived, or have complex needs. In these circumstances, the amount of money set aside for care would likely be substantial.

"The disposition of noble dogs is to be gentle with people they know and the opposite with those they don't know... How, then, can the dog be anything other than a lover of learning since it defines what's its own and what's alien."
– **PLATO** (427-347 BC), GREEK PHILOSOPHER

"I am because my little dog knows me."
– **GERTRUDE STEIN** (1874-1946), AMERICAN WRITER

"Dogs love their friends and bite their enemies, quite unlike people, who are incapable of pure love and always have to mix love and hate."
– **SIGMUND FREUD** (1856-1939), AUSTRIAN PSYCHOLOGIST

CHAPTER 11

Setting up a statutory pet trust

OVERVIEW

- If you live in one of the 42 U.S. states that permit it, you can set up a simple trust arrangement for the benefit of your pet.
- You would be the settlor, your pet benefits from the property you place into the trust, and the trustee could either be the person you named as caregiver or, preferably, someone else. You might also name a protector to ensure your pet is being properly cared for and to act on its behalf.
- Like other trusts, a statutory pet trust may be subject to the rule against perpetuities. This rule forbids property owners from setting up trusts that never end – or that go on for decades. Many jurisdictions have now modernized or repealed the rule against perpetuities.
- Most people arm their trust with about $25,000 for each animal. Some people fund these trusts with property, such as a house or apartment, which is then used by the pet and its caregiver. Some transfer both money and property to the trust. Many people also use insurance payable-on-death (POD) accounts, or other non-probate assets, to fund a pet trust.
- If you set up a testamentary trust, either as a conditional gift in trust for a pet, or as a statutory pet trust in one of the states that permit them, you will need another instrument to bridge the gap between the time you become disabled or die and the time your will has been probated.

Only in America, apparently

Over the past decade, a significant number of American states have enacted laws allowing pet owners to set up trust funds for the care of their animals after the owners have died. At the time of writing, these states were the only places in the world that that could be found as recognizing pet trusts. *Lawyers Weekly U.S.A.* notes that the average amount left in such trusts for pet care is about $25,000.

If you live in a country, or one of the U.S. states that does *not* have a pet trust statute, creating a trust for an animal without naming a human beneficiary whose receipt of funds is conditioned on taking care of the pet is risky. If human heirs launch a court challenge, most judges would rule it invalid because there is no human beneficiary, because its duration is not based on a human life, or for other reasons.

Even if a judge does not invalidate such a trust, he or she may decide that it is unenforceable, leaving it up to the trustee to decide whether to implement it. In one state that authorizes pet trusts, Wisconsin, the trustee may refuse to carry out its terms.

In pet-trust states where a trustee is legally required to fulfill the terms of the trust, the trust is essentially treated like a trust for a minor child, and the person appointed to enforce it is treated like a guardian. On the other hand, your dog is unlikely to complain to anyone if he is shortchanged on kibble or rabies shots. Presumably, a child might tell someone about negligent care. (For the wording of the individual state statutes pertaining to pet trusts, see *Appendix H.*)

Why the trend toward pet trusts?

New pet laws, including statutory pet trusts, recognize that many of us no longer believe that our children or other surviving relatives will necessarily carry out our final wishes. They may or may not be willing, or able, to take care of a surviving pet. The only option we have for peace of mind is to establish a legal instrument, such as a pet trust, to get the job done.

The trend toward a kinder, more careful attitude toward pet care and survival has been reflected in the U.S. by a rapid increase in the number of states with laws authorizing statutory pet trusts, which gained momentum when they were included in both the Uniform Probate Code and the Uniform Trust Code. (Uniform laws are statutes suggested by the National Conference of Commissioners on Uniform States Laws, and statute legislatures often given them favorable consideration.)

The statutory pet trust laws typically provide that the trust may be enforced by someone named in the trust instrument. If no one has been named, the court may appoint someone (an individual who has formally applied to the court for the job). The court may also reduce the amount of property in the trust if it finds it excessive.

Although the states that permit statutory pet trusts have enacted similar provisions, there are significant differences. Generally, you can set up a trust for your pet. Your pet would receive the benefits of the property placed into the trust, and the trustee could either be the person you named as caregiver or, preferably, someone else. You might also name a protector (or enforcer) to ensure your pet is being properly cared for and to act on its behalf. Again, be sure to name alternates for each position of trustee, protector and caregiver.

As mentioned in the previous chapter, to establish such a pet trust, your lawyer may need to deal with the rule against perpetuities or some other provision limiting the length of time a pet trust is enforceable. This rule forbids property owners from setting up trusts, including trusts with human beneficiaries, that never end – or go on for what may appear to be forever.

Many jurisdictions have modernized or repealed this rule with respect to pet trusts, so your lawyer will need to ascertain how long a pet trust may last in your jurisdiction. In many jurisdictions, a pet trust can run for the life of the pet and perhaps its offspring.

"I've seen a look in dogs' eyes, a quickly vanishing look of amazed contempt, and I am convinced that basically dogs think humans are nuts." – JOHN STEINBECK (1902-1968), AMERICAN NOVELIST

"You can say any fool thing to a dog, and the dog will give you this look that says, 'My God, you're RIGHT! I NEVER would've thought of that!' " – DAVE BARRY, U.S. COLUMNIST & HUMORIST

"The dog has got more fun out of Man than Man has got out of the dog, for the clearly demonstrable reason that Man is the more laughable of the two animals." – JAMES THURBER (1894-1961), AMERICAN AUTHOR, CARTOONIST, HUMORIST & SATIRIST

Assuming your jurisdiction applies the rule against perpetuities to pet trusts, the rule will probably pose no problem for most pets, such as dogs and cats, if the trust is properly drafted. Your lawyer should anticipate, and prepare for its potential effect on longer-lived animals, such as parrots, making certain the trust ends only with the death of the last pet or 21 years after the death of the measuring life, whichever comes first.

(Note that the life you choose to measure against need not be connected with the trust, the trustee or even with your family. For example, you could use Prince William of England as the measuring life.)

While Colorado permits a trust to run until the death of a pet's offspring *in gestation* at the time of the owner's death, some of the states that permit pet trusts, such as New York and New Jersey, do not allow them to run for more than 21 years, period. That can present problems even to horse owners. As mentioned in an earlier chapter, if you live in one of these states, and if you want to provide for a long-lived animal, such as a parrot or horse, you might forego the statutory pet trust and opt for a traditional pet trust.

Funding your pet trust

While $25,000 is the average amount left in a pet trust, you might put in more for a young horse and less for an old dog or cat. Some people fund these trusts with property, such as a house or apartment, which is then used by the pet and its caregiver. Other pet owners may decide to fund the trust with a life insurance policy, a joint account with survivorship rights, a pay on death bank account, or by some other method.

As with some of the other instruments we have discussed, you should plan carefully. Be vigilant about choosing your human representatives. Provide adequate funds for your pet's care. Set out how the funds are to be distributed and whether the caregiver is to be paid a fee. And provide guidelines for your pet's care.

Here is how one California woman used the pet trust laws of her state to help ensure care for her Shar-Pei dogs, if and when she predeceases them.

Because she lives in California, a state that allows her to name dogs to benefit from the trust property, she has left her house for her dogs, as well as money to support them for 10 years. In addition, she has given a rent break to a suitable caregiver who would live there.

She established the trust when she was 42 years old because she was worried about what would happen to her dogs if she died suddenly. She said her mother's death prompted her to set up a living trust, because she had watched the courts put her sister through probate hell for their mother's tiny estate.

The trust, she said, gave her peace of mind.

Although she hopes her dogs end up in a permanent home with someone, the trust relieves the pressure to find a home quickly. She explained that the dogs will be comfortable in their own environment instead of frightened to be somewhere they've never been before. She hopes anyone who lives with them for awhile to take care of them might end up giving them a permanent home, either at her house or elsewhere.

She named her sister trustee, but she has asked the staff at her vet's office to find someone to stay at the house to care for the dogs.

She says she updates notes on each dog every six months, covering diet, handling, likes and dislikes and so on. She has also noted the kind of home they might be able to go to.

> *"There has never been a cat*
> *Who couldn't calm me down*
> *By walking slowly*
> *Past my chair"*
>
> – **ROD MCKUEN,** AMERICAN POET,
> SONGWRITER & SINGER

> *"The trouble with a kitten is that...*
> *Eventually....*
> *It becomes a cat!"*
>
> – **OGDEN NASH** (1902-1971),
> AMERICAN HUMORIST & POET

Some final words about trusts

Whether you set up a traditional pet trust or a statutory pet trust, there are several points to consider.

- The cost to set up a trust for your dog will be similar to the cost of setting up a trust for your daughter. The amount of time your lawyer will spend is similar in both cases.
- You will need documents to deal with your pets if you become incapable of looking after them through physical or mental disability.
- The more complicated you make the conditions of the trust, the more it will cost in legal fees to set up and administer.
- If you have a large estate with no, or few, relatives and friends, resist the temptation to leave your entire estate in trust to your pets. Judges may see such behavior as a sign that your mental faculties were slipping. Instead, leave enough to care for your pets and the remainder to charities – perhaps charities that will benefit a large number of animals.

If you fear that a relative or other would-be beneficiary may challenge your last wishes on the grounds of competency, you may want to obtain notarized statements from medical professionals who would attest to your state of mind at the present time and on the date you signed your testamentary documents. You may also want your attorney to make a video recording in which you clearly restate the wishes expressed in your will and powers of attorney.

You may also slip in a paragraph stating that any beneficiary who challenges your last will and testament will automatically forfeit his or her inheritance. That usually makes most people think twice about launching a challenge, assuming you left them enough property that they see a contest as not worth the risk.

Tax issues

Remember that, even though most American states recognize pet trusts, the U.S. Internal Revenue Code does not give them special treatment. That means that a trust with a pet as beneficiary, or with an animal as the life-in-being, does not receive any of the estate and income tax benefits that accrue to a trust which is charitable in nature.

Needless to say, the tax laws in most other countries also require that both the beneficiary and the life in being be human.

A special note about dogs adopted through agencies devoted to saving abused, neglected or unwanted dogs of certain specific breeds

There are organizations that serve as champions for almost every type of popular breed of dogs. They rescue animals that are in trouble for one reason or another, and care for them until they can find them suitable homes.

For example, there are organizations that take in and then adopt out greyhounds that are past their racing prime and are unwanted by their previous owners. These animals would likely be destroyed, were it not for the kind and dedicated people who staff these groups.

Some of these organizations ask the people who adopt their animals to sign a special contract when they receive an animal.

Said Lynda Seed, Executive Director of Adopt-A-Greyhound of Central Canada:

> *"In the case of our organization, greyhound adopters sign a contract, at the time of adoption stipulating that if at any time during the life of their greyhound they are unable to keep the dog, it cannot be given to someone else, sold or turned over to a shelter, but must be returned to our program. This is to ensure that none of these greyhounds fall between the cracks and perhaps end up going into situations with people who are unfamiliar with the unique needs and requirements of these retired athletes."*

> *"To the best of my knowledge, this contract policy is fairly 'standard' among greyhound adoption groups."*

Other groups of this type may require adopters to sign a similar agreement. Anyone who has received an animal through such an organization will have to take any such contract into account when planning for their pet's future.

CHAPTER 12

Planning for your pet's death

SUMMARY

- If you want your pet cremated, buried or immortalized on the Internet, make the arrangements yourself, consider prepaying any costs involved, and pass along to your caregiver the information needed to carry out your plans.
- Make plans assuming you will die before your pet. Such plans will likely be modest. If you happen to outlive your pet and wish to do more, you can obviously expand on your plans.
- Be aware of the wide variety of options for dealing with your pet after it has died.
- If you leave your pet's body for disposal with someone else, such as a veterinarian or animal control organization, ask how they deal with it (unless you don't care).
- Question the proprietors of pet cemeteries and investigate their business to ensure your pet's remains will not be disturbed or the site abandoned.
- There are a variety of cremation services for pets, including individual, group or mass cremation. Decide which option you want.

What do you want to happen when your pet dies?

At some point your pet is going to die. In most states and countries, there are few, if any, regulations or laws governing the disposition of pet animal bodies. (Farm animals are a different matter, and if your pet is a donkey or goat, there may indeed be government regulations to consider.) In any case, it is your responsibility, or the responsibility of the caregiver, to make after-death arrangements for your pet.

It is unfair to ask a caregiver to make complex after-death arrangements that require time and effort, even if you have left sufficient funds to pay for them. If you want to have your pet cremated, buried or immortalized in poetry on an Internet virtual pet cemetery site, make these arrangements yourself and consider prepaying any costs involved. Just make sure your caregiver is aware of these arrangements and has the information needed to carry them out. If you think it's necessary, you can detail your plans in your will or pet trust.

The type of arrangements you make, or ask your caregiver to execute, will depend on several factors – your beliefs about an afterlife and whether animals are part of that afterlife, your values in terms of respect for animals, the type of pet you have, your financial limitations, how your arrangements will be perceived by friends and family, and so on. Everyone is different and only you can decide how you want to handle the matter.

> *"If there are no dogs in Heaven, then*
> *when I die I want to go where they went."*
> – **WILL ROGERS** (1879-1935), AMERICAN HUMORIST
>
> *"The dog is a gentleman; I hope to go*
> *to his heaven, not man's."*
> – FROM A LETTER TO W. D. HOWELLS FROM
> **MARK TWAIN** (1835-1910), AMERICAN HUMORIST,
> NOVELIST, SHORT STORY AUTHOR & WIT

Remember too, if you are still relatively young, but are prudently setting up a safety net to provide for your pet just in case, you may actually outlive your pet. That means any final arrangements you make and prepay now will be in place while you are still alive. The problem is this: you might have made different arrangements, had you known you would outlive your pet.

How can you cover both eventualities? Why not make your arrangements assuming that you will die first? That suggests your arrangements will be modest. After all, there would be little point in planning an expensive cremation and arranging to purchase a fancy urn in which to house your cat's ashes if you could not attend the ceremony and claim the urn. If you happen to outlive your pet, you can always expand your minimal arrangements to reflect the fact that you are alive to celebrate a more elaborate goodbye to an old friend.

Keeping in mind that everyone's views on the subject of after-death arrangements for a pet are individual, and remembering that you may want to upgrade a basic set of arrangements to something more elaborate if you outlive your pet, you should be aware of the various options open to you. You might, for example:

- Allow a veterinarian to dispose of your pet's body.
- Ask your local animal control organization to dispose of the body.
- Bury your pet in a pet cemetery.
- Have your pet cremated at a pet cremation facility and its ashes either returned to you (or someone you designate), buried in a pet cemetery, or scattered at an outdoor columbarium.
- Bury your pet on private property (where allowed by law).
- Commemorate your pet on a virtual pet cemetery or commemorative Internet web page.

Let's look at each of these alternatives in more detail.

Allow a veterinarian to dispose of your pet's body

Many pets die or are put to sleep at a veterinarian's clinic. Owners often ask the vet to dispose of the remains. Even if a pet dies at home, many pet owners will request that their vet pick up the body and provide this service. For some people, it is a matter of economy. The vet provides the least expensive option, short of burying their pet themselves in their back yard, if they have one.

A few pet owners may find the vet to be the least emotionally painful option. A burial and ceremony can be draining. Others may go the vet route for the opposite reason – they may have formed no sentimental bond to a large caiman or python, and see no problem having their vet dispose of its body.

Remember, however, that veterinarians generally have a several options themselves for disposing of deceased pets that have been left at their clinics or hospitals. The bodies may be sent to:

- local land fill sites,
- rendering plants,
- incinerators,
- cremation facilities for communal or individual cremation, or
- local pet cemeteries for communal or individual burial.

The final decision is yours. If you care about what will happen to your pet's remains, ask your vet how he or she normally handles the disposal of deceased animals and what options are available. It is then up to you to decide if one of the options is acceptable. If not, you have the right to claim your pet's body and have someone else deal with it as you wish.

Ask your local animal control organization to dispose of the body

Some animal control organizations will dispose of a dead pet. Again, these organizations may have a number of disposal options. You need to ask questions about how the remains are handled by the organizations in your area. If you are uncomfortable with the answers you get, or if the organizations are evasive or unclear on the subject, you may want to look at other options.

Bury your pet in a pet cemetery

Many people think the idea of burying pets in their own cemeteries is a relatively new one, tied to a society where pets occupy an increasingly important place in the lives of their owners. Not true. The pharaohs of ancient Egypt established a memorial resting place for cats at the time the Old Testament was being written. Cats were sometimes mummified and buried with mummified mice to snack on in the afterlife.

Indeed, the oldest recorded cat name is *Bouhaki*, which dates back to Egyptian writings of 2000 B.C. In the hieroglyphics of the period, *bou* was the symbol for house and *haki* signified divine ruler. Many cat owners can attest to the fact that all modern cats believe they are descended from old *Bouhaki*, the "divine ruler of the house."

Chinese emperors maintained a dog cemetery in Beijing, with tombstones of marble, ivory and precious metals. Pet cemeteries are found throughout Europe, several dating back hundreds of years. The oldest known pet cemetery in the Americas was reportedly uncovered in Green County, Illinois, by archaeologist Dr. Stewart Schrever, who thinks pets were buried there by native Americans in about 6500 B.C.

At present, there are commercial pet cemeteries in many countries of the world, with between 600 and 700 operating in the United States alone, offering a variety of services and products, including memorial grave stones, pet photo frames, pet caskets, pet loss books, lifelike animal figurines and stuffed animals, clothing, jewelry, flowers and more.

The oldest operating American pet cemetery is the Hartsdale Pet Cemetery in New York State, established in 1896. The largest pet cemetery in the

- **300,000 mummified cats.**
Ancient Egyptians believed cats were sacred animals and the entire family would shave off their eyebrows as a sign of mourning when the family cat died. In 1888, an estimated 300,000 mummified cats were found at Beni Hassan, Egypt. They were sold at $18.43 per ton, and shipped to England to be ground up and used for fertilizer.

- **Cat most popular pet.**
According to recent studies, the domestic cat is the world's most popular pet. In the United States alone there are approximately 73 milion owned cats. Three in 10, or 34.7 million U.S. households own at least one cat. One half of cat-owning households (49%) own one cat; the remaining households own two or more cats.

- **Catnip leads to catnapping.**
Roughly three-quarters of all cats respond to catnip, an herb known to humans for at least two millennia. Cats generally find catnip pleasant and become more playful under its influence. Its effects last about 15 minutes after, which it stops affecting the cat. Cats usually appear relaxed and often take a catnap after playing with catnip.

- **Fraidy cats.** Julius Caesar, Henry II, Charles XI and Napoleon were all ailurophobes, which means they were afraid of cats.

country is Bide-A-Wee Home Association, also located in New York. The Bide-A-Wee organization incorporates satellite pet cemeteries and has more than 5,000 pets in one site alone. One of the Bide-A-Wee sites is the final resting place of *Checkers*, former U.S. President Richard Nixon's dog.

Most cemeteries operate in conjunction with other pet-related businesses – boarding kennels, grooming salons, training centers and veterinarian hospitals. Some human cemeteries have set aside a portion of their grounds for pet burials.

What should you look for in a pet cemetery? For one thing, it should be *deeded* to assure pet owners that their pet's remains will not be disturbed by land development. Access to the cemetery should be guaranteed, should development occur on surrounding lands. And the cemetery should also maintain a care fund (as do human cemeteries), so money will be available for ongoing maintenance of the grounds and roadways.

It would also be wise to investigate any site you are looking at and apply some common sense. If the cemetery is owned by an elderly couple with no offspring, perhaps they will be unable to sell the business when they can no longer carry on.

In one such instance, the 78-year-old owner of a pet cemetery in Florida told customers in 2001 that she would close the 30-year-old facility in June of that year because she could not find help to maintain it. The cemetery was the final resting place of thousand of pets. She gave her clients a choice: transfer the remains and headstones, etc., by the fall of the year or lose the right to do so. A feud broke out between the owner and some customers, who decided to fight the closing.

One family, who had invested $1,300 in memorials for four pets, accused the owner of violating her agreement to watch over the graves. Now they were being asked to move them. Since the cemetery is still listed in a number of online directories, a solution may have been found.

> *"You think dogs will not be in heaven? I tell you, they will be there long before any of us."*
> – **ROBERT LOUIS STEVENSON** 1850-1894, SCOTTISH-BORN WRITER

> *"When a human dies, there is a bridge they must cross to enter into heaven. At the head of that bridge waits every animal that human encountered during his or her lifetime. The animals, based upon what they know of these persons, decide which humans may cross the bridge – and which are turned away."* – NATIVE AMERICAN LEGEND

The costs for burial in a pet cemetery vary, depending on where you live, the size of the animal you want buried, and whether or not you want, or need, to use a casket. Most pet cemeteries insist on caskets. To give you an idea of what to expect in the United States, the price for burial of a small pet ranges from $350 to $600, depending on the type of casket and grave marker selected.

The range for large animals is $425 to $800 or more, depending on the actual size of the animal. Some cemeteries base their price on the pet's weight; others on its length.

Have your pet cremated at a pet cremation facility and its ashes returned to you, buried in a pet cemetery or scattered at an outdoor columbarium

Most pet cemeteries offer cremation services for pets. The ashes, called cremains, may be buried in the cemetery or returned to you (or someone you designate) in an urn or other container. Some cemetery operators have set aside a part of their property on which clients can scatter the cremains of their pet if they don't want to take them home or buy a burial plot.

A wide range of cremation services are available, although not all are offered by all cremation facilities. These include:

Individual cremation: The top of the line is the individual cremation service. Pets are cremated one at a time, the ashes are removed and the cremation chamber is cleaned, ready for the next pet.

Group cremation: Fifteen or more deceased pets, separated by a few inches, are cremated at the same time in an extra large cremation chamber. The ashes can be divided among the pets' owners.

Mass cremation: The bodies of as many pets as possible are placed into the cremation chamber without any separation. They are cremated together.

Some cremation services offer additional services, such as delivering your pet's ashes to your home, burial at sea, and so on. If you chose to have your pet's ashes returned, you can keep them in an urn or other memorial container, bury them, scatter them over an area favored by your pet, or make use of a commercial service which buries or scatters ashes at an outdoor columbarium.

Or you may want to try something more creative. One man, for example, placed the ashes of his Labrador retriever inside a bigfoot goose decoy "so she can continue to hunt with us."

If a bigfoot goose decoy isn't your thing, a Chicago company, LifeGem Memorials, has developed a method of applying heat and pressure to ashes (animal or human) to turn them into diamonds.

Like burial in a cemetery, costs for cremation vary according to the weight or size of your pet, and whether you want it cremated individually or as part of a group. You will be looking at anywhere from $100 for a small pet to $400 or more for a large animal.

Bury your pet on private property (where allowed by law)

Local or county ordinances determine what types of animals can or cannot be buried on private property. Authorities sometimes pass laws prohibiting the burial of larger animals, such as cats and dogs, to reduce the health hazards caused by other animals digging them up. If you are in doubt, check with your lawyer or local health authorities to find out whether it is legal to bury your pet in the back yard. If your pet is a small animal, such as a hamster, it is doubtful you need worry about such laws.

If you do decide to bury your pet at home, place the body in a thick plastic bag and then in a metal or wood box. Place the box in a hole that is at least three feet (one meter) deep. These steps will prevent other animals from digging around the area of the grave. Be certain the area is clear of drains, underground pipes and utility lines, wells, springs and the like.

Many bereaved pet owners mark their pet's grave with a gravestone or memorial plaque, and perhaps bury it in a special place in the yard, such as under a tree or near a flower bed. One person used a smooth rock from a beach and wrote her own memorial on it in black paint, placing it atop her pet's grave in the backyard.

The services and trappings associated with pet burial and cremation help pet owners pay respect to their animal friends and provide an outlet for their sorrow. If you happen to outlive your pet, you may want to take advantage of some of them. But if you die before your pet, many of these extras will be lost on you. That's why it is wise to make some basic arrangements with the idea you will die first and, if you wish, upgrade later if your pet dies before you do.

Marking your pet's grave

Regardless of where you bury your pet's remains, you may want a headstone or marker to denote the spot. Companies that make headstones for human remains would likely consider making them for pets as well. If not, you might check the Internet or the yellow pages for suppliers in your area.

Commemorate your pet on a virtual pet cemetery or commemorative Internet web page

Internet sites that offer pet owners a place where they can commemorate their pets are hugely popular. These are places where people can write epitaphs for favorite pets: cats, dogs, birds or even rabbits. These heart-felt personal stories, memorials and poems run the gamut of emotion, from sad to funny.

Many of the virtual sites are extensions of real pet cemeteries, or tied to other pet-related businesses. Some charge a fee for the service they offer; many more ask for a donation, and others are free.

One of the first Internet sites, the Virtual Pet Cemetery (www.mycemetery. com) was created as an experiment in 1995 by LavaMind, a San Francisco-based software development company. The response? An avalanche of visitors within the first few weeks. People loved the idea of immortalizing their recently deceased pets on the World Wide Web.

The Virtual Pet Cemetery went on to grab media attention around the world. It has been featured on PBS, the Discovery Channel, ZDTV, NHK TV, as well as many European television stations. *Entertainment Weekly*, *LA Times*, *New York Times*, *London Independent*, *Newsweek*, and many other magazines and newspapers have written it up.

Over the years, the Virtual Pet Cemetery has become the world's best known and most loved online burial ground. Thousands of visitors from around the globe visit the site every day to read and share the epitaphs. It provides an outlet for this very personal experience, allowing pet owners to bond with others, leave epitaphs and find friends with similar interests.

Final thoughts on the death of a pet

A few final thoughts on the death of a pet: if, indeed, you outlive your pet and find it difficult to cope with the loss, there are pet loss support centers or grief counselors who can help you. Your vet or local animal shelter or humane society branch should be able to put you in touch. If not, check out (www.petloss.com) on the Internet, or see *Appendix M* for more information.

Don't feel silly or shy away from getting help with your grief. Society is becoming increasingly aware of the important role pets play in our lives and the emotional pain involved in a pet's death. In some cases, a beloved dog or cat may be all the family a person has.

A Canadian man, for instance, felt so strongly about the death of his dog that he placed a six-inch death notice, complete with photograph, in the front section of a local newspaper. He told a reporter for the *Toronto Star* that he wished it could have run on the births and deaths page.

"He had just as much right to be in the deaths column as anyone else in it," the man said in an October 19, 2002 article. *"In fact I would argue that he was better than lots of people in there."*

> *"If I have any beliefs about immortality, it is that certain dogs I have known will go to heaven, and very, very few persons."* – **JAMES THURBER** (1894-1961), AMERICAN AUTHOR, CARTOONIST, HUMORIST & SATIRIST

> *"Heaven goes by favor. If it went by merit, you would stay out and your dog would go in."*
> – **MARK TWAIN** (1835-1910), AMERICAN HUMORIST, NOVELIST, SHORT STORY AUTHOR & WIT

CHAPTER 13

Dealing with exotic pets

OVERVIEW

- Some people believe they can bequeath their exotic pet to the local zoo. In fact, most zoos refuse such gifts.
- If you do not have a plan in place for the care of your exotic pet after you die or become disabled, chances are it will end up in an animal shelter and be put down.
- In the United States, a patchwork of federal, state, and local laws regulate the keeping of certain species of animals.
- If your pet is simply unusual (rather than one that is banned in your area), the major challenge you face in arranging for its care should you die or lose capacity is finding a willing and competent caregiver.
- If you are keeping an animal in violation of the laws in your area, you will need to find a caregiver willing to risk fines and perhaps jail time to care for your pet. The caregiver will also have to ensure security (if the pet is dangerous) and find a veterinarian willing to provide routine and emergency services.
- Anyone who cannot find a caregiver for an exotic pet can check the Internet for organizations that will adopt or find homes for such animals.

The controversy about exotic pets

Although animal activists discourage the buying, selling and keeping of exotic pets, the fact is many people ignore their advice. Scorpions, tarantulas, caimans, poisonous and constricting snakes, big cats of all kinds, wolves – you name it and someone likely has one as a pet. There are arguments for and against exotic pets. And there are plenty of books and websites dedicated to both sides of the debate. Regardless of the arguments, one thing is clear: any animal kept as a pet deserves to be looked after properly, should its owner die or become incapacitated.

But unless an exotic pet owner belongs to a club or society composed of like-minded individuals, he or she may have difficulty finding a willing and competent caregiver for, say, a leopard or a rattlesnake.

Some people believe they can solve the problem by bequeathing their exotic pet to the local zoo. In fact, most zoos will refuse such gifts. They have limited space, tight operating budgets, and rigid acquisition policies and programs that generally exclude accepting abandoned or survivor animals. They may also be concerned that such animals may harbor communicable diseases or have other physical or psychological problems. Besides, all the zoos and accredited institutions in existence could not accommodate the thousands of exotic pets that are cast off each year, either because they are unwanted or because they are survivors of deceased humans.

If you have an exotic pet and do not have a plan in place for its care after you are no longer able to look after it, chances are it will end up in an animal shelter that will put it down, either because it cannot find new home for it, or because it feels there is no place for exotic animals in human society. Many would argue that adopting out such animals could suggest that the shelter or organization approved of exotic pets; most don't. Rightly or wrongly, shelter organizations feel that private individuals cannot provide the proper care and environment for most exotic animals.

> *"I think dogs are the most amazing creatures; they give unconditional love. For me they are the role model for being alive."* – **GILDA RADNER** (1946-1989), AMERICAN COMEDIAN

> *"I like pigs. Dogs look up to us. Cats look down on us. Pigs treat us as equals."* – **SIR WINSTON CHURCHILL** (1874-1965), BRITISH POLITICIAN, PRIME MINISTER & WAR LEADER

Exotic pets and the law

There is another aspect to exotic animal ownership you need to consider as well. In the United States, a patchwork of federal, state and local laws regulate the keeping of certain species of animals.

U.S. federal laws. Three federal laws regulate exotic animals – the *Endangered Species Act*, the *Public Health Service Act* and the *Lacey Act*.

Under the *Endangered Species Act* (ESA) it is illegal to possess, sell or buy any animal that is a member of an endangered species.

The *Public Health Services Act* prohibits anyone from importing non-human primates and their offspring into the United States after October 1975, other than for scientific, educational or exhibition purposes. But, unless it can be proved that a specific primate or its ancestors entered the country after October 1975, the act is unenforceable. Most people are unaware of their animal's heritage and it is nearly impossible to trace its origin.

The *Lacey Act* allows the U.S. government to prosecute anyone who owns an animal that has been illegally obtained in a foreign country or another state.

U.S. state laws. State governments can also regulate exotic animals held privately. Laws vary among states regarding the type of regulation imposed and the specific animals regulated. A number of states ban private possession of exotic animals (including large cats, bears, wolves, non-human primates and dangerous reptiles). Others have a partial ban (some define exotic animals but not all). A few require a license or permit to possess certain exotic animals. The remaining states neither prohibit nor require a license, but they may require some information from the possessor (veterinarian certificate, certification that an animal was legally acquired, etc.).

U.S. local laws. Many cities and counties in the United States have adopted ordinances that are tougher than state laws, forbidding their residents from owning certain exotic species that might threaten the health, safety and/or welfare of other residents. They usually base their determinations on the physical attributes or natural behavior of a certain species, or on whether an individual of the species has attacked someone in the community.

While it is understandable that various levels of government are involved in regulating the trade and ownership of exotic animals, the result can be confusion for ordinary pet owners.

Take, for example, the U.S. laws that apply to domesticated ferrets. Under federal law, and the laws of 48 states, you may keep ferrets as pets. Only California and Hawaii have banned this member of the weasel family outright. But even if you live in a state that permits ferrets, your county or city ordinances may prohibit them. For instance, if you live in any of the five boroughs of New York City, or in Minneapolis, Indianapolis or Dallas, local laws forbid you to keep ferrets, despite federal and state laws permitting them.

While restrictive laws may deter some folks, others simply thumb their noses at them. People who are determined to obtain an animal that has been banned in their area may purchase one locally on the black market, buy one in a jurisdiction where the animals are not banned and bring it home or, increasingly, make their purchase over the Internet and have it shipped by special courier.

Let's look again at California. Despite the ban on ferrets, an estimated half a million or more of the little creatures live with their human owners in the state. Many of those owners paid as much as $800 for a pet that can sell for as little as $60 in other states.

The scope of the exotic pet phenomenon

And if you think such activities are rare, think again. Although accurate statistics on exotic animals, legally or illegally kept, are understandably difficult to come by, research suggests the figures are astounding. Lions, tigers, cougars, bears, monkeys, snakes and other reptiles, wallabies and obscure rodents live in bedrooms, basements and backyards across much of the world. Unfortunately, many of their owners are astonishingly ignorant of their needs.

Estimates for the number of one species alone – tigers – held privately in the United States run from 6,000 to 7,000 animals. If that estimate is accurate, there are more privately held tigers in the United States than there are wild tigers in all of Asia. The Save the Tiger Fund estimates there are fewer than 5,000 tigers left in the wild in Asia, and only about 1,000 tigers held in accredited zoos worldwide.

Many exotic pets are available cheaply and conveniently. In some instances, a tiger cub may cost about the same as a purebred puppy. But as it grows, it loses its cuteness and becomes a huge, wild, ferocious beast. Should its owner die or become too ill to care for it, who will assume responsibility for it? Likely no one, and it will be euthanized.

It takes only a few moments of browsing on the Internet to realize that the commerce in exotic creatures is big business in the United States and worldwide. Hundreds, if not thousands, of websites, domestic and international, are dedicated to the buying, selling, trading and care of exotics. Others sell specialized food and equipment for a wide variety of such animals.

Yet there are justifiable concerns associated with the keeping of exotic pets. Early in 2009, for example, a 14-year-old, 200-pound (90-kilogram) pet chimpanzee in Stamford, Connecticut, left a woman in critical condition after attacking her and mutilating her face and hands. The chimp's owner, tried to stop the attack and was also injured and briefly hospitalized. The victim was in critical condition and required extensive surgery.

While large exotic animals often grab the headlines because their owners have done something irresponsible or stupid, there is good reason to suspect that most exotic pets are rather small. The growth in ownership of exotic pets is often attributed to the fact that more and more people live in buildings that are too small for traditional pets or where larger animals, such as dogs and cats, are banned. Smaller animals and exotics have become an alternative.

In Canada, the Pet Industry Joint Advisory Council (PIJAC) has developed a list of animals it feels should not be kept as pets (See *Appendix M*), but the issue is being discussed at the municipal level across the country. To date, certain exotic animals are banned in some municipalities in several provinces (British Columbia, Newfoundland, Nova Scotia and Quebec).

Many countries are becoming wary of imported exotic animals because of their potential for carrying dangerous diseases. In 2005, for example, two parrots that had been imported into the U.K. from South America were found to have had a deadly strain of avian flu. Fortunately, their illness was discovered while they were being held in quarantine and did not have a chance to mingle with other birds in the U.K.

Today, many countries are reviewing their regulations governing the importation of exotic animals, especially those captured in the wild, and are devising new ways to control their movement and, by extension, the spread of possibly harmful pathogens. In July 2003, the British medical journal *Lancet* stated: "The practice of taking animals from the wild for the pet trade should swiftly be brought to an end."

The U.S. Center for Disease Control has said some exotic species could pose "a significant threat" to public health, domestic animals, agriculture and wildlife.

Most Australian states and territories regulate the private keeping of exotic animals within their borders. Those laws set out the number of animals, types of animals, and conditions under which animals can be kept. If you live in Australia and wish to acquire an exotic animal, indigenous or import, check first with local, state and national officials.

New Zealanders should heed the same advice. The country's pre-human environment was largely devoid of land animals, although there were plenty of bird and fish species. Today, domestic animals, such as sheep, pigs, cattle, horses, dogs, cats and other imports are widespread. While New Zealanders are enthusiastic pet owners, private ownership of most exotic animals, particularly reptiles and big cats, is prohibited. And snakes, which are not native to New Zealand, are not even permitted in zoos, because they would damage the ecosystem if they escaped.

In the U.K., laws governing the keeping of exotic animals are weakly drafted and enforced, according to the Royal Society for the Prevention of Cruelty to Animals. Perhaps as a result, the trade in exotic pets is flourishing, especially in reptiles and amphibians. Iguanas are the most commonly traded exotic reptiles. It is estimated that a single legal shipment of green iguanas entering the U.K. can contain 2,000-5,000 animals. Boas, pythons, chameleons and geckos are imported and traded privately and in pet shops. By some counts, the U.K. imports more than one million live reptiles and amphibians annually.

And in 2005, one of these reptiles, a boa constrictor named *Keith*, demonstrated why governments, animal activists and the general population are, or should be, concerned about exotic pets. *Keith* was apparently abandoned when its owner was evicted from his flat in Manchester. For nearly three months, *Keith* slithered in and out of toilet bowls throughout flats in the building, and was spotted by several terrified tenants, who put bricks on toilet seats to keep the 3.5 meter (10-foot) animal from popping out of the bowl.

 FACTOIDS

- **Cheetahs.** The Sumerians were the first people known to tame cheetahs while the Egyptians actually deified them. Marco Polo noted that many were kept as pets in the Orient, far beyond their native range. Three historical figures are documented as having pet cheetahs: Genghis Khan, Akbar the Great of India and Charlemagne. During his 45-year reign (1555-1600 AD) Akbar reportedly kept 9,000 cheetahs and attempted to breed them. But, for all his efforts, only one litter was produced.

- **Llamas.** In addition to being good pets, llamas can make great livestock guardians, protecting herds against dog and fox attacks.

- **Hmmmmm.** Llamas communicate by humming and through a series of ear, body and tail postures. If threatened they may issue a distinctive alarm to alert other llamas or humans.

- **Ferrets.** Ferrets make great pets, but require more time and attention than a dog or a cat, and are not recommended as pets for children under eight unless older family members are helping out.

Firefighters eventually began to believe the agitated tenants and responded with high-tech fiber optics to check sewer lines. They found no trace of *Keith*, but one bleary-eyed resident came face-to-face with him on his bathroom floor late one night and managed to trap him.

Local RSPCA officials said snakes can swim well, hold their breath for more than 20 minutes and have no problem living in sewer pipes and eating rats. Most such snakes, however, are not as large as *Keith*.

Other exotic wildlife commonly featured in the U.K. pet trade includes birds and tropical fish. Bird keeping has long been popular, and exotic parrots and finches are traded in large numbers. Falconry, in particular, has steadily increased. Again, the fear of bird flu may cause U.K. authorities to tighten import and trade regulations.

The tropical fish and aquarium trade is also very large in the U.K., but it is mostly unregulated and, therefore, its extent is difficult to quantify.

> *"A dog is not almost-human, and I know of no greater insult to the canine race than to describe it as such."*
> – **JOHN HOLMES** (1904-1962), ENGLISH POET

> *"The dog has seldom been successful in pulling man up to its level of sagacity, but man has frequently dragged a dog down to his."* – **JAMES THURBER** (1894-1961), AMERICAN AUTHOR, CARTOONIST, HUMORIST & SATIRIST

Finding care for your exotic (but legal) pet

If you keep a pet that is simply unusual (rather than one that is banned in your area), the major challenge you may face in arranging for its care should you die or lose capacity, will be finding a willing and competent caregiver. In addition to the points listed under choosing a caregiver in Chapter 2, you should also consider the following:

Legal status of your pet in the caregiver's jurisdiction. While a specific pet may be legally kept in your area, it may be banned where your prospective caregiver lives. If it is, you will be asking your caregiver to break the law. You need to check the law carefully in the area where your chosen caregiver lives.

Special traits. Your caregiver must be familiar with the species of animal you are asking him or her to look after and be prepared to deal with any of its special traits. Kangaroos, for example, can jump long distances; tigers eat huge quantities of meat (and can jump long distances); adult raccoons are smart and destructive; some snakes only eat live food.

Veterinarian services. If you chose a caregiver who lives some distance from you, that person must have access to a veterinarian who is willing and competent to deal with your animal. Not all vets are qualified to treat a 6-foot-long alligator or a 400-pound tiger. Not all want to.

Consider the case of *Houdini*, a 12-foot (3.5-meter) Burmese python who swallowed a queen-size electric blanket, complete with electrical cord and control box, in July 2006. The blanket's wiring extended through about 8 feet (2.5 meters) of the 60-pound (27-kilogram) reptile's digestive tract.

Local veterinarians had to call up several specialists for advice on where to operate on the snake to remove the blanket. The snake's owner (not to mention *Houdini* himself) was fortunate there were vets willing to take the trouble.

Proper accommodation. If your exotic pet is large, or has special exercise needs, its caregiver will need to provide proper accommodation for it. A monkey, for example, will need an area where it can climb and swing.

Security. If your pet can be construed as dangerous, review safety considerations with the caregiver and put important points in writing. For example, write down how high a fenced enclosure must be to prevent your jaguar from leaping over the top. Wolf-dogs are notorious escape artists and are particularly adept at digging their way out of a standard dog run. Write down the types of barriers that will be needed to prevent your pet from hitting the road.

What to do with an illegal animal

If you are keeping an animal in deliberate violation of national or local laws, you have additional problems if you want to provide for its future. To start with, you will need to find a caregiver willing to risk legal penalties, should local authorities discover the prohibited animal. Given the possible penalties for keeping such an animal, will that person risk taking it to a vet for routine care, such as checkups and shots, or to treat it for diseases or injury? While many vets will not report an illegal pet (because they know what the authorities will do with it), they may not want to treat it anyway.

If you die or suffer a stroke or other physically disabling problem, the authorities may find your pet before it is transferred to your caregiver. It would likely be confiscated and destroyed. You, or your estate, could be fined.

Technically, when you die, your executor takes charge of your estate and discharges all of the duties normally associated with the job. Any illegal animal you own at the time of your death would become part of your estate and the responsibility of the executor, who would be obliged to take all appropriate legal steps to deal with it. These steps may not be in keeping with the plans you have made for the pet. In other words, the six-foot-crocodile you raised from a baby could wind up at the local animal control shelter, living on borrowed time.

> *"If a dog will not come to you after having looked you in the face, you should go home and examine your conscience."* – **WOODROW WILSON** (1913-1921), 28th PRESIDENT OF THE UNITED STATES

> *"When a man's dog turns against him, it is time for his wife to pack her trunk and go home to mamma."*
> – **MARK TWAIN** (1835-1910), AMERICAN HUMORIST, NOVELIST, SHORT STORY AUTHOR & WIT

If you can't find a caregiver

If you are unable to find a suitable permanent caregiver for your exotic pet (legal or otherwise), you still have some options that may keep it safe.

For example, there is an Internet website that provides free exotic animal adoption/placement services. Located at www.altpet.net/adopt.html, the site provides a listing for people with unwanted exotic pets and people willing to take in unwanted exotic pets. This site is heavily weighted toward the United States, Canada and the United Kingdom, but covers other parts of the world as well. The service is free, but donations or purchases from the bookstore are appreciated to help defray operating costs.

You may be able to contact someone through this site to serve as caregiver for your pet, or you might ask a family member or your estate's executor to use the site to find a home for your pet, should you die or become incapacitated. Unfortunately, it will likely be difficult to verify that the home chosen for your pet is a good one and that it is receiving proper care.

Other organizations you, or someone you designate, might contact to make arrangements for an exotic pet are:

- **East Coast Exotic Animal Rescue.** A non-profit haven for unwanted exotic animals. Located in Fairfield, Pennsylvania. www.eastcoastrescue.org
- **Ferret & Reptile Rescue Sanctuary.** Located in Utah, also rescues some domestic animals. www.petfinder.com/shelters/ferretreptile.html
- **Just Skunks.** Non-profit shelter specializing in the domestic skunk. Information on Skunkfest, information about skunk care, photographs and membership application. Located in Avon Lake, Ohio. www.justskunks.com
- **Love of Animals.** Exotic pet information, photographs, rescue information and links. http://members.tripod.com/loveanimals0/index.htm
- **Rattie Ratz:** Rescue, Resource and Referral. Provides rescue, rehabilitation and adoption services for rats, mice, guinea pigs, hamsters, rabbits and chinchillas. www.rattieratz.com
- **Scalesandtails.** A non-profit online animal adoption and animal rescue place for ferrets, iguanas, reptiles and snakes. www.scalesandtails.org
- **Triad Exotic Animal Rescue.** A federally and state licensed, non-profit organization dedicated to the rescue and rehabilitation of small exotic animals. www.allcreaturesrescue.org/rescue.php

If you live in Australia, New Zealand, the U.K. or Canada, turn to Exotic Animal/Alternative Pet Shelter, Rescue and/or Adoption Groups, respectively for a short list of organizations that will help you with exotic pet placement.

www.altpet.net/Rescue/Australia.html,
www.altpet.net/Rescue/NewZealand.html,
www.altpet.net/Rescue/UK.html, and
www.altpet.net/Rescue/CANADA.html.

You might also check Rescue Groups/Shelters/Sanctuaries (listed by location) at: www.altpet.net/Rescue/index.html.

It should be pointed out that these represent only a fraction of the organizations that exist for the purpose of rescuing or finding homes for exotic animals. If you have access to the Internet, either at home or at a local library, you should be able to find many others in your area.

Some people believe they can simply turn their exotic pets loose. To do so may have negative impacts on the animal, the environment and other people. Consider the following:

- If the animal is not native to the area where it is turned loose, it may (but not always) be condemned to die of starvation or the elements.
- In the United States, it is against federal law to turn any animal loose into the wild, unless it is native to the area and you have permits for rehabilitating it into the wild. Laws in other jurisdictions may be similar.

The reasons for such laws are obvious. Aside from the cruelty to some animals let loose in an unfamiliar and even hostile environment, releasing exotics can also endanger indigenous wild animals, local pets, and even people.

For example, in the year 2000, the British Broadcasting Corporation reported that an estimated 100 leopards and pumas were roaming the British countryside. These were apparently the offspring of animals released by owners in the 1970s after the introduction of stringent laws governing the private keeping of wild and dangerous animals.

And almost everyone in North America is aware of the problem of the Burmese pythons in the Florida Everglades. Presumably the result of released pets, the snakes can grow to over 20 feet long and more than 250 pounds. According to state wildlife managers, they pose a danger to state- and federally listed threatened and endangered species, as well as to humans. Some estimates put their numbers in the 50,000 range in Florida.

Florida began a program in 2009 to eradicate the snakes before they eradicate the local wildlife and spread beyond the state's borders.

"There are two means of refuge from the misery of life – music and cats." – ALBERT SCHWEITZER
(1875-1965), GERMAN PHILOSOPHER, PHYSICIAN & HUMANITARIAN

"Until one has loved an animal, a part of one's soul remains unawakened." – ANATOLE FRANCE (1844-1924),
FRENCH AUTHOR & WINNER OF THE NOBEL PRIZE IN LITERATURE IN 1921

In conclusion, if you keep an exotic pet, be aware of the special challenges you face in preparing for its care if and when you can no longer look after it. Plan ahead with these challenges in mind, and make certain your plans are documented and in the hands of someone you trust to carry them out.

CHAPTER 14

Pet retirement homes and sanctuaries

O V E R V I E W

- Retirement homes and sanctuaries for pets are becoming increasingly popular in the United States. They may become available in other countries in the near future.
- Such facilities come in many forms – non-profit, for-profit, private and shelter-operated.
- It is generally much more expensive to send your pet to one of these retirement homes or sanctuaries than it is to provide funds to a relative or friend to care for your pet.
- You will need to do considerable research and ask a lot of questions before committing money and your pet to any of these establishments.

Gaining in popularity

Some people find retirement homes for pets a frivolous indulgence, especially because good, affordable, long-term care facilities for elderly people are scarce or non-existent in many parts of the world. Nevertheless, retirement homes for animals, operated by a variety of non-profit and for-profit organizations, are gaining in popularity, especially in the United States.

Pet retirement homes, notably those dedicated to cats and dogs, will likely become common as America's affluent baby boomers become too old, or too ill, to care for their pets and have nowhere else to send them.

Who can argue with the idea of allowing a loyal, well-loved pet to live out what is left of its life with similar animals – and with humans who will love and care for them? In many cases, the animals are free to ramble throughout a house or other living area, unconfined by chains or cages.

Remember, however, that some pets, especially older dogs, may be perpetually miserable in the care of strangers. If *Fido* has made it quite clear that he is hopelessly unhappy without you, make every effort to find a family member or friend that he knows to become his caregiver. At least he will have the comfort of being with a human with whom he is familiar and who has a connection to you. If you are disabled, he may even be able to visit with you occasionally.

Pet retirement facilities and sanctuaries come in several forms. Many are located in the country, where land may be less expensive and there is room to build dog runs, horse pastures and out-buildings. There are also such facilities in suburban areas and even cities. Some facilities will try to find new homes for pets; others will provide care until the end comes for their charges.

"If you pick up a starving dog and make him prosperous, he will not bite you. This is the principal difference between a dog and a man." – **MARK TWAIN** (1835-1910), AMERICAN HUMORIST, NOVELIST, SHORT STORY AUTHOR & WIT

"Dogs are our link to paradise. They don't know evil or jealousy or discontent. To sit with a dog on a hillside on a glorious afternoon is to be back in Eden, where doing nothing was not boring – it was peace." – MILAN KUNDERA, AWARD-WINNING CZECH NOVELIST

Homes operated by animal shelters

In the United States, some humane society shelters in the larger urban areas use separate buildings to house cats and dogs whose owners have entered retirement homes or have died. Most of the owners of these animals were either long-standing shelter members, or they gifted money to a specific shelter (before they died or in their wills) to look after their pets for the remainder of their lives.

This type of arrangement is beneficial to pet owners, pets and the shelters. The benefit to pets and their owners is obvious. Many shelters now see such arrangements as providing a steady stream of funds to contribute to their day-to-day operations. As a result, more shelters are developing or setting aside facilities for these trust-fund animals.

The experience of one well-off Texas couple illustrates how such an arrangement can be a win-win-win experience for all involved. To provide their seven dogs with lifetime protection, they donated a 4,500-square-foot luxury home near Lewisville to the SPCA of Texas.

In exchange, they have requested that, after their death, the SPCA provide around-the-clock care and medical attention to their dogs. The dogs will live in the home for the rest of their lives, and will be permitted to roam freely in the home and surrounding two-acre grounds. The home and property will also be used to house other dogs for the SPCA of Texas.

The couple feels they have a serious responsibility to their pets and want someone to look after them when they are gone, rather than having them institutionalized.

Such arrangements (willing an estate or large gift to an animal welfare group) are becoming more common, say officials in these organizations. As baby boomers get older, they worry about the future of their pets and are solving the problem through creative estate planning, rather than by relying on friends or family members to provide lifetime pet care.

Veterinarian-affiliated homes

Also in the U.S., pet retirement homes are sometimes operated in conjunction with veterinarian schools. This idea is another win-win-win situation. Pets can live out their lives in a friendly, homelike atmosphere with good medical attention; the schools receive funds through endowments; and students often obtain scholarships, accommodations and a number of animals with which to work and study.

Pets may live in family homes near the school or in special facilities attached to the school. One school suggests that potential donors bequeath their homes to the school to help build a network of pet retirement homes across the state. Any pets would continue to live in their homes but would have to share the premises with other animals during their lifetimes.

For example, Texas A&M University and the University of Minnesota College of Veterinary Medicine both operate such retirement homes for pets.

Sanctuaries for specific breeds or pets

Retirement homes for birds and horses, sometimes known as sanctuaries, have been around in many countries for much longer than similar facilities for dogs and cats. Why? Many tropical birds are long-lived and often survive their owners. Horses, too, live for several decades. Generally, such pets have been relatively expensive (to buy and maintain) and people who could afford them could also afford to make arrangements for their care.

Since it is often difficult to find an individual caregiver for a horse or a parrot, retirement homes or sanctuaries were a natural solution.

Today, the number of sanctuaries dedicated to looking after one species or one breed of animal is on the rise. Those of us who have had to temporarily board pets at mixed animal facilities know that cats are often traumatized by the experience of being in close proximity to dozens of dogs.

Similarly, some dogs become overly excited and agitated for extended periods of time when they can hear or smell cats nearby. Temporary boarding for a few days or a few weeks is one thing; a permanent retirement that may last years is quite another, and a good case can be made for species specialization under such circumstances, especially if your pet is uncomfortable with other species. Only you will know this. Some cats and dogs could care less.

Also, some owners of very small breeds of dogs may not feel comfortable retiring them to a home where Rottweilers or other large dogs roam at will. The operators of some facilities may segregate their charges by size or temperament, but if you have concerns along these lines, ask the people who run your prospective retirement home how they handle mixing the breeds. Better yet, visit the facility and see for yourself.

Privately run non-profit homes

Many non-profit retirement homes or shelters for animals are not planned as such, but simply evolve as soft-hearted animal shelter volunteers take home pets that have been left behind by deceased or institutionalized owners. These animals are usually old, sad, unwanted, and destined to be euthanized.

As the volunteers dedicate part of their houses or yards to more and more pets that they hope to place in new homes, the cost of food and vet bills grows.

What to do?

The next logical step for the volunteers is to find and persuade older pet owners, who themselves have to enter retirement homes, to pay them a sum of money in exchange for looking after their pets in the hope that it will offset their total operating expenses.

If successful, they have created a non-profit retirement home for animals.

Privately run for-profit homes

Privately run, for-profit retirement homes are often extensions of professionally operated animal boarding kennels or pet-sitting businesses, which is why they are the most common of all of the homes we have discussed. They usually accept the animals of regular clients, whose pets they have known and grown fond of over the years.

Generally, they integrate the pets into their homes so they become part of their family. Animals that are used to being part of a group will feel comfortable in such surroundings; animals that have been the sole pet in a household may not be able to adjust successfully.

Despite the for-profit label, such arrangements tend to be an informal extension of the owner's main business. If he or she agrees to take your pet, should you be unable to care for it, you should be able to come to a suitable financial arrangement and put the paperwork in place to ensure that the entire deal goes smoothly at the appropriate time.

Making a choice

How do you choose a retirement home or sanctuary for your pet? The most important factors to consider are:

- Will it be around for the entire lifespan of your pet?
- Is there financial and managerial stability?
- Is there a plan for long-term survival?

As you might imagine, facilities run by established animal shelters or universities will likely be in play for some time. They will also be well-staffed, provide good medical services, and possess a genuine commitment to the well-being of their retirement charges.

Nevertheless, do not discount the smaller establishments or their owners' dedication to animals. We suggest you research and visit as many facilities (and as many types of facilities) as you can. Ask questions, meet any staff that may be involved and try to get a feel for their qualifications and commitment.

Some points to cover in your research:

- Can you afford to send your pet to this establishment? If you can't, all other points are irrelevant. Costs can range from $5,000 to $25,000 or more, depending on the species, age and special needs of your pet and the type of establishment you select.

- How long has the operator been in business with this retirement home, or any other animal-related activity? This shouldn't necessarily be a deciding factor, but one to consider.
- How are the animals accommodated during the day? Are they allowed to roam a section of the home or property? How are they housed at night? Avoid establishments that confine pets to cages or very small areas for long periods of time.
- Are outdoor activity areas fenced against escape artists and predators?
- How are sick or injured animals handled? Which veterinary clinic is used and how far away is it? What type of illness or injury would trigger a visit by the vet? Are records kept on veterinary visits?
- How much daily interaction is there between animals and humans? Most pets, especially dogs, need some human contact every day.
- What kind of food do the animals receive? If your pet is on a special diet, can this be accommodated?
- How are the pets exercised?
- Does the establishment try to find new homes for residents? If a new owner is found for your pet, what happens to the remainder of the fee you paid to the retirement home? What if you do not want your pet to be adopted?
- What would happen to the animals should the business have to close down? Is there a plan to ensure their continued care?
- What will happen to your pet after it dies? Can you decide beforehand what you want done (and pay for it, if necessary)?

You must also consider factors that relate to any specific attributes of your pet. For example, if your pet is particularly long-lived, as are some tropical birds, you need to pay particular attention to factors pertaining to adoption, to the retirement home or sanctuary having to go out of business and the cost of what may turn out to be decades of care.

"No man can be condemned for owning a dog. As long as he has a dog, he has a friend; and the poorer he gets, the better friend he has." – WILL ROGERS
(1879-1935), AMERICAN HUMORIST

"When a man's best friend is his dog, that dog has a problem." – EDWARD ABBEY
(1927-1989), AMERICAN ENVIRONMENTALIST

To find the closest suitable retirement facility for your pet, search the Internet. If you do not have Internet access, your vet does. Ask for help. A starter list of pet retirement homes in the United States is given in **Appendix N**. Research suggests that pet retirement homes are uncommon in most other countries. If you live outside of the U.S., turn to local veterinarians, animal shelters and welfare groups, and local business directories for help locating such facilities.

Retiring with your pet

As a corollary to the concept of separate pet retirement homes, remember that, should you be forced to enter a retirement home or community due to physical or mental incapacity, you might look for one that will allow you to bring your pet along with you. Generally, pets must be small dogs, cats or birds (no snakes or rodents, please) and are subject to a variety of rules and restrictions.

Again, the Internet is your best friend in helping to find a suitable facility.

Some final words:

Hopefully, this book has helped you put together a plan to provide ongoing care for your pet, regardless of what happens to you. Some final words of advice of a general nature:

First, if you are entering anything except a very informal agreement with a friend or relative, always retain professional legal advice. Your pet's life may depend on it.

Second, do as much research as you can about the choices you are making, from the selection of a caregiver to the signing of a legal document. Ask questions, make lists, and consult with friends and relatives.

Third, review your plans on a regular basis, in case circumstances have changed. People get married and divorced, have children, move away, become rich, fall into poverty, get sick, or become unemployed – it all matters.

> *"Animals have these advantages over man: they have no theologians to instruct them, their funerals cost them nothing, and no one starts lawsuits over their wills."*
> – **VOLTAIRE** (1694–1778) FRENCH AUTHOR & PHILOSOPHER

Pampered pets of the past

Over the last four or five decades, pets have become increasingly important to many people. Yet there is much anecdotal evidence to support the argument that they have played a significant role in our lives for centuries.

While researching material for this book, we came across dozens of stories that illustrate how important pets have been for people throughout history, including many of the rich and/or famous. Here are some of those stories:

About dogs

Showered with love. The late bathroom fixture magnate, Sidney Altman of Beverly Hills, California, died at age 60 in 1996. Sidney's friends and family were astounded to discover that, in his will, he had left $350,000 and his Beverly Hills mansion, valued at $5 million, for the care of his 15-year old cocker spaniel, *Samantha*.

Altman left his long-time human companion, 32-year-old Marie Dana, an annual stipend of $60,000. She was also to be allowed to remain living in the mansion, provided she continued to care for *Samantha*. The will also stated that, upon the death of the dog, Dana would lose her stipend and the house was to be sold – all proceeds going to animal charities. Dana sued for half the estate.

The judge who heard the case suggested an out-of-court settlement.

***Toby* the $15-million poodle.** According to the *Guinness Book of World Records (1999)*, *Toby*, a standard poodle, was left $15 million when his mistress, Ella Wendel of New York City, died in 1931. Ella apparently came from an unconventional family where dogs were served lamb chops by personal butlers and slept in their own bedrooms in hand-carved miniature four-poster beds with silk sheets.

Mini smokes the executor. Tobacco heiress Doris Duke left a $1.5 billion estate when she died in 1993. Of that amount, she bequeathed $100,000 in a trust fund for the care of her dog, *Mini*. The executor of the Duke estate went to court to dispute the trust, a move *Mini's* new owner opposed. New York judge Eve Preminger ruled in favor of *Mini* and her new owner. If you have Internet access, you can read Doris' will in its entirety at www.doyourownwill.com/duke.asp.

General Patton and *Willy the Conqueror*. U.S. General George Patton's bull terrier (and his second in command) was named *Willy*, short for William the Conqueror. *Willy* had Patton's icy stare, and it was rumored that people who had to appear before Patton would also appear before *Willy*, thereby facing four of the steeliest eyes ever seen. When the general died, *Willy* retired and went to live with Patton's wife and daughters.

The Prime Minister and *Pat*, the Irish terrier. William Lyon Mackenzie King, the 10th prime minister of Canada (three terms in the 1920s, 1930s and 1940s) was a strange, lonely man. He never married and had few close friends other than his mother and his Irish terrier, *Pat*.

The prime minister could sometimes be found in the corridors of power whispering in *Pat's* ear. King was also a spiritual man and believed he could communicate with his late mother through *Pat*.

When *Pat* also died, it is said that Prime Minister King conducted daily séances to try to communicate with the little terrier.

Christine Norman and her grave instruction. In 1930, the beautiful and talented Broadway actress, Christine Norman, stunned her followers when she leaped to her death from the 20th floor of a New York City hotel.

While her suicide was big news, the headlines grew bigger when her will was probated. As one newspaper announced: "Miss Christine Norman's Will, Disposing of $150,000, Fails to Mention Mother."

The gist of the story was that, along with bequests to a number of friends, her will instructed that a certain amount of money be put aside for the upkeep of her Japanese terrier's grave at the Hartsdale Pet Cemetery in Hartsdale, New York.

Her mother went to court in an effort to have the instruction put aside, but Arthur Garfield Hayes, a well-known lawyer and civil libertarian, argued that Ms. Norman's will reflected a caring, loving woman of integrity. The court agreed and ruled the will valid. Her dead terrier had won, and the actress' wishes were carried out.

The legal precedent set in the lawsuit over Christine Norman's will has protected others in a similar situation. According to the Hartsdale Pet Cemetery website on the Internet:

- In 1946, Mrs. Cornelia Polhemus Meserole left $10,000 for the repair and preservation of a monument at Hartsdale to her dogs.

- Three years later, Marion C. Robinson died, and her will instructed her executors to scatter her ashes over the grave of her German shepherd, *Chief*, and to pay a sum of money to Hartsdale for perpetual care for *Chief's* resting place.

- In 1979, the ashes of Brigitte Riffaterre, a psychologist, were placed, at her request, between her two dogs, *Puce* and *Filo*, and 75% of her estate went to various animal organizations.

These women, unlike Christine Norman, had their wishes fulfilled without court battles.

Liberace and his children.

Pop pianist Liberace was known for his flamboyant lifestyle, highly affected mannerisms, sequined costumes and over-the-top stage shows, but he was also a dog lover.

In 1987, it is reported that he owned a West Highland white terrier (*Lady Di*); a chow chow (*Suzie Wong*); two shar-peis (*Wrinkles* and *Prunella*); and a keeshond (*Gretal*), all of whom lived in Palm Springs. In his Las Vegas home, he had three Yorkshire terriers (*Bernadette, Lady* and *Tramp*); three Maltese (*Solo, Charmin'* and *Leah*); five poodles (*Peaches, Coco, Minuet, Noel* and *Snuffy*); two cocker spaniels (*Chow Mein* and *Blondie*); a schnauzer (*Precious*); a Shetland sheepdog (*Lassie*); a Lhasa apso (*Chop Suey*); and a much-loved mutt named *Southern Comfort*.

Liberace is also said to have owned two borzoi dogs that he incorporated into his Las Vegas act. The pianist referred to his dogs as his children and spared no expense to keep them in luxury.

After he had died, a photo spread of Liberace and his children appeared in *Globe Magazine*. The headline screamed: Liberace's dying plea: Look after my children. The sub-text read: "Surrounded for years by beauty and wealth & adoring admirers – all he can think of as he lay gasping for air was what would become of his 24 children – his dogs."

Rudolph Valentino and *Kabar*.

Although silent film actor Rudolph Valentino (1895–1926) was renowned as one of the world's great lovers, he was also a man who adored children and animals. He was devoted to *Kabar*, a Doberman pinscher/Great Dane cross. *Kabar*, in turn was devoted to his movie star master. When Valentino died suddenly at the age of 31, *Kabar* was distraught. When the dog died six months after his master, Valentino's brother had *Kabar* autopsied. The findings? *Kabar* was physically fine. The conclusion? He had likely died of a broken heart.

Kabar is buried at the Los Angeles Pet Cemetery with a headstone that reads: "*Kabar*, My Faithful Dog, Rudolph Valentino, Owner."

Sigmund Freud and *Jo-Fi*.

The father of psychoanalysis believed dogs can detect a person's state of mind. Consequently, he used one of his three chow chows, *Jo-Fi*, in his therapy sessions. *Jo-Fi* tipped his master off as to how a patient was feeling by lying close to those who were calm and relaxed and far away from any who were tense and uncomfortable.

The pampered pugs of royalty.

The Duke and Duchess of Windsor owned 12 pugs who lived the high life with their human family, drinking from solid silver bowls, sleeping on monogrammed sheets, and sporting silver collars with 14-karat Cartier leashes.

The Duchess would invite the pugs onto her bed each evening to feed them special biscuits prepared each day by her chef. And invited or not, at least some of the pugs accompanied the royal pair to social events, to the consternation of guests who knew that the Windsor dogs would run about on their own and relieve themselves wherever they chose.

Jack and *Bobby*. Edinburgh policeman John Gray, also known as Jack, died of tuberculosis in 1858, but was survived by *Bobby*, his little Skye terrier. After Gray's death, *Bobby* took up residence at his master's grave at the Greyfriars kirkyard. Some of the locals helped the faithful little dog by building him a shelter near his master's grave and giving him food and water.

Bobby spent the next 14 years living in the kirkyard and, by the time he finally died in 1872, his name was almost synonymous with loyalty in the minds of the people of Edinburgh, who erected a bronze statue to him in front of a pub just near the entrance of the kirkyard.

The faithful dog *Hachi-ko*. In 1923, a white, Akita male puppy, later named *Hachi*, was born in the city of Odate in the Akita Prefecture of Japan. The pup was brought to Tokyo in 1924. From the start, he and his new owner, Dr. Eisaburo Ueno, a professor at the Imperial University, became inseparable friends. To the name *Hachi*, the professor added the suffix – *ko*, a term of endearment.

Each day, *Hachi-ko* would accompany Dr. Ueno to the Shibuya railroad station when he left for work at the university. Upon returning to the station in the evening, the professor would find his dog waiting patiently, tail wagging. Their daily ritual continued until one day in 1925, when the professor became ill on the job and died before he could return home. *Hachi-ko* was only 18 months old.

Nevertheless, the faithful dog continued to wait each day at Shibuya station for a friend who was never going to come back. At times, he wouldn't return home for days at a stretch. The Akita became a familiar sight to commuters as he kept his vigil for more than 10 years. On March 8, 1935, *Hachi-ko* finally returned to his master. He died on the very same spot he last saw his friend alive.

People who passed the dog each day were so touched they commissioned the famous artist, Ando Teru, to create and erect a bronze sculpture at the rail station in his honor in 1934. The statue was melted down during the war but, in 1948, The Society For Recreating The Hachi-ko Statue commissioned Ando Tekeshi, son of the original artist (who had since passed away), to make a second statue. *Hachi-ko* had not been forgotten.

Despite its small size amidst the massive and busy surroundings of the train station and city, the statue isn't difficult to find. Millions of Tokyo's citizens have been meeting at the landmark since 1934 and continue to do so today. Though *Hachi-ko* was only a dog, he left a message about the meaning of loyalty and the importance of good friends. His life has been immortalized in a book and a motion picture (*The Hachi-ko Story*).

Hachi-ko may be gone but he will never be forgotten. Each year on April 8, at a solemn ceremony in Tokyo's Shibuya railroad station, hundreds of dog lovers pay homage to the devotion of *Hachi-ko.*

Napoleon Bonaparte and his dachshunds. Napoleon Bonaparte loved his little dachshunds, owning more than 20 of them over his lifetime. Although he was a tough, tenacious warrior, Napoleon wept openly at the passing of one of his beloved dogs and mourned for extensive periods of time. When the great general passed away himself, he left instructions to have his surviving dachshunds entombed with him – after they had died, of course.

Rin Tin Tin. Some dogs have been credited with saving people from drowning, or from being trapped in a fire, or from being lost in the woods. *Rin Tin Tin* is sometimes credited with saving the Warner Brothers film studio from oblivion.

The famous German shepherd was found in September 1918 when some U.S. airmen, including Corporal Lee Duncan, were scouting for a new headquarters. They stumbled upon an abandoned German war dog station and, in one corner, discovered a female German shepherd and five puppies.

Duncan took two puppies home with him and named one *Rin Tin Tin* after a popular toy of the day. He apparently decided then and there that his dog would become a movie star. *Rin Tin Tin* appeared in 24 films and was known as an extraordinary stunt dog. Duncan said the reason *Rin Tin Tin* could accomplish amazing feats was because he and the dog had an understanding based on a strong, loving bond. No word on what happened to the second puppy.

What rhymes with *Boatswain*?
Lord Byron, the romantic English poet, shared his estate, Newstead Abbey, with a tame bear, a wolf, a tortoise, a hedgehog, horses, monkeys and cats, to name a few of the animals on the grounds. But his most beloved companion was *Boatswain*, his Newfoundland dog. One day, when *Boatswain* was following the post-boy (letter carrier) to town, he was bitten by a rabid dog. As the Newfoundland foamed at the mouth, it is said Byron gently wiped away the foam with his bare hands. Lord Byron erected a monument on the dog's grave that read:

"One who possessed beauty without vanity, Strength without insolence, Courage without ferocity and all the virtues of man without his vices."

Oh, that nasty little *Nipper*.
Nipper was the dog portrayed in the picture *His Master's Voice*. He was born in 1884 in Bristol, England, and died 11 years later. After his death, Francis Barraud, his former owner, painted a picture of his dog with his head cocked to one side, listening to a wind-up record player. A modified version of this picture became the trademark of Victor and HMV records, HMV music stores and RCA.

Although the painting and its derivative trademark depicted a little canine cutie, in fact, the dog was named *Nipper* because he liked to bite people's legs.

Owney the globetrotter. When U.S. postal workers found a mutt abandoned near an Albany, N.Y., post office in 1888, they brought him inside and bundled him up in mail bags for warmth. That was the beginning of *Owney's* career as an unofficial mascot for the postal system.

He traveled more than 140,000 miles over the following decade, following postal workers wherever they traveled. Said the curator of the National Postal Museum: "American postal workers were his family. He liked anyone who smelled like a mail bag."

When *Owney* died in 1897, he was stuffed and put on display in a glass case at the postal museum, where he can still be seen wearing a small doggy vest festooned with medals and mail bag tags.

Old Drum died, and he died so hard. *Old Drum*, a hound dog, was shot dead in 1870 in or near Warrensburg, Missouri, by Samuel Dick Ferguson, nephew and ward of Leonidas Hornsby, an irate neighbor, who thought *Drum* had been killing his sheep.

Charles Burden, *Drum's* owner, sued Hornsby, who was also his brother-in-law, and the case wound up in the Missouri Supreme Court. Burden won the case, but it was in the courtroom in Warrensburg that his lawyer, future senator George Graham Vest, delivered his famous tribute to a dog: "The one absolutely unselfish friend that a man can have in this selfish world... is his dog."

While no record was kept of the last half of Vest's tribute, the first half has been preserved. This speech is credited with originating the saying, "A man's best friend is his dog."

Said George Graham Vest to the courtroom that day:

"Gentlemen of the Jury: The best friend a man has in this world may turn against him and become his enemy. His son or daughter that he has reared with loving care may prove ungrateful. Those who are nearest and dearest to us, those whom we trust with our happiness and our good name, may become traitors to their faith. The money that a man has, he may lose. It flies away from him, perhaps when he needs it the most.

"A man's reputation may be sacrificed in a moment of ill-considered action. The people who are prone to fall on their knees to do us honor when success is with us may be the first to throw the stone of malice when failure settles its cloud upon our heads. The one absolutely unselfish friend that a man can have in this selfish world, the one that never deserts him and the one that never proves ungrateful or treacherous is his dog."

"Gentleman of the Jury, a man's dog stands by him in prosperity and in poverty, in health and in sickness. He will sleep on the cold ground, where the wintry winds blow and the snow drives fiercely, if only he may be near his master's side. He will kiss the hand that has no food to offer, he will lick the wounds and sores that encounters the roughness of the world. He guards the sleep of his pauper master as if he were a prince. When all other friends desert, he remains. When riches take wings and reputation falls to pieces, he is as constant in his love as the sun in its journey through the heavens."

"If fortune drives the master forth an outcast in the world, friendless and homeless, the faithful dog asks no higher privilege than that of accompanying him to guard against danger, to fight against his enemies. When the last scene of all comes, and death takes the master in its embrace and his body is laid away in the cold ground, no matter if all other friends pursue their way, there by his graveside will the noble dog be found, his head between his paws, his eyes sad but open in alert watchfulness, faithful and true even to death."

Bum and his friend Shorty. *Shorty* was a burro, and the much-loved town mooch of Fairplay, Colorado, in the early 1950s. *Bum* was his doggie pal. When *Shorty* died and was buried on the courthouse lawn, the grief-stricken *Bum* lay down on the grave and refused to move or eat until he died as well. *Shorty* was then dug up, and *Bum* was laid to rest alongside his friend.

Richard Nixon's dog, *Checkers*. If it hadn't have been for a cute cocker spaniel named *Checkers*, Richard Nixon may never have become president of the United States and the Watergate scandal would never have happened.

Checkers touched the hearts of Americans when vice-presidential candidate Nixon was accused of financial skullduggery. Nixon appeared on television, pleading that the only gift he had taken from political cronies was *Checkers*, the cocker spaniel. Nixon said his children loved the dog and he wasn't going to return it.

America bought the entire performance. Nixon became VP under President Dwight Eisenhower and went on to become president. *Checkers* died in 1964, and is buried alongside 50,000 other dogs, cats, chimpanzees, etc., in Long Island's Bide-a-Wee Pet Cemetery.

Congratulations to the happy couple! In the more recent past, Brazilian socialite Vera Loyola arranged a wedding for some friends, complete with flowers and a banquet for 1,000 guests in the year 2000. Nothing unusual in that, except the bride and groom were dogs. Vera's female shih-tzu, *Pepezinha,* was married to *Winner*, a cairn terrier. Ms. Loyola, an animal lover who made her fortune running a chain of bakeries, shrugged off all criticism of the event in a country where the average monthly wage is about $100.

Miss Ritchey's millions. Eleanor Ritchey, a spinster granddaughter of Philip John Bayer, who founded the Quaker State Refining Company, adopted 150 dogs, most of them stray or unwanted.

When the heiress died in 1968 in Fort Lauderdale, Florida, each and every dog was well provided for in her will – as was Auburn University... sort of.

Miss Ritchey left her entire fortune, including her home, numerous real estate holdings, bonds, Treasury bills and 113,328 shares of Quaker Oil common stock, for the care of her pack of stray dogs.

The will named the university as her chief beneficiary and chief caregiver of the dogs. Under the terms of her will, Auburn could collect interest on the heiress' millions, provided the funds were used, at least in part, to care for her dogs, but the capital could not be touched until the last pet had died.

It is said that Auburn officials were overjoyed when *Musketeer*, the last surviving mutt, moved into the great doggie house in the sky. With *Musketeer's* death, the university collected a windfall of $11 million.

The only catch? All the money had to be used for small-animal research.

About cats

Tinker's **spiffy apartment.** In 1984, Anna Morgan of Seattle left half a million dollars to care for *Tinker*, her 11-year old Angora cat. The money was used to hire a caregiver to pamper little *Tinker* in the late Ms. Morgan's apartment.

Nicholas **and** *Dusty*. 1960s British pop singer Dusty Springfield provided in her will that her cat, *Nicholas*, was

to listen to Dusty's recordings each night at bedtime and, for the first year after Dusty's death, was to be fed only imported baby food. Furthermore, *Nicholas'* bed was to be lined with Dusty's nightgown. According to an article written by Colin Randall in *The Telegraph* (London) in 1999, Dusty was philosophical about her own death sentence as a result of breast cancer.

"It was only when I came home one night and saw my cat lying asleep that I thought, 'Who's going to look after you?' It was as if somebody had run a train through me. I wept and wept and wept because then I realized: it is you. Yes, it might kill you."

Dusty's concerns for her pet were met, the *Telegraph* article continued. She arranged for the cat, a 12-year-old Californian ragdoll, to be adopted by Lee Everett-Alkin, widow of the late disc jockey Kenny Everett. Ms. Wickham said: "*Nicholas* had been in the home of Lee many times. We can be sure he will be looked after splendidly."

Apparently he was. *Nicholas* died at age 21.

Humphrey **of Downing Street.** *Humphrey* was a well-known and popular longhaired black-and-white cat who lived at No. 10 Downing Street in London for eight years. He had arrived at the home of the prime minister as a stray when Margaret Thatcher held the office and remained throughout the term of her successor, John Major. Officially, *Humphrey* was Mouser to the Cabinet Office.

In 1995, the cat disappeared for three months until he was found at his new digs – the Royal Army Medical College. But the cat came back, returning to No. 10 Downing Street in short order.

In 1997, Tony Blair took office as a Labour Prime Minister. When in November of that year *Humphrey* retired from Downing Street for health reasons, a Conservative Party wag claimed that *Humphrey* was voting with his paws to leave Downing Street.

"After eight happy years under a Conservative government, he could only take six months of Labour before he lost interest in living," said the Tory opposition member.

Humphrey retired to a civil servants' home in south London.

Edgar Allan Poe and the black cat.

While Edgar Allan Poe loved all cats, one was special – his black cat, *Catarina*. She became his sole companion during his many battles with depression. It is said that Poe based his short story, *The Black Cat*, on his beloved *Catarina*. It was likely inevitable that cemetery workers would claim to have seen a black cat sitting at his headstone after his death in 1849.

Nero and *Phoebe*, his pet tigress.

Nero ruled the Roman Empire with a tigress at his at his side – no, not an aggressive human mate. His tigress, *Phoebe*, was a true feline who entered his life when he saved her from death in the Coliseum. She became his constant companion, even taking part, apparently, in deciding how to discipline and punish alleged traitors to the empire.

Florence Nightingale's Persian cats.

Over her lifetime, Florence Nightingale owned more than 60 Persian cats, naming each one after a political figure she either liked or disliked, depending on an animal's personality. By the end of her life, the famous nurse was spending most of her time at home with her cats.

Winston Churchill and *Jock*.

Britain's wartime prime minister, Winston Churchill, adored ginger cats. He was fond of one in particular – *Jock* – named after his private secretary, Sir John Colville.

Jock lived a lavish life with Churchill, even taking meals with the PM at the dining room table. He also had his own reserved chair at wartime cabinet meetings. *Jock* was at Churchill's deathbed the whole time the old man lay dying. In return, Churchill provided for his feline friend in his will, and *Jock* lived on at the family home until his death in 1974.

In his will, Churchill also asked that there always be a ginger cat living at the family home in Chartwell. His request has been honored.

Cardinal Richelieu, Prime Minister of France.

In the 16th and early 17th centuries, cats were persecuted throughout most of Europe as the embodiment of evil. Cardinal Richelieu dismissed this notion and adopted dozens of stray cats. Richelieu hired two maidservants to feed the felines expensive *foie gras* twice daily, and occasionally allowed the cats at his table. When he died in 1642, he left pensions for the care of his remaining cats, but his wishes were ignored and the cats came to a bad end.

Ernest Hemingway and his six-toed cats. At one point in his life, American novelist Ernest Hemingway owned more than 30 cats. He respected all cats because of their independence, but he was particularly fond of *polydacts*, cats with six toes. He acquired a number of them, having been given his first by a ship's captain. Today more than 50 cats live at his former Key West, Florida, home, which has been converted into a Hemingway museum. They are cared for by the museum staff through a provision in the writer's will.

The lion that roared to fame. Did you ever wonder about the MGM lion that has roared at the start of thousands of the studio's movies? His name was *Leo,* and he was taught to roar on cue by Volney Phifer, Hollywood's premier animal trainer.

What happened to *Leo?*

Sometime during the 1930s, Volney bought a farm in Gillette, NJ, where he boarded animals used in Broadway shows and Manhattan vaudeville acts. Both man and cat lived out their lives on the farm.

When *Leo* died in 1936, Volney buried him in the front yard, marking the grave with a small block of granite. He also planted a pine tree over *Leo's* body, insisting that its roots would "hold down the lion's spirit."

It was reported in 1997 that the new owners of the Phifer farm removed the granite block marking *Leo's* grave, but the 60-year-old pine was still on the site.

Goodbye, *Mrs. Chippy*. When Harry McNeish boarded the *Endurance* as ship's carpenter on Sir Ernest Shackleton's ill-fated 1914 expedition to Antarctica, he brought with him a pet tabby cat aptly named *Mrs. Chippy.*

(It was later discovered that the little carpenter's mate was actually a tomcat, but everyone continued to call him *Mrs. Chippy* or just *Chippy*.)

There is little doubt that *Mrs. Chippy* was a real character, and one that amused the ship's crew and expedition members.

On the voyage out, *Mrs. Chippy* fell overboard and was dredged out of the South Atlantic by the biologist Robert Clark's net. The event was recounted by one of the other members of the expedition in his diary:

"13 September, 1914. An extraordinary thing happened during the night. The tabby cat – Mrs. Chippy – jumped overboard through one of the cabin portholes and the officer on watch Lt. Hudson, heard her screams and turned the ship smartly round & picked her up. She must have been in the water 10 minutes or more."

Expedition photographer Frank Hurley captured *Mrs. Chippy's* whiskered chops and bold look of confidence in several pictures, while diary entries from the other expedition members paid tribute to the cat's outstanding character.

Capt. Frank Worsley described *Mrs. Chippy's* habit of climbing the rigging "exactly after the manner of a seaman going aloft," and Leonard Hussey, the meteorologist, recalled how *Mrs. Chippy* took provocative strolls across the roofs of the sled dogs' kennels.

But after the sea ice crushed the *Endurance* and then sank the ship, Shackleton ordered McNeish's cat shot, along with the pups on board and, later, the rest of the sled dogs.

McNeish then became one of five men who accompanied Shackleton in a 22-foot-long open boat on a 800-mile voyage through the South Atlantic to South Georgia Island in search of help for the rest of the crew. Indeed, McNeish had made the voyage to South Georgia possible, since he refitted the boat for its remarkable ordeal.

Yet *Mrs. Chippy's* death affected McNeish greatly, as it had most of those who had been aboard the *Endurance,* where the mouser had become a well-loved and most popular shipmate. And those who had known McNeish, from his days on the Wellington docks until his death in 1930 at age 56, knew that he never forgave Shackleton for the death of his handsome tabby tomcat, which he had originally acquired from friends in his hometown of Cathcart, Scotland.

Yet the story doesn't end here.

In 1959, when the New Zealand Antarctic Society learned that McNeish had received only a pauper's burial, it raised funds for a headstone to stand on his unmarked grave. Later, it decided to unite the carpenter with his feline friend. With funds raised through public subscription, it had a life-size bronze statue of a watchful *Mrs. Chippy* cast for McNeish's grave.

So it came to be that on a blustery, gray day in June 2004, 100 people gathered in the Karori Cemetery, in a suburb of Wellington, New Zealand, at McNeish's grave site for a solemn ceremony that involved tributes for both the carpenter and his cat.

Said one of the researchers looking into the Shackleton voyage: "From an early stage in my research, I was struck by the number of amused and affectionate references to this characterful (sic) explorer – *Mrs. Chippy.*"

And the artist who created *Mrs. Chippy's* bronze figure commented: "I was impressed by *Mrs. Chippy's* adventurous nature, and the friendship between the cat and his mate on such an arduous voyage. I would like people to come upon the grave to be surprised to find a cat resting, its face alert, its body relaxed as if he were lying on McNeish's bunk."

The inscrutable cat. According to the *Guinness Book of Records* (1992), when Grace Alma Patterson of Joplin, Montana, died in January 1978, she left her entire estate, worth $250,000, to her white alley cat, *Charlie Chan.* When the cat died, the estate, which included a three-bedroom house, a 7-acre pet cemetery and a collection of antiques, was auctioned and the proceeds donated to humane societies

Other critters

General Lee and *Traveler*. General Robert E. Lee's favorite horse, *Traveler*, was a familiar figure in Confederate camps and helped Lee through many battles. After the Civil War, the general took *Traveler* with him when he took up his post at Washington College. The horse is reputed to have lost many tail hairs to admirers and souvenir seekers. When Lee died, *Traveler* walked behind the hearse at his funeral. Today the horse's remains are buried near Lee's on the campus of Washington and Lee College in Lexington, Virginia.

Mozart and his pet starling. Some of the world's greatest musicians, including Wolfgang Amadeus Mozart, have admired starlings because of their strong mimicry abilities and their two-part larynx, which allows them to sing two songs at the same time. In fact, Mozart had a starling as both a pet and as a musical companion. When the starling died in 1784, all of Mozart's friends were required to attend the funeral.

Dr. Albert Schweitzer and his African menagerie. In addition to his status as a Nobel prizewinner and renowned Alsatian medical missionary, Dr. Albert Schweitzer was also known as a lover of animals. It is said that *Sizi*, one of his cats, would often fall asleep on his left arm. Rather than moving her (Schweitzer was left handed), the good doctor became ambidextrous so he wouldn't disturb her while he wrote prescriptions. Schweitzer also had many exotic animals as companions, including antelopes, pelicans, chimpanzees and gorillas. He raised his two antelopes, *Leonie* and *Theodore*, from infancy and enjoyed strolling with them in the evening.

***You'll Do Lobelia* (AKA *Elsie* the cow).** *Elsie* started out as a cartoon drawing in 1938 and became one of the most powerful and recognized advertising symbols in the world. *Elsie's* head on packaging immediately identified it as a Borden Milk product. But *Elsie* didn't become a real cow until the following year, when Borden decided to put a dairy exhibit into the 1939 New York World's Fair.

The company built a Rotolactor, a giant, glass-enclosed turntable on which cows were milked by automated machines for the edification of fair goers. When Borden's ad agency scanned a list of questions asked by exhibit visitors, they were amazed that six out of every ten people asked, "Which cow is *Elsie*?"

The agency quickly found a good-natured, big-eyed Jersey cow named *You'll Do Lobelia* in Borden's herd of fair cows. Renaming her *Elsie*, they put her on the Rotolactor between milkings. A star was born.

By the time the fair closed in 1940, Borden was milking *You'll Do Lobelia* for every quart of good will she could give, but on a cross-country series of appearances in 1941, her custom 18-wheeler (dubbed the Cowdillac) was hit from behind by another truck. *Elsie* was injured and her veterinarians decided she had to be *put to sleep*. She was buried on a farm, and a headstone was placed at the farm's entrance, praising her as "one of the great *Elsies* of our time." Borden discreetly found a new *Elsie,* and the advertising program moved on.

Strictly speaking, *Elsie* was not a pet, but she was loved and revered by thousands of people, especially children, who saw her. She was a national pet.

Sounds like an excuse for a party. It is said that the Roman poet Virgil spent the equivalent of $100,000 on his pet fly's funeral. No word on the fly's name or whether it was buried or cremated.

You named your parrot what? According to the *The Ultimate Irrelevant Encyclopaedia*, American writer and rapier wit, Dorothy Parker, had a dog called *Cliché*. She also had a parrot named *Onan* because it spilt its seed on the ground.

The priceless Pekinese. In 1907 Clarice Ashton Cross of Ascot, Great Britain, turned down an offer of £32,000 (equivalent to more than $1 million today) from American financier and industrialist J.P. Morgan for her Pekinese *Ch. Ch êrh* of Alderbourne. Morgan later returned with an open cheque, but was rebuffed yet again.

Byron and the bear. British poet Lord Byron was a noted animal lover and, wherever he settled, his household always included a menagerie. As a student at Cambridge, the young Byron was annoyed that university rules ruled out the keeping of dogs. But the rules said nothing about bears, and Byron soon found and installed one. In one of his letters he suggested that his bear should "sit for a fellowship."

APPENDIX B

Pound seizure

𝒯his is what the U.S. organization known as Last Chance for Animals (www.lcanimal.org), has said about pound seizure:

> "Pound seizure is the practice which refers to the taking of cats and dogs from shelters and pounds to supply the biomedical research industry. When dogs and cats are obtained for research, their fate is terminal. Some animals die quickly, while others are allocated for long-term, agonizing studies. Once the animal is turned over to the research facility, the Animal Welfare Act and anti-cruelty laws are close to nonexistent. Although there is no law pertaining to pound seizure, thirteen (now 14) states prohibit it. Most other states have no declaration regarding pound seizure and leave it up to the county or town governments to decide. Several anti-pound seizure bills have been presented before Congress, but [have] yet to be ratified.

> "AB 588, as introduced 2/18/03 by Assemblyman Paul Koretz, (D-West Hollywood), is intended to prohibit the pain and suffering of animals who are sold or given away by animal shelters to entities that perform biomedical research, product development and safety testing, and educational demonstrations."

Last Chance For Animals names the 14 states prohibiting pound seizure as Connecticut, Delaware, Hawaii, Maine, Maryland, Massachusetts, New Hampshire, New Jersey, New York, Pennsylvania, Rhode Island, South Carolina, Vermont and West Virginia.

The organization rightly calls the practice "the ultimate betrayal of companion animals."

To learn more about pound seizure and its status in your state, visit the American Anti-Vivisection Society (www.aavs.org) on the Internet.

Pound seizure has been banned in the United Kingdom, Sweden, Denmark, the Netherlands, and in several Japanese jurisdictions, but is alive elsewhere, including New Zealand, Australia and Canada, where it is being fought by the Animal Alliance of Canada, which complains that the practice of selling unclaimed stray dogs and cats for medical research is a "deep, dark secret that happens in shelters across Canada." Provincially, Atlantic Canada has the lowest percentage of strays sold for research, and Quebec has the highest.

And the Animal Alliance of Canada (www.animalalliance.ca) weighs in on the subject on its website:

"According to the Canadian Council on Animal Care, more than 4,400 dogs and 3,300 cats from 'random sources' – generally pounds and animal shelters – were used in Canadian experiments in 2001. Researchers generally prefer to experiment on pound animals because, as former human companions, they have come to trust people and are easy to handle. In addition to being a horrible betrayal of trust, these animals make extremely poor research subjects because their age, genetic makeup, and past medical history are not known. Ignorance of these important variables severely undermines the validity of the research.

Pound seized dogs are most commonly used in 'curiosity driven' research and teaching, while the vast majority of pound seized cats are used in teaching exercises. By definition, 'curiosity driven' research is not intended to find treatments or cures for human diseases. Likewise, the use of animals in teaching does not advance scientific knowledge, but instead is intended to demonstrate well-established scientific facts, which could often be demonstrated just as easily without the use of animals.

A number of scientific organizations, including the Canadian Veterinary Medical Association and the Physicians Committee for Responsible Medicine, have called for an end to pound seizure, and Animal Alliance of Canada is campaigning to make this goal a reality. In the meantime, Animal Alliance has created Project Jessie (www.projectjessie.ca), a network of foster homes that rescue animals from pounds before they are sold for experimentation."

Power of attorney

When you grant power of attorney to someone, you are giving that person the legal right to act for you. Note that, in this context, *attorney* does not mean lawyer; instead, it means *agent*, that is, a person to act in your stead. In the power of attorney document, you can stipulate exactly what your attorney can do and under what circumstances. If you are giving your son power of attorney to act for you on all property matters, should you become physically or mentally unable to act competently for yourself, you could include provisions in the document allowing him to look after your pet, as well as access your bank accounts to pay bills, etc.

On the other hand, you could exclude pets from the terms of your son's power of attorney, and give another family member, or friend, a special power of attorney that deals specifically with pets if you are unable to look after them for any reason.

Some things to consider:

- Where you want your pet to live (at your home, providing you are there, or somewhere else, should you be hospitalized or moved into long-term care).

- Whether you want to authorize the person who holds your power of attorney to (1) select alternate living arrangements for your pet, should you be moved out of your home, or (2) make decisions according to your pre-planned written instructions.

- The amount of money you are authorizing your agent to spend for care – food, board, medical services, exercise, etc. (In circumstances where you have created two powers of attorney for property, you may be wise to specify in the one dealing with your pet which fund of money your attorney has access to and what is to become of any money remaining, once the pet dies.)

- Whether you want to include options that might permit your pet to visit you during your incapacity, subject to approval by the facility where you reside.

- Should you prepare a special limited power of attorney for the sole purpose of authorizing your agent to procure emergency veterinary care while you are on vacation, or while you are away on business?

There have been instances in which people who have failed to make these provisions have returned home from an extended hospital or nursing home stay to discover their beloved pet has been given away, placed in a shelter, euthanized, or has died from lack of care.

The following is an example of the type of language you could ask your lawyer to include in your power of attorney to instruct your attorney on how you wish your pets treated. It is meant as a guide for interest and information only. Have your lawyer prepare a power of attorney document that meets the requirements and conventions of your state or jurisdiction

My agent may expend my money or other property for the care of my pets.

My agent may pay veterinarian and other medical expenses of my [dogs] not to exceed $XX.

My agent may select one or more of the persons to receive one or more of my [i.e. dogs] who agree to care for such [dogs] and to treat them as companion animals.

My agent may give [$XX or a sum at my agent's discretion not to exceed $XX] to each person selected by my agent and who accepts one or more of my dogs.

Sample wording for wallet cards

Every pet owner should carry a wallet card to alert emergency workers, police and medical personnel that he or she has an animal at home that may need care, should a situation arise that prevents its owner from looking after it. The following sample wording for such a card covers most such situations.

Pet alert

In any situation in which I am unable to return home to feed my pets, such as my institutionalization, hospitalization or death, please immediately call [name of primary contact who has agreed to provide emergency care for your pet] at [address and phone number of contact] and [name of alternate contact] at [address and phone number of alternate], to arrange for the feeding and care of my [specified by name or my cats, dogs and other animals] located in my home at [your address].

The superintendent of my apartment building [name, address and phone number], and/or my executor [name, address and phone number], and/or my neighbor [name, address and phone number] and/or my brother [name, address and phone number] have a copy of this document, with instructions and with my full permission and authority to provide complete access to my home and/or any location and/or property where my [specified by name or my cats, dogs and other animals] for [name of primary contact] or [alternate contact] to arrange for the feeding and care of my [specified by name or my cats, dogs and other animals].

Regarding the last paragraph of this document, if you do not live in an apartment (and therefore do not have a superintendent), or if you do not have a brother, simply name whoever would have the authority (and a key) to grant entry into your home to the emergency pet caregiver if the caregiver is someone who would not normally have access under an emergency situation. Eliminate the last paragraph if the caregiver is a close relative.

Average lifespan of animals

For people who are establishing long-term pet plans, the question of how many years their animal can be expected to live is extremely important. An animal's lifespan determines the amount of money needed to support it until it dies. In some jurisdictions, lifespan also ties into the law against perpetuities, which may limit the length of time a pet trust may run.

Unfortunately, estimating the exact length of time a specific animal will live is a tricky business. A number of factors may be in play. A cat's lifespan, for example, can vary depending on whether it is an indoor or outdoor animal, its diet, the quality of medical care it receives, its overall activity level and its genes.

What is certain, however, is that in developed countries we have extended the lifespan of our pets, especially our dogs and cats, over the last 30 years or so, largely because of better medical care, diet and living conditions. Cats have fared especially well, according to recent studies. Thirty years ago, cats lived for about seven or eight years on average. Now,

because many cats live indoors most of their lives, receive high-quality medical attention and eat nutritious food, a 7-year-old cat is a young cat.

Some animals, such as small rodents (mice, hamsters, gerbils, etc.) are more predictable, but even their life spans can vary by a year or more. Lifespan data for a few animals, even some commonly kept as pets, such as certain birds, are often poorly documented and may be blurred by injury and disease. The lifespan for the Pionus parrot, for example, is given by some authorities as 15 years and by others as 40 years. The estimated lifespan of the red-eared slider turtle ranges from seven to 40 years, depending on who you ask.

For some of the wild animals people sometimes keep as pets, such as skunks and raccoons, there are really two lifespan figures: in the wild and in captivity. For example, a cheetah can expect to live only three to four years in the wild (because man will find some way of ending its life early). In captivity, the lifespan expectation rises to 10–15 years. In most cases, the figures used here are for captive animals.

Use the figures given in the following tables as guides only. Consult your veterinarian for a more informed opinion on the life expectancy of your own animal.

Birds commonly kept as pets

African Grey Parrot	60 + years
Amazon Parrot	80 years
Canary	20 years
Chicken	15 years
Cockatiels	20–25 years
Cockatoos	60 + years
Conures	10–25 years
Finches	10–12 years
Macaw	50 years
Mynah	8 years
Parakeets	15–20 years
Pionus Parrot	25–40 years
Rainbow Lorikeet	15–20 years
Toucan*	6–15 years

* There are about 40 known species of toucans. Some live longer than others.

Fish commonly kept as pets

Carp	100 years
Goldfish	20 + years
Koi	40–70 + years

Reptiles and amphibians commonly kept as pets

American Alligator	50 + years
American Newt	3 years
American Toad	15 years
Anole	4 years
Ball Python	40 years
Bearded Dragon	4–10 years
Leopard Frog	6 years
Leopard Gecko	Up to 20 years
Lizards (large)	8–10 years
Lizards (small)	3–4 years
Painted Turtle	10 + years
Red-Eared Turtle	15–25 years
Snakes (large)	25 years
Snakes (small)	10–15 years

Miscellaneous small mammals commonly kept as pets

Chinchilla	14 + years
Ferret	6–8 years
Gerbil	2–4 years
Guinea Pig	5–8 years
Hamster	2–3 years
Hedgehog	5–7 years
Mouse	2–3 years
Rabbit	9–12 years
Rat	2–3 years
Sugar Glider	10–15 years

Larger mammals commonly kept as pets

Cat (indoor)	12–20 years
Cat (outdoor)	4–5 years
Dog (large)	10–12 years
Dog (small)	12–15 years
Donkey (Ass)	30–40 years
Donkey (miniature)	25–35 years
Goat	15 years
Horse	40 years

A more detailed estimation of lifespan for specific breeds of popular dogs is given below. All bets are off, however, for mutts.

Afghan Hound	11–12 years	German Shepherd	10–13 years
Airedale Terrier	10–12 years	Golden Retriever	10–13 years
Basset Hound	11–13 years	Great Dane	7–10 years
Beagle	13–16 years	Greyhound	12–14 years
Bloodhound	9–11 years	Irish Setter	14–16 years
Border Collie	12–13 years	Newfoundland	7–10 years
Boxer	9–11 years	Papillion	12–15 years
Chihuahua	15–18 years	Pomeranian	12–15 years
Chow Chow	9–11 years	Rottweiler	8–11 years
Cocker Spaniel	14–16 years	Schnauzer	14–16 years
Collie	12–15 years	Standard Poodle	11–13 years
Dachshund	15–18 years	St. Bernard	9–11 years
Dalmatian	10–13 years	Terriers	10–16 years
Doberman	12–15 years	Toy Poodle	14–16 years
English Bulldog	7–9 years		

Exotic animals kept as pets

African Bush Baby	16 years		Emperor Scorpion	6–8 years
Alpaca	15–29 years		Fennec Fox	Up to 12 years
American Box Turtle	120 years		Giant Millipedes	7–10 years
Ant (queen)	3 years		Hellbender	29 years
Ant (worker)	6 months		Jaguar	12–16 years
Bat	24 years		Kinkajou	20–25 years
Bear	40 years		Lion	35 years
Beaver	20 years		Llamas	30–50 years
Binturong	18 years		Madagascar Hissing Cockroach	2–5 years
Blackbird	18 years			
Bull	28 years		Mule	30–35 years
Bull Frog	16 years		New Guinea Singing Dog***	15–20 years
Caiman	28 years		Pot Belly Pig	12–15 years
Camel	50 years		Puma	10–15 years
Canada Goose	33 years		Rosella	15 years (est.)
Cane Toad*	6–40 years		Raccoon	Up to 17 yeas
Canvasback Duck	19 years		Skunk	5–8 years
Capybara	12 years		Snapping Turtle	57 years
Caracals	Up to 18 years		Tarantula (Female)	Up to 30 years, depending on species
Cheetah	10–15 years			
Chinchilla	14 + years		Tarantula (Male)	2–3 years, any species
Civit	13 years		Tiger	22 years
Crocodile	45 years		Tiger Salamander	10–25 years (est.)
Dingo**	20 + years		White's Tree Frog****	15–20 years
Elephant	60–70 years		Wolf	18 years

*   No one seems to have a definitive lifespan figure for cane toads in captivity.

**   The dingo is native to Australia and Australians must obtain a permit to keep it, or any other native fauna, in captivity.

***   Although these dogs are kept as pets by a few fanciers, they are endangered. Several zoos in Australia are trying to ensure the survival of the species.

**** There are many species of tree frogs aside from this native Australian type, including the North American Red Eyed Tree Frog, but few experts will estimate how long they might live in captivity, where they are safe from predators or environmental degradation.

A longer life for your pet

You can help extend the life of any pet but, in particular, your dog or cat, by making certain you feed it the correct amount of high-quality food. You may, indeed, find that you need much less high-quality food to satisfy your pet's needs than poorer-quality alternatives. Why? Low-quality foods usually contain more indigestible ingredients, such as wheat, or gluten, that an animal's digestive system cannot easily absorb.

Talk with your veterinarian, especially if you have an exotic or unusual pet, or if your dog or cat has special dietary needs. You can do your bit by checking the labels of prospective foods. Here are some pointers relative to dogs and cats:

- Look for food that contains a high percentage of high-quality meat ingredients. Cats and dogs are carnivores. A basic meat-based diet means they can digest their meals more easily and absorb more nutrients from it than they could from vegetable protein. Avoid foods with meat ingredients such as meat meal or animal tallow.

- Unless advised otherwise by your veterinarian, avoid foods with high percentages of starches such as rice, corn or wheat. This is particularly important for cats. If rice, corn or wheat is a food's first ingredients, it is likely a poorer quality product.

- Avoid foods with wheat, glutens or soy products. Wheat can cause upset stomach and allergies; gluten and soy are vegetable-based protein sources that are less digestible than meat.

- If you want your pet to enjoy optimum health with a boosted, disease-fighting immune system, look for foods that contain vitamins and minerals at levels above minimum recommendations.

- Look for extra ingredients in the food that will improve the health of your pet and extend its life – omega 3 fatty acids from flax or fish for better skin and coat, and improved immune function; oligosaccharides for good digestive tract health; and chelated minerals for improved absorption and utilization. There may also be nutrients such as glucosamine for healthier joints; L carnitine to aid fat digestion, and chromium yeast for blood sugar control in diabetic animals.

Sample will provisions for pets

The following wording is meant to provide guidance for you and your attorney in drafting pet provisions for inclusion in your will. Your attorney will want to use it in accordance with local law and practices.

Note that these provisions do NOT create binding arrangements. A pet trust, either traditional or statutory, is needed to create a binding and enforceable arrangement. See **Appendix I** for sample pet trust provisions.

Sample will provision 1 (simple gift of animal(s) and money to a single beneficiary with provision for backups)

I give my [**dog, Rover**], and all other animals that I own at the time of my death, to [**Jane Doe**], currently residing at [**address**], and trust that she shall treat them as companion animals. If [**Jane Doe**] does not survive me, or is, or becomes, unwilling or unable to accept my animals, I give such animals to [**John Smith**], currently residing at [**address**] and trust that he shall treat them as companion animals.

If [**John Smith**] does not survive me or is, or becomes unwilling or unable to accept my animals, my executor shall select a suitable person and/or persons to accept my [**dog, Rover**] and all other animals that I own at the time of my death and trust that said person and /or persons shall treat them as companion animals.

I direct my executor to give [**$XXXX**] from my estate to the person and/or persons who accept my [**dog, Rover**] and all other animals that I own at the time of my death, in such amount or amounts of the [**$XXXX**] that my trustee in the exercise of an absolute discretion considers appropriate and I request (but do not direct) that these funds be used for the care of my animals.

Sample will provision 2 (gift of one or more animals and money to one or more named persons at discretion of executor)

My executor shall give my [**dog, Rover**] or my [**dogs, Rover and King – as the case may be**] to one or more of the following persons who agree to care for such [**dog or dogs – as the case may be**] and to treat them as companion animals.

[**Jane Doe**], presently residing at [**address**].
[**John Smith**], presently residing at [**address**].
[**Jill Jones**], presently residing at [**address**].

My executor shall have the discretion to select one or more of the persons named above to receive one or more of my [**dog, Rover, or my dogs, Rover and King – as the case may be**]. If none of such persons are willing or able to take my [**dog, Rover, or my dogs, Rover and King – as the case may be**], my executor shall have the discretion to give my [**dog, Rover, or my dogs, Rover and King – as the case may be**] to another person, persons, individual and/or individuals who agree to care for my [**dog, Rover, or my dogs, Rover and King – as the case may be**] and to treat them as companion animals.

My executor shall give [**$XXXX**] to each person selected by my executor and who accepts one or more of my [**dogs, Rover and King**]. My executor shall give up to twice as much money [**not to exceed $XXXX**] if one person selected by my executor accepts both of my [**dogs, Rover and King**].

Note: The last paragraph can also read:

My executor shall give, in my executor's complete and absolute discretion, the sum of [**$XXXX**] to each person selected by my executor and who accepts one or more of my [**dogs, Rover and King**]. My executor shall, in my executor's complete and absolute discretion, give up to twice as much money [**not to exceed $XXXX**] if one person selected by my executor accepts both of my [**dogs, Rover and King**].

Sample will provision 3 (interim care)

My [**cat, Harry**] shall at the time of my death be delivered to [**Jane Doe**], currently residing at [**address**] for temporary holding and trust that she shall, during that time, treat it as a companion animal. The executor shall determine the amount from the estate to go with my [**cat, Harry**] for such temporary care and feeding.

The executor shall advertise and otherwise make diligent efforts to find a good permanent home for my [**cat, Harry**] taking reasonable amount of money for this purpose from the estate.

Sample will provision 4 (wide executor discretion to deal with pets and funds for their care)

I direct my executor to pay, as an administration expense out of my estate, all expenses associated with the feeding and care, including veterinary costs, of [**pets specified by name** or *my cats, dogs and other animals*] until [**pets specified by name** or *my cats, dogs and other animals*] are placed with the persons that I or my executor have selected to care for [**pets specified by name** or *my cats, dogs and other animals*] for the duration of their lives, whether or not these expenses are deductible for estate tax purposes.

Sample will provision 5 (shelter care)

Upon my death, I give all my animals to the [**name of shelter, humane society, or other institution**], presently located at [**address**] with the following requests:

The shelter will attempt to find homes for my animals – together or separately – with persons who have successfully adopted pets from the shelter;

If suitable homes cannot be found for one or all of my pets, the shelter will house them on the shelter premises, uncaged, and separated from new intakes and animals under veterinary care;

The shelter will provide them with adequate top-quality food and regular veterinary checkups. Should any of my pets become ill, adequate veterinary care will be administered. Should any of my pets become terminally ill, no heroic measures should be taken to keep them alive.

I direct my executor to give the shelter [**amount of money per pet that has been pre-arranged with shelter**] to cover the expenses involved.

Sample will provision for people leaving their pet to a shelter or similar organization

I give all of my [**pets** *specified by name* or *my cats, dogs and other animals that I own at the time of my death*] to the [**name of humane society or shelter or other willing and acceptable institution**], presently located at [**address**], with the following requests:

- that the [**named institution**] take possession of and care for all my animals and search for good homes for them, where they will be treated as companion animals;

- that until homes are found for my animals [**specified by name** or *my cats, dogs and other animals*] that I own at the time of my death – the animals be placed in foster homes where they should be treated as companion animals, rather than in cages in the shelter;

- that if it is necessary to keep some of the [**specified by name** or *my cats, dogs and other animals*] in cages while making arrangements to find permanent homes, in no event should any animal [**specified by name** or *my cats, dogs and other animals*] stay more than a total of [**X days**] in a cage;

- that after attempts have been made for three months to place an animal [**specified by name** or *my cats, dogs and other animals*] my [**brother or mother or father or other close relative with whom this was discussed and agreed in advance**], presently residing at [**address**], be contacted if it is not possible to place an animal [**specified by name** or *my cats, dogs and other animals*] so that my [**brother or mother or father or other close relative with whom this was discussed and agreed in advance**] can assist with finding a home for the animal;

- that the [**name of shelter or other institution**] make every effort to assure that none of my animals [**specified by name** or *my cats, dogs and other animals*] are ever used for medical research or product testing or painful experimentation under any circumstances;

- that after placement, [**name shelter or other institution**] personnel make follow-up visits to assure that my animals [**specified by name** or *my cats, dogs and other animals*] are receiving proper care in their new home.

If the [**name of shelter or other institution**] is in existence at the time of my death and is able to accept my animals [**specified by name** or *my cats, dogs and other animals*] I give [**$XXXX**] to the [**name of shelter or other institution**]. If the [**name of shelter or other institution**] is unable to accept my animals [**specified by name** or *my cats, dogs and other animals*] I give my animals [**specified by name** or *my cats, dogs and other animals*] and [**$XXXX**] to one or more similar [**shelter, shelters or other willing and acceptable institution or charitable organization or charitable organizations**] as my executor shall select, subject to the requests made above.

Uniform statutes on pet trusts

$\mathcal{I}$n the United States the National Conference of Commissioners on Uniform State Laws revised the country's Uniform Probate Code in 1990. More than 300 lawyers, judges and law professors, selected by state government, make up the conference. Its main task is to propose legal statutes for uniform and model laws in specific subjects and help state legislatures put the statutes into law.

The following is a sample code drafted and accepted by the Conference in 1990 and amended in 1993. Approximately 10 states have enacted this provision. **See Appendix H.**

§ (section)* 2-907. Honorary trusts, trusts for pets; conditions

A. If a trust is for a specific lawful non-charitable purpose or for lawful non-charitable purposes to be selected by the trustee and there is no definite or definitely ascertainable beneficiary designated, the trust may be performed by the trustee for not longer than twenty-one years whether or not the terms of the trust contemplate a longer duration.

B. A trust for the care of a designated domestic or pet animal is valid. The trust terminates when no living animal is covered by the trust. A governing instrument shall be liberally construed to bring the transfer within this subsection, to presume against the merely precatory or honorary nature of the disposition and to carry out the general intent of the transferor. Extrinsic evidence is admissible in determining the transferor's intent.

C. In addition to the provisions of subsection A or B, a trust created under this section is subject to the following:

1. Except as expressly provided otherwise in the trust instrument, no portion of the principal or income may be converted to the use of the trustee or to any use other than for the trust's purpose or for the benefit of a covered animal.

2. On termination, the trustee shall transfer the unexpended trust property in the following order:

(a) As directed in the trust instrument.

(b) If the trust was created in the non-residuary clause in the transferor's will or in a codicil to the transferor's will, under the residuary clause in the transferor's will.

(c) If no taker is produced by the application of subdivision (a) or (b) of this paragraph, to the transferor's heirs under section 2-711.

* This symbol "§" refers to the *section* number of a legal reference.

3. For the purposes of section 2-707, the residuary clause is treated as creating a future interest under the terms of a trust.

4. The intended use of the principal or income can be enforced by a person who is designated for that purpose in the trust instrument or, if none, by a person appointed by a court on application to it by any person.

5. Except as ordered by the court or required by the trust instrument, no filing, report, registration, periodic accounting, separate maintenance of funds, appointment or fee is required by reason of the existence of the fiduciary relationship of the trustee.

6. A court may reduce the amount of the property transferred if it determines that amount substantially exceeds the amount required for the intended use. The amount of the reduction, if any, passes as unexpended trust property under paragraph 2 of this subsection.

7. If no trustee is designated or no designated trustee is willing or able to serve, a court shall name a trustee. A court may order the transfer of the property to another trustee if this is necessary to assure that the intended use is carried out and if no successor trustee is designated in the trust instrument or if non-designated successor trustee agrees to serve or is able to serve. A court may also make other order and determinations that it determines advisable to carry out the intent of the transferor and this section.

§ 408. Trust for Care of Animal.

Likewise, the section 408 of the Uniform Trust Code completed in 2000 provides that a "trust may be created to provide for the care of an animal alive during the settlor's lifetime." Approximately twenty states (See *Appendix H*) have enacted this Code which contains the following pet trust provision:

(a) A trust may be created to provide for the care of an animal alive during the settlor's lifetime. The trust terminates upon the death of the animal or, if the trust was created to provide for the care of more than one animal alive during the settlor's lifetime, upon the death of the last surviving animal.

(b) A trust authorized by this section may be enforced by a person appointed in the terms of the trust or, if no person is so appointed, by a person appointed by the court. A person having an interest in the welfare of the animal may request the court to appoint a person to enforce the trust or to remove a person appointed.

(c) Property of a trust authorized by this section may be applied only to its intended use, except to the extent the court determines that the value of the trust property exceeds the amount required for the intended use. Except as otherwise provided in the terms of the trust, property not required for the intended use must be distributed to the settlor, if then living, otherwise to the settlor's successors in interest.

U.S. state pet trust statutes
(current as of October 2009)

The following U.S. states have passed statutes that recognize trusts created for the care of animals. Some of these specify domestic or pet animals; some do not, referring simply to "animals."

Some of the states have used the Uniform Probate Code Statute on Pet Trusts (**Appendix G**) as a paradigm for their statutes; others have developed their own laws.

If no specific statute was located for your state, check to see if your state has brought in new legislation regarding pet trusts since this book was written. Discuss your state's relevant statute with your lawyer to get up-to-date professional legal advice on how to take maximum advantage of any trust law that will benefit your pet.

Alabama

In brief

This law validates a trust created to provide care for an animal alive during the trust-maker's lifetime. The trust ends with the death of the specified animal or the last surviving animal if the trust were created to care for more than one animal. The court can reduce the amount of trust property to be used for the care of an animal or animals, if it determines that the amount in the trust is excessive to the requirements.

In full

Alabama Uniform Trust Code
§19-3B-408. Trust for care of animal.

(a) A trust may be created to provide for the care of an animal alive during the sett-lor's lifetime. The trust terminates upon the death of the animal or, if the trust was created to provide for the care of more than one animal alive during the settlor's lifetime, upon the death of the last surviving animal.

(b) A trust authorized by this section may be enforced by a person appointed in the terms of the trust or, if no person is so appointed, by a person appointed by a court. A person having an interest in the welfare of the animal may request the court to appoint a person to enforce the trust or to remove a person appointed.

(c) Property of a trust authorized by this section may be applied only to its intended use, except to the extent the court determines that the value of the trust property exceeds the amount required for the intended use. Except as otherwise provided in the terms of the trust, property not required for the intended use must be distributed to the settlor, if then living, otherwise to the sett-lor's successors in interest.

Added by 2006 Alabama Laws Act 2006-216 (H.B. 49), § 1, eff. Jan. 1, 2007.

Alaska

In brief

This statute states that trusts for the continuing care of designated domestic animals are valid, so long as they are for a duration of 21 years or less. Such a trust ends when a living animal is no longer covered by the trust. Funds remaining in the trust do not go to the trustee, but rather transfer by the order stipulated in the statute.

In full

Alaska Statutes § 13.12.907.
Honorary trusts; trusts for pets.

a) Subject to (c) of this section, a trust may be performed by the trustee for 21 years but not longer, whether or not the terms of the trust contemplate a longer duration, if

(1) the trust is for a specific lawful, noncharitable purpose or for a lawful, noncharitable purpose to be selected by the trustee, and

(2) there is not a definite or definitely ascertainable beneficiary designated.

(b) Except as otherwise provided by this subsection and (c) of this section, a trust for the care of a designated domestic or pet animal is valid. The tust terminates when a living animal is not covered by the trust. A governing instrument shall be liberally construed to bring the transfer within this subsection, to presume against the merely precatory or honorary nature of the disposition, and to carry out the general intent of the transferor. Extrinsic evidence is admissible in determining the tranferor's intent.

(c) In addition to the provisions of (a) or (b) of this section, a trust covered by either of those subsections is subject to the following provisions:

(1) except as expressly provided otherwise in the trust instrument, a portion of the principal or income may not be converted to the use of the trustee or to a use other than for the trust's purposes or for the benefit of a coveted animal;

(2) upon termination, the trustee shall transfer the unexpended trust property in the following order:

(A) as directed in the trust instrument;

(B) if the trust was created in a nonresiduary clause in the transferor's will or in a codicil to the transferor's will, under the residuary clause in the transferor's will; and

(C) if a taker is not produced by the application of (A) or (B) of this paragraph, to the transferor's heirs under AS 13.12.711;

(3) for the purpose of AS 13.12.707, the residuary clause is treated as creating a future interest under the terms of a trust;

(4) the intended use of the principal or income may be enforced by an individual designated for that purpose in the trust instrument or, if none, by an individual appointed by a court upon application to the court by an individual;

(5) except as ordered by the court or required by the trust instrument, a filing, report, registration, periodic accounting, separate maintenance of funds, appointment, or fee is not required by reason of the existence of the fiduciary relationship of the trustee;

(6) a court may reduce the amount of the property transferred if it determines that amount substantially exceeds the amount required for the intended use; the amount of the reduction, if any, passes as unexpended trust property under (2) of this subsection;

(7) if a trustee is not designated or a designated trustee is not willing or able to serve, a court shall name a trustee; a court may order the transfer of the property to another trustee, if required to assure that the intended use is carried out and if a successor trustee is not designated in the trust instrument or if

a designated successor trustee does not agree to serve or is unable to serve; a court may also make other orders and determinations as are advisable to carry out the intent of the transferor and the purpose of this section.

Added by 1996 Alaska Laws Ch. 75 (H.B. 308), § 3, eff. Jan. 1. 1997.

Arizona

In brief

The Arizona statute allows a trust to be created for a designated domestic or pet animal. The trust cannot run for more than 90 years and ends when no living animal is covered by the trust. Any remaining property is distributed according to statute and cannot be converted by the trustee.

In full

Arizona Revised Statutes § 14-2907. Honorary trusts; trusts for pets; conditions.

A. If a trust is for a specific lawful noncharitable purpose or for lawful noncharitable purposes to be selected by the trustee and there is no definite or definitely ascertainable beneficiary designated, the trust may be performed by the trustee for not longer than ninety years whether or not the terms of the trust contemplate a longer duration.

B. A trust for the care of a designated domestic or pet animal is valid. The trust terminates when no living animal is covered by the trust. A governing instrument shall be liberally construed to bring the transfer within this subsection, to presume against the merely precatory or honorary nature of the disposition and to carry out the general intent of the transferor. Extrinsic evidence is admissible in determining the transferor's intent.

C. In addition to the provisions of subsection A or B, a trust created under this section is subject to the following:

1. Except as expressly provided otherwise in the trust instrument, no portion of the principal or income may be converted to the use of the trustee or to any use other than for the trust's purposes or for the benefit of a covered animal.

2. On termination, the trustee shall transfer the unexpended trust property in the following order:

(a) As directed in the trust instrument.

(b) If the trust was created in a nonresiduary clause in the transferor's will or in a codicil to the transferor's will, under the residuary clause in the transferor's will.

(c) If no taker is produced by the application of subdivision (a) or (b) of this paragraph, to the transferor's heirs under section 14-2711.

3. For the purposes of section 14-2707, the residuary clause is treated as creating a future interest under the terms of a trust.

4. The intended use of the principal or income can be enforced by a person who is designated for that purpose in the trust instrument or, if none, by a person appointed by a court on application to it by any person.

5. Except as ordered by the court or required by the trust instrument, no filing, report, registration, periodic accounting, separate maintenance of funds, appointment or fee is required by reason of the existence of the fiduciary relationship of the trustee.

6. A court may reduce the amount of the property transferred if it determines that amount substantially exceeds the amount required for the intended use. The amount of the reduction, if any, passes as unexpended trust property under paragraph 2 of this subsection.

7. If no trustee is designated or no designated trustee is willing or able to serve, a court shall name a trustee. A court may order the transfer of the property to another trustee if

this is necessary to assure that the intended use is carried out and if no successor trustee is designated in the trust instrument or if no designated successor trustee agrees to serve or is able to serve. A court may also make other orders and determinations that it determines advisable to carry out the intent of the transferor and this section.

Added by 1994 Arizona Laws Ch. 290 (H.B. 2536), § 6, eff. Jan. 1, 1995. Amended by 2009 Arizona Laws Ch. 85 (H.B. 2333), § 3, eff. Sept. 30, 2009.

Arkansas

In brief

Arkansas' pet trust law says that a trust may be created to provide for the care of an animal alive during the trust maker's lifetime. The trust ends when the animal dies (or, if the trust was created to care for more than one animal alive during the trust maker's lifetime, when the last surviving animal dies).

In full

Arkansas Trust Code § 28-73 408. Trust for care of animal.

(a) A trust may be created to provide for the care of an animal alive during the settlor's lifetime. The trust terminates upon the death of the animal or, if the trust was created to provide for the care of more than one (1) animal alive during the settlor's lifetime, upon the death of the last surviving animal.

(b) A trust authorized by this section may be enforced by a person appointed in the terms of the trust or, if no person is so appointed, by a person appointed by a court. A person having an interest in the welfare of the animal may request the court to appoint a person to enforce the trust or to remove a person appointed.

(c) Property of a trust authorized by this section may be applied only to its intended use,

except to the extent a court determines that the value of the trust property exceeds the amount required for the intended use. Except as otherwise provided in the terms of the trust, property not required for the intended use must be distributed to the settlor, if then living, otherwise to the settlor's successors in interest.

Added by 2005 Arkansas Laws Act 1031 (S.B. 336), § 1, eff. Sept. 1, 2005.

California

In brief

A person can create a trust for the care of a domestic or pet animal for the life of the animal. The trust will endure only for the life of the pet, even if the trust contemplates a longer duration. Note that the statute uses the singular form *animal* and the term *domestic* or *pet*.

In full

California Probate Code § 15212. Trusts for care of animals; duration; requirements; accountings; beneficiaries.

(a) Subject to the requirements of this section, a trust for the care of an animal is a trust for a lawful noncharitable purpose. Unless expressly provided in the trust, the trust terminates when no animal living on the date of the settlor's death remains alive. The governing instrument of the animal trust shall be liberally construed to bring the trust within this section, to presume against the merely precatory or honorary nature of the disposition, and to carry out the general intent of the settlor. Extrinsic evidence is admissible in determining the settlor's intent.

(b) A trust for the care of an animal is subject to the following requirements:

(1) Except as expressly provided otherwise in the trust instrument, the principal or income shall not be converted to the use of the

trustee or to any use other than for the benefit of the animal.

(2) Upon termination of the trust, the trustee shall distribute the unexpended trust property in the following order:

(A) As directed in the trust instrument.

(B) If the trust was created in a nonresiduary clause in the settlor's will or in a codicil to the settlor's will, under the residuary clause in the settlor's will.

(C) If the application of subparagraph (A) or (B) does not result in distribution of unexpended trust property, to the settlor's heirs under Section 21114.

(3) For the purposes of Section 21110, the residuary clause described in subparagraph (B) of paragraph (2) shall be treated as creating a future interest under the terms of a trust.

(c) The intended use of the principal or income may be enforced by a person designated for that purpose in the trust instrument or, if none is designated, by a person appointed by a court. In addition to a person identified in subdivision (a) of Section 17200, any person interested in the welfare of the animal or any nonprofit charitable organization that has as its principal activity the care of animals may petition the court regarding the trust as provided in Chapter 3 (commencing with Section 17200) of Part 5.

(d) If a trustee is not designated or no designated or successor trustee is willing or able to serve, a court shall name a trustee. A court may order the transfer of the trust property to a court-appointed trustee, if it is required to ensure that the intended use is carried out and if a successor trustee is not designated in the trust instrument or if no designated successor trustee agrees to serve or is able to serve. A court may also make all other orders and determinations as it shall deem advisable to carry out the

intent of the settlor and the purpose of this section.

(e) The accountings required by Section 16062 shall be provided to the beneficiaries who would be entitled to distribution if the animal were then deceased and to any nonprofit charitable corporation that has as its principal activity the care of animals and that has requested these accountings in writing. However, if the value of the assets in the trust does not exceed forty thousand dollars ($40,000), no filing, report, registration, periodic accounting, separate maintenance of funds, appointment, or fee is required by reason of the existence of the fiduciary relationship of the trustee, unless ordered by the court or required by the trust instrument.

(f) Any beneficiary, any person designated by the trust instrument or the court to enforce the trust, or any nonprofit charitable corporation that has as its principal activity the care of animals may, upon reasonable request, inspect the animal, the premises where the animal is maintained, or the books and records of the trust.

(g) A trust governed by this section is not subject to termination pursuant to subdivision (b) of Section 15408.

(h) Section 15211 does not apply to a trust governed by this section.

(i) For purposes of this section, "animal" means a domestic or pet animal for the benefit of which a trust has been established.

Added by 2008 California Laws Ch. 168 (S.B. 685), § 2, eff. Jan. 1, 2009.

Colorado

In brief

This statute validates a trust established for the care of designated domestic or pet animals and their offspring in gestation. In Colorado, the determination of the "animals' offspring in gestation" is made when the animals become beneficiaries of the trust. Unless the trust provides for an earlier termination, the trust terminates when no living animal is covered by the trust (but no longer than 21 years). Any remaining trust property is then transferred as provided by statute.

In full

Colorado Revised Statutes § 15-11-901. Honorary trusts; trusts for pets.

(1) Honorary trust. Subject to subsection (3) of this section, and except as provided under sections 38-30-110, 38-30-111, and 38-30-112, C.R.S., if (i) a trust is for a specific, lawful, noncharitable purpose or for lawful, noncharitable purposes to be selected by the trustee and (ii) there is no definite or definitely ascertainable beneficiary designated, the trust may be performed by the trustee for twenty-one years but no longer, whether or not the terms of the trust contemplate a longer duration.

(2) Trust for pets. Subject to this subsection (2) and subsection (3) of this section, a trust for the care of designated domestic or pet animals and the animals' offspring in gestation is valid. For purposes of this subsection (2), the determination of the "animals' offspring in gestation" is made at the time the designated domestic or pet animals become present beneficiaries of the trust. Unless the trust instrument provides for an earlier termination, the trust terminates when no living animal is covered by the trust. A governing instrument shall be liberally construed to bring the transfer within this subsection (2), to presume against the merely precatory or honorary nature of the disposition, and to carry out the general intent of the transferor. Extrinsic evidence is admissible in determining the transferor's intent. Any trust under this subsection (2) shall be an exception to any statutory or common law rule against perpetuities.

(3) Additional provisions applicable to honorary trusts and trusts for pets. In addition to the provisions of subsection (1) or (2) of this section, a trust covered by either of those subsections is subject to the following provisions:

(a) Except as expressly provided otherwise in the trust instrument, no portion of the principal or income may be converted to the use of the trustee, other than reasonable trustee fees and expenses of administration, or to any use other than for the trust's purposes or for the benefit of a covered animal or animals.

(b) Upon termination, the trustee shall transfer the unexpended trust property in the following order:

(I) As directed in the trust instrument;

(II) If the trust was created in a nonresiduary clause in the transferor's will or in a codicil to the transferor's will, under the residuary clause in the transferor's will; and

(III) If no taker is produced by the application of subparagraph (I) or (II) of this paragraph (b), to the transferor's heirs under part 5 of this article.

(c) (Reserved)

(d) The intended use of the principal or income can be enforced by an individual designated for that purpose in the trust instrument, by the person having custody of an animal for which care is provided by the trust instrument, by a remainder beneficiary, or, if none, by an individual appointed by a court upon application to it by an individual.

(e) All trusts created under this section shall be registered and all trustees shall be subject to the laws of this state applying to trusts and trustees.

(f) (Reserved)

(g) If no trustee is designated or no designated trustee is willing or able to serve, a court shall name a trustee. A court may order the transfer of the property to another trustee, if required to assure that the intended use is carried out and if no successor trustee is designated in the trust instrument or if no designated successor trustee agrees to serve or is able to serve. A court may also make such other orders and determinations as shall be advisable to carry out the intent of the transferor and the purpose of this section.

Repealed and reenacted by 1994 Colorado Laws S.B. 94-93, § 3, eff. July 1, 1995; subsec. (2) amended by 1995 Colorado Laws S.B. 95-43, § 15, eff. July 1, 1995.

Connecticut

In brief

This statute permits a settler or testator to create a trust for an animal or group of animals. Upon the death of the last surviving animal, the trust terminates. A trust protector must be designated by the trust. The Superior Court and Probate Court have exclusive jurisdiction over matters resulting from this statute. The trustee must render an annual account of the trust. Trust property may only be applied towards its intended use. The statute provides for the distribution of property that remains after the termination of the trust.

In full

[not yet codified]

(a) A testamentary or inter vivos trust may be created to provide for the care of an animal or animals alive during the settlor's or testator's lifetime. The trust shall terminate upon the death of the last surviving animal. A trust created pursuant to this section shall designate a trust protector in the trust instrument whose sole duty shall be to act on behalf of the animal or animals provided for in the trust instrument. A trust protector shall be replaced in the same

manner as a trustee under section 45a-474 of the general statutes.

(b) Except as otherwise provided in this section, the provisions of the laws of this state that govern the creation and administration of trusts shall apply to a trust created to provide for the care of an animal or animals pursuant to this section.

(c) (1) The Superior Court, or a probate court described in subdivision (2) of this subsection, shall have jurisdiction over any trust created pursuant to this section.

(2) A probate court shall have jurisdiction over any trust created pursuant to this section if the trustee of the trust is otherwise subject to the jurisdiction of such probate court, or the trust is an inter vivos trust and the trust is or could be subject to the jurisdiction of such probate court for an accounting pursuant to section 45a-175 of the general statutes.

(d) The trustee of a trust created pursuant to this section shall annually render an account for the trust, signed under penalty of false statement, to the trust protector.

(e) Any individual identified as a trust protector pursuant to this section may file a petition in the Superior Court or a probate court having jurisdiction pursuant to subsection (c) of this section to enforce the provisions of the trust, remove or replace any trustee of the trust, or require a trustee to render an account as required under subsection (d) of this section. The court may award costs and attorney's fees to the trust protector, from the trust property, if the trust protector prevails on a petition filed under this subsection and the court finds that the filing of the petition was necessary to fulfill the trust protector's duty to act on behalf of the animal or animals provided for in the trust instrument.

(f) If the trust protector determines that the trustee has used trust property for personal use or has otherwise committed fraud with respect to the trust, the trust protector may request the Attorney General to file a petition in the Superior Court or a probate court having jurisdiction pursuant to subsection (c) of this section to enforce the provisions of the trust, remove or replace any trustee of the trust or seek restitution from the trustee with respect to such trust property. The Attorney General may file such petition if the Attorney General determines that the circumstances warrant such filing.

(g) Trust property may be applied only to its intended use, subject to proper trust expenses including trustee fees, except to the extent the Superior Court or a probate court having jurisdiction pursuant to subsection (c) of this section, upon application by the trustee or trust protector, determines that the value of the trust property exceeds the amount required for its intended use. Trust property not required for its intended use, including trust property remaining upon termination of the trust, shall be distributed in the following order of priority:

(1) As directed by the terms of the trust instrument;

(2) To the remainder beneficiaries identified in the trust instrument, under the same terms provided in the trust for the remainder interest;

(3) To the settlor, if then living;

(4) Pursuant to the residuary clause of the settlor's or testator's will; or

(5) To the settlor's or testator's heirs in accordance with the laws of this state governing descent and distribution.

Added by 2009 Connecticut Laws Public Act No. 09-169 (S.S.B. 650), § 1, eff. Oct. 1, 2009.

Delaware

In brief

This statute allows a trustor to create a trust for one or more animals. The term "animal" includes any nonhuman member of the animal kingdom, but does not include plants or inanimate objects. The trust terminates with the death of the last remaining animal. Property of the trust may only be used for its intended use.

In full

Delaware Code § 3555.
Trust for care of an animal.

(a) A trust for the care of 1 or more specific animals living at the trustor's death is valid. The trust terminates upon the death of all animals living at the trustor's death and covered by the terms of the trust.

(b) A trust authorized by subsection (a) of this section shall not be invalid because it lacks an identifiable person as beneficiary.

(c) A trust authorized by subsection (a) of this section may be enforced by a person appointed in the terms of the trust or, if there is no such person or if the last such person no longer is willing and able to serve, by a person appointed by the Court of Chancery. A person who has an interest in the welfare of the animal or animals other than a general public interest may petition the Court of Chancery for an order that appoints a person to enforce the terms of the trust or to remove that person.

(d) Property of a trust authorized by this section may be applied only to its intended use. Upon the termination of the trust, any property of the trust remaining shall be distributed in accordance with the terms of the trust or, in the absence of such terms, as provided in § 3592 of this title.

(e) In the case of a trust created in accordance with subsection (a) of this section, a trustor or other owner of an animal for whose benefit the trust was created may transfer ownership of the animal to the trustee at or subsequent to the creation of the trust. Subject to any contrary provision in the trust or other instrument by which ownership of the animal is given or bequeathed, if the person to whom ownership of the animal is given or bequeathed disclaims or releases such ownership, ownership of the animal shall pass to the trustee upon such disclaimer or release.

(f) The trustee of a trust created in accordance with subsection (a) of this section shall provide care for the benefit of the animal in accordance with the terms of the trust or, in the absence of any such terms, shall provide care that is reasonable under the circumstances. The trustee may employ agents or contractors to provide any such care and pay for such care from the assets of the trust.

(g) For purposes of this section, the term "animal" shall include any nonhuman member of the animal kingdom but shall exclude plants and inanimate objects.

Added by 2006 Delaware Laws Ch. 301 (S.B. 312), § 3, eff. Aug. 1, 2006. Amended by 2008 Delaware Laws Ch. 254 (S.B. 247), § 11, eff. Aug. 1, 2008.

District of Columbia

In brief

In DC, a trust maker can create a trust for an animal or animals alive during his or her lifetime; the trust ends when the animal (or the last of several animals covered by the trust) dies. A person named in the trust document, or someone appointed by the court, can enforce such a trust. The court can reduce the amount of the trust property if it believes it is excessive to the intended requirements and will return any money not required for the care of the named animals to the trust maker, if alive, or to his or her heirs.

In full

District of Columbia Official Code §19-1304.08. Trust for care of animal.

(a) A trust may be created to provide for the care of an animal alive during the settlor's lifetime. The trust terminates upon the death of the animal or, if the trust was created to provide for the care of more than one animal alive during the settlor's lifetime, upon the death of the law surviving animal.

(b) A trust authorized by this section may be enforced by a person appointed in the terms of the trust or, if no person is so appointed, by a person appointed by the court. A person having an interest in the welfare of the animal may request the court to appoint a person to enforce the trust or to remove a person appointed.

(c) Property of a trust authorized by this section may be applied only to its intended use, except to the extent the court determines that the value of the trust property exceeds the amount required for the intended use. Except as otherwise provided in the terms of the trust, property not required for the intended use must be distributed to the settlor, if then living, otherwise to the settlor's successors in interest.

Added by 2003 District of Columbia Laws 15-104 (Act 15-286), §2(b), eff. Mar. 10, 2004.

Florida

In brief

A trust maker in Florida can create a trust for an animal or animals alive during his or her lifetime; the trust ends when the animal (or the last of several animals covered by the trust) dies. The provisions of the statute apply to trusts created after January 1, 2003. The court can reduce the amount of the trust property if it believes it is excessive to the intended requirements and will return any money not required for the care of the named animal(s) to the trust-maker if alive, or to his or her heirs.

In full

Florida Trust Code § 736.0408. Trust for care of an animal.

(1) A trust may be created to provide for the care of an animal alive during the settlor's lifetime. The trust terminates on the death of the animal or, if the trust was created to provide for the care of more than one animal alive during the settlor's lifetime, on the death of the last surviving animal.

(2) A trust authorized by this section may be enforced by a person appointed in the terms of the trust or, if no person is appointed, by a person appointed by the court. A person having an interest in the welfare of the animal may request the court to appoint a person to enforce the trust or to remove a person appointed.

(3) Property of a trust authorized by this section may be applied only to the intended use of the property, except to the extent the court determines that the value of the trust property exceeds the amount required for the intended use. Except as otherwise provided in the terms of the trust, property not required for the intended use must be distributed to the settlor, if then living, otherwise as part of the settlor's estate.

Added by 2006 Florida Law Ch. 2006-217 (C.S.S.B. 1170), § 4, eff. July 1, 2007.

Georgia

No specific statute located.

Hawaii

In brief

This statute states that pet trusts are valid and that such instruments are to be liberally interpreted to carry out the intent of the pet owner. The transferor's intent can be determined using extrinsic evidence. This law also provides for the order of disbursement of and assets remaining in the trust and it excludes these trusts from Hawaii's rule against perpetuities law.

In full

Hawaii Revised Statute §560: 7-501. Trusts for domestic or pet animals.

(a) A trust for the care of one or more designated domestic or pet animals shall be valid. The trust terminates when no living animal is covered by the trust. A governing instrument shall be liberally construed to bring the transfer within this section, to presume against a merely precatory or honorary nature of its disposition, and to carry out the general intent of the transferor. Extrinsic evidence shall admissible in determining the transferor's intent.

(b) A trust for the care of one or more designated domestic or pet animals is subject to the following provisions:

(1) Except as expressly provided otherwise in the instrument creating the trust, and notwithstanding section 554A-3, no portion of the principal or income of the trust may be converted to the use of the trustee or to a use other than for the trust's purposes or for the benefit of a covered animal;

(2) Upon termination, the trustee shall transfer the unexpended trust property in the following order:

(A) As directed in the trust instrument;

(B) If there is no such direction in the trust instrument and if the trust was created in a non-residuary clause in the transferor's will, then under the residuary clause in the transferor's will; and

(C) If no taker is produced by the application of subparagraph (A) or (B), then to the transferor's heirs, determined according to section 560:2-711;

(3) The intended use of the principal or income may be enforced by an individual designated for that purpose in the trust instrument or, if none, by an individual appointed by a court having jurisdiction of the matter and parties, upon petition to it by an individual;

(4) Except as ordered by the court or required by the trust instrument, no filing, report, registration, periodic accounting, separate maintenance of funds, appointment, or fee is required by reason of the existence of the fiduciary relationship of the trustee;

(5) The court may reduce the amount of the property transferred if it determines that the amount substantially exceeds the amount required for the intended use and the court finds that there will be no substantial adverse impact in the care, maintenance, health, or appearance of the designated domestic or pet animal. The amount of the reduction, if any, shall pass as unexpended trust property under paragraph (2);

(6) If a trustee is not designated or no designated trustee is willing and able to serve, the court shall name a trustee. The court may order the transfer of the property to another trustee if the transfer is necessary to ensure that the intended use is carried out and if a successor is not designated in the trust instrument or if no designated successor trustee agrees to serve and is able to serve. The court may also make other orders and determinations as are advisable to carry out the intent of the transferor and the purpose of this section; and

(7) The trust is exempt from the operation of chapter 525, the Uniform Statutory Rule Against Perpetuities Act.

Added by 2005 Hawaii Laws Act 160 (H.B. 1453), § 1, eff. June 24, 2005.

Idaho

Note: Effective on July 1, 2005, Idaho adopted the unique concept of a "purpose trust," which apparently includes trusts for pets.

In brief

This Idaho statute, while not termed a pet trust law, allows a person to create a "purpose trust." Instead of requiring a beneficiary, the law says this type of trust may just name a person to enforce the trust.

In full

Idaho Code §15-7-601. Purpose trust.

(1) A trust may be created for any purpose, charitable or noncharitable, under the terms of a trust agreement or will. A noncharitable trust so created is a purpose trust and shall exist to serve a purpose.

(2) A purpose trust does not need a beneficiary.

(3) A purpose trust shall be enforceable on the terms set forth in the trust agreement by the person named to enforce the trust; provided however, that the failure to name a person to enforce the trust shall not void the trust or otherwise cause it to be unenforceable.

(4) A person named to enforce a purpose trust may resign or be removed or replaced in accordance with the trust.

(5) If the person named to enforce the trust resigns, or is removed, or is unwilling or unable to act, and if no successor is named in accordance with the trust, the trustee shall forthwith apply to the court having jurisdiction of the purpose trust for directions or for a person to be appointed by the court to enforce the trust. The court having jurisdiction of the purpose trust shall be empowered to make an order appointing a person to enforce the trust on such terms as it sees fit and to designate how successors will be named.

(6) During any period of time when no person is named or acting to enforce a purpose trust, the court having jurisdiction of the purpose trust shall have the right to exercise all powers necessary to enforce the trust in order to serve the purpose for which it was created.

(7) Any interested person, as defined in section 15-1-201(24), Idaho Code, may bring an action under law or equity to enforce a purpose trust.

(8) Charitable trusts are not governed by this section.

(9) A purpose trust created prior to July 1, 2005, shall be valid and enforceable from the date of the trust's creation.

Added by 2005 Idaho Laws Ch. 99 (S.B. 1070), § 1, eff. July 1, 2005.

Illinois

In brief

This law permits a person to create a trust to care for one or more designated domestic animals. Such a trust ends when the last named animal dies. These trusts are liberally interpreted under the law. Extrinsic evidence is admissible to prove a trust-maker's intent. This law also furnishes a distribution schedule for any excess property that remains in the trust. A clause in the statute exempts such a trust from the common law rule against perpetuities.

In full

760 Illinois Compiled Statutes 5/15.2. Trusts for domestic or pet animals.

(a) A trust for the care of one or more designated domestic or pet animals is valid. The trust terminates when no living animal is covered by the trust. A governing instrument shall be liberally construed to bring the transfer within this Section, to presume against a merely precatory or honorary nature of its disposition, and to carry out the general intent of the transferor. Extrinsic evidence is admissible in determining the transferor's intent.

(b) A trust for the care of one or more designated domestic or pet animals is subject to the following provisions:

(1) Except as expressly provided otherwise in the instrument creating the trust, no portion of the principal or income of the trust may be converted to the use of the trustee or to a use other than for the trust's purposes or for the benefit of a covered animal.

(2) Upon termination, the trustee shall transfer the unexpended trust property in the following order:

(A) as directed in the trust instrument;

(B) if there is no direction in the trust instrument and if the trust was created in a non-residuary clause in the transferor's will, then under the residuary clause in the transferor's will; or

(C) if no taker is produced by the application of subparagraph (A) or (B), then to the transferor's heirs, determined according to Section 2-1 of the Probate Act of 1975.

(3) The intended use of the principal or income may be enforced by an individual designated for that purpose in the trust instrument or, if none, by an individual appointed by a court having jurisdiction of the matter and parties, upon petition to it by an individual.

(4) Except as ordered by the court or required by the trust instrument, no filing, report, registration, periodic accounting, separate maintenance of funds, appointment, or fee is required by reason of the existence of the fiduciary relationship of the trustee.

(5) The court may reduce the amount of the property transferred if it determines that the

amount substantially exceeds the amount required for the intended use. The amount of the reduction, if any, passes as unexpended trust property under paragraph (2).

(6) If a trustee is not designated or no designated trustee is willing and able to serve, the court shall name a trustee. The court may order the transfer of the property to another trustee if the transfer is necessary to ensure that the intended use is carried out, and if a successor trustee is not designated in the trust instrument or if no designated successor trustee agrees to serve and is able to serve. The court may also make other orders and determinations as are advisable to carry out the intent of the transferor and the purpose of this Section.

(7) The trust is exempt from the operation of the common law rule against perpetuities.

Added by 2005 Illinois Laws Public Act 93-668, § 5, eff. Jan. 1, 2005.

Indiana

In brief

This statute says a person can create a trust to provide care for an animal or animals alive during that person's lifetime. Such a trust can be enforced by a person named in the trust or appointed by the court. The court can reduce the amount of the trust property if it believes it is excessive to the intended requirements, and will return any money not required for the care of the named animals according to provisions in the statute. A trust of this type ends when the last named animal dies.

In full

Indiana Code § 30-4-2-18. Trust to provide for care of an animal alive during settlor's lifetime.

(a) A trust may be created to provide for the care of an animal alive during the settlor's lifetime.

(b) A trust authorized by this section terminates as follows:

(1) If the trust is created to provide for the care of one (1) animal alive during the settlor's lifetime, the trust terminates on the death of the animal.

(2) If the trust is created to provide for the care of more than one (1) animal alive during the settlor's lifetime, the trust terminates on the death of the last surviving animal.

(c) A trust authorized by this section may be enforced by the following:

(1) A person appointed in the terms of the trust.

(2) A person appointed by the court, if the terms of the trust do not appoint a person.

(d) A person having an interest in the welfare of an animal for whose care a trust is established may request the court to:

(1) appoint a person to enforce the trust; or

(2) remove a person appointed to enforce the trust.

(e) Property of the trust authorized by this section may be applied only to the trust's intended use, except to the extent the court determines that the value of the trust property exceeds the amount required for the trust's intended use.

(f) Except as provided in the terms of the trust, property not required for the trust's intended use must be distributed to the following:

(1) The settlor, if the settlor is living.

(2) The settlor's successors in interest, if the settlor is deceased.

Added by 2005 Indiana Laws Public Law 238-2005, § 26, eff. July 1, 2005.

Iowa

In brief

In Iowa, a person can create a trust for the continuing care of an animal (the text does not say domestic or pet animal) living at the time of the trust maker's death. This type of trust is valid for up to 21 years, even if the trust contemplates a longer duration. The trust ends when no living animal is covered by its terms.

In full

Iowa Trust Code § 633A.2105. Honorary trusts – trusts for pets.

1. A trust for a lawful noncharitable purpose for which there is no definite or definitely ascertainable beneficiary is valid but may be performed by the trustee for only twenty-one years, whether or not the terms of the trust contemplate a longer duration.

2. A trust for the care of an animal living at the settlor's death is valid. The trust terminates when no living animal is covered by its terms.

3. A portion of the property of a trust authorized by this section shall not be converted to any use other than its intended use unless the terms of the trust so provide or the court determines that the value of the trust property substantially exceeds the amount required.

4. The intended use of a trust authorized by this section may be enforced by a person designated for that purpose in the terms of the trust or, if none, by a person appointed by the court.

Added by 1999 Iowa Laws Ch. 125, § 12, eff. July 1, 2000. Transferred by 2005 Iowa Laws Ch. 38 (S.F. 379), § 54, eff. July 1, 2005.

Kansas

In brief

This Kansas statute states that a person may create a trust for the care of an animal alive during the trust maker's lifetime. It does not specify that the animal must be a "domestic" or a "pet" animal. The trust ends when the animal (or the last of several animals covered by the trust) dies. Property in such a trust must be used for the intended purpose only. Furthermore, the court can reduce the amount of property in the trust, if it feels that that amount greatly exceeds the amount needed to adequately care for the animal or animals named.

In full

Kansas Uniform Trust Code § 58a-408. Trust for care of animal.

(a) A trust may be created to provide for the care of an animal alive during the settlor's lifetime. The trust terminates upon the death of the animal or, if the trust was created to provide for the care of more than one animal alive during the settlor's lifetime, upon the death of the last surviving animal.

(b) A trust authorized by this section may be enforced by a person appointed in the terms of the trust or, if no person is so appointed, by a person appointed by the court. A person having an interest in the welfare of the animal may request the court to appoint a person to enforce the trust or to remove a person appointed.

(c) Property of a trust authorized by this section may be applied only to its intended use, except to the extent the court determines that the value of the trust property exceeds the amount required for the intended use. Except as otherwise provided in the terms of the trust, property not required for the intended use may be distributed to the settlor, if then living, otherwise to the settlor's successors in interest.

Added by 2002 Kansas Laws Ch. 133 (S.B. 297), § 29, eff. Jan. 1, 2003.

Kentucky

No specific statute located.

Louisiana

No specific statute located.

Maine

In brief

This statute states that a trust may be created to provide for the care of an animal alive during the trust maker's lifetime. Such a trust ends upon the death of the animal or, if the trust was created to provide for the care of more than one animal alive during the trust-maker's lifetime, upon the death of the last surviving animal. A comment at the end of statute's text clarifies the kinds of animal-related activities that qualify as charitable versus non-charitable trusts.

In full

Maine Uniform Trust Code tit. 18-B, §408. Trust for care of animal.

1. To provide for animal; termination. A trust may be created to provide for the care of an animal alive during the settlor's lifetime. The trust terminates upon the death of the animal or, if the trust was created to provide for the care of more than one animal alive during the settlor's lifetime, upon the death of the last surviving animal.

2. Enforcement. A trust authorized by this section may be enforced by a person appointed in the terms of the trust or, if no person is so appointed, by a person appointed by the court. A person having an interest in the welfare of the animal may request the court to appoint a person to enforce the trust or to remove a person appointed.

3. Intended use of property. Property of a trust authorized by this section may be applied only to its intended use, except to the extent the court determines that the value of the trust property exceeds the amount required for the intended use. Except as otherwise provided in the terms of the trust, property not required for the intended use must be distributed to the settlor, if then living, otherwise, to the settlor's successors in interest.

The following are the "Maine Comments" that appear in the text of the enacting bill:

This section is new Maine law. The question of the validity of a trust for the care of a specific animal or animals has not previously been addressed in Maine. These types of arrangements are distinguishable from trusts having broader objectives such as the prevention of cruelty to animals or the benefit of animals generally such as through the maintenance of wildlife sanctuaries or animal habitat. Maine case law has indirectly addressed the question of whether arrangements for the care of animals generally qualify as charitable activities. See, e.g., Holbrook Island Sanctuary v. Inhabitants of Town of Brooksville, 214 A.2d 660, 161 Me. 476 (1965), a case concerning the charitable exemption for property taxes. Citing the Restatement (Second) of Trusts, Section 374 (1959), the Law Court stated: "A trust to prevent or alleviate the suffering of animals is charitable. Thus, a trust for the prevention of cruelty to animals, or a trust to establish a home for animals, or a trust for the prevention or cure or treatment of diseases or of injuries to animals, is charitable." However, the Law Court held that the operation of a wildlife sanctuary or preserve was not a charitable purpose.

Section 408 does not address these broader animal-related and wildlife-related arrangements, but section 409 may be applicable to those animal-related activities that do not qualify as charitable in nature.

Added by 2004 Maine Laws Ch. 618 (H.P. 678) (L.D. 921), § A-1, (eff. July 1, 2005.)

Maryland

In brief

This statute allows a settlor to create a trust for an animal alive during the lifetime of the settlor. The trust terminates on the death of the last surviving animal. A court may determine that the amount in the trust exceeds the amount required to satisfy intended use of the trust and order the excess to be distributed to the settlor or the successors in interests of the settlor. Maryland Estate and Trust § 11-102(b)(12) states that the Rule Against Perpetuities does not apply to pet trusts.

In full

Maryland Estate and Trusts § 14-112.

(A) A trust may be created to provide for the care of an animal alive during the lifetime of the settlor.

(B) A trust authorized by this section terminates:

(1) if created to provide for the care of one animal alive during the lifetime of the settlor, on the death of the animal; or

(2) if created to provide for the care of more than one animal alive during the lifetime of the settlor, on the death of the last surviving animal.

(C) (1) A trust authorized by this section may be enforced by a person appointed under the terms of the trust or, if no person is appointed, by a person appointed by the court.

(2) a person having an interest in the welfare of an animal the care for which a trust is established may request the court to appoint a person to enforce the trust or to remove a person appointed.

(D) (1) Except to the extent that the court may determine that the value of a trust authorized by this section exceeds the amount required for the use intended by the trust,

the property of the trust may be applied only to the intended use of the trust.

(2) Except as otherwise provided under the terms of the trust, property not required for the intended use of the trust shall be distributed:

(i) to the settlor, if living; or

(ii) if the settlor is deceased, to the successors in interest of the settlor.

Added by 2009 Maryland Laws Ch. 132 (H.B. 149), § 1, eff. Oct. 1, 2009.

Massachusetts

No specific statute located.

Michigan

In brief

The statute validates a trust for the care of a designated domestic or pet animal. Such a trust follows the terms for a non-charitable trust and can endure up to 21 years, terminating when no living animal is covered by the trust. The statute provides for the transfer of unexpended trust property when the trust is terminated.

In full

Michigan Compiled Laws § 700.2722. Honorary trusts; trusts for pets.

Sec. 2722. (1) Except as provided by another statute and subject to subsection (3), if a trust is for a specific lawful noncharitable purpose or for lawful noncharitable purposes to be selected by the trustee, and if there is no definite or definitely ascertainable beneficiary designated, the trust may be performed by the trustee for 21 years, but no longer, whether or not the terms of the trust contemplate a longer duration.

(2) Subject to this subsection and subsection (3), a trust for the care of a designated domestic or pet animal is valid. The trust

terminates when no living animal is covered by the trust. A governing instrument shall be liberally construed to bring the transfer within this subsection, to presume against the merely precatory or honorary nature of the disposition, and to carry out the general intent of the transferor. Extrinsic evidence is admissible in determining the transferor's intent.

(3) In addition to the provisions of subsection (1) or (2), a trust covered by either of those subsections is subject to the following provisions:

(a) Except as expressly provided otherwise in the terms of the trust, no portion of the principal or income may be converted to the use of the trustee or to a use other than for the trust's purposes or for the benefit of a covered animal.

(b) Upon termination, the trustee shall transfer the unexpended trust property in the following order.

(i) As directed in the terms of the trust.

(ii) To the settler, if then living.

(iii) If the trust was created in a nonresiduary clause in the transferor's will or in a codicil to the transferor's will, under the residuary clause in the transferor's will.

(iv) If no taker is produced by the application of subparagraph (i), (ii), or (iii), to the transferor's heirs under section 2720.

(c) For the purposes of sections 2714 to 2716, the residuary clause is treated as creating a future interest under the terms of a trust.

(d) The intended use of the principal or income may be enforced by an individual designated for that purpose in the terms of the trust or, if none, by an individual appointed by a court upon petition to it by an individual. A person having an interest in the welfare of the animal may request the court to appoint a person to enforce the trust or remove a person appointed.

(e) Except as ordered by the court or required by the terms of the trust, no filing, report, registration, periodic accounting, separate maintenance of funds, appointment, or fee is required by reason of the existence of the fiduciary relationship of the trustee.

(f) The court may reduce the amount of the property transferred if it determines that that amount substantially exceeds the amount required for the intended use. The amount of the reduction, if any, passes as unexpended trust property under subdivision (b).

(g) If a trustee is not designated or no designated trustee is willing or able to serve, the court shall name a trustee. The court may order the transfer of the property to another trustee if the transfer is necessary to ensure that the intended use is carried out, and if a successor trustee is not designated in the terms of the trust or if no designated successor trustee agrees to serve or is able to serve. The court may also make other orders and determinations as are advisable to carry out the intent of the transferor and the purpose of this section.

(h) The trust is not subject to the uniform statutory rule against perpetuities, 1988 PA 418, MCL 554.71 to 554.78.

Added by 1998 Michigan Laws Public Act 386 (S.B. 209), § 2722, eff. Apr. 1, 2000. Amended by 2009 Michigan Laws Public Act 46 (S.B. 387), § 2722, eff. Apr. 1, 2010.

Minnesota
No specific statute located.

Mississippi
No specific statute located.

Missouri

In brief

This law declares that a trust may be created to provide for the care of an animal alive during the trust maker's lifetime. The trust ends upon the death of the animal, or the last surviving animal, if it had been created for the care of more than one animal alive during the trust maker's lifetime.

In full

Missouri Revised Statutes § 456.4-408. Trust for care of animal.

1. A trust may be created to provide for the care of an animal alive during the settlor's lifetime. The trust terminates upon the death of the animal or, if the trust was created to provide for the care of more than one animal alive during the settlor's lifetime, upon the death of the last surviving animal.

2. A trust authorized by this section may be enforced by a person appointed in the terms of the trust or, if no person is so appointed, by a person appointed by the court. A person having an interest in the welfare of the animal may request the court to appoint a person to enforce the trust or to remove a person appointed.

3. Property of a trust authorized by this section may be applied only to its intended use, except to the extent the court determines that the value of the trust property exceeds the amount required for the intended use. Except as otherwise provided in the terms of the trust, property not required for the intended use must be distributed to the settlor, if then living, otherwise to the settlor's successors in interest.

Added by 2004 Missouri Laws H.B 1511, § A, eff. Aug. 28, 2004.

Montana

In brief

This law states that a trust for the care of a specified domestic or pet animal is valid, but for no longer than 21 years. The trust ends when all animals originally covered have died. Unless the trust document states otherwise, no part of the principal or income may be used for anything other than the trust's original purpose. If the court determines that the amount of property in such a trust significantly exceeds the amount needed to adequately care for the animal or animals, it may reduce the trust property.

In full

Montana Code § 72-2-1017. Honorary trusts – trusts for pets.

(1) Subject to subsection (3), a trust may be performed by the trustee for 21 years but no longer, whether or not the terms of the trust contemplate a longer duration if:

(a) a trust is for a specific lawful noncharitable purpose or for lawful noncharitable purposes to be selected by the trustee; and

(b) there is no definite or definitely ascertainable beneficiary designated.

(2) Subject to the provisions of subsection (3) and this subsection, a trust for the care of a designated domestic or pet animal is valid. The trust terminates when no living animal is covered by the trust. A governing instrument must be liberally construed to bring the transfer within this subsection, to presume against the merely precatory or honorary nature of the disposition, and to carry out the general intent of the transferor. Extrinsic evidence is admissible in determining the transferor's intent.

(3) In addition to the provisions of subsection (1) or (2), a trust covered by either of those subsections is subject to the following provisions:

(a) Except as expressly provided otherwise in the trust instrument, no portion of the principal or income may be converted to the use of the trustee or to any use other than for the trust's purposes or for the benefit of a covered animal.

(b) Upon termination, the trustee shall transfer the unexpended trust property in the following order:

(i) as directed in the trust instrument;

(ii) if the trust was created in a nonresiduary clause in the transferor's will or in a codicil to the transferor's will, under the residuary clause in the transferor's will; and

(iii) if no taker is produced by the application of subsection (3)(b)(i) or (3)(b)(ii), to the transferor's heirs under 72-2-721.

(c) For the purposes of 72-2-717, the residuary clause is treated as creating a future interest under the terms of a trust.

(d) The intended use of the principal or income may be enforced by an individual designated for that purpose in the trust instrument or, if none, by an individual appointed by a court upon application to it by an individual.

(e) Except as ordered by the court or required by the trust instrument, no filing, report, registration, periodic accounting, separate maintenance of funds, appointment, or fee is required by reason of the existence of the fiduciary relationship of the trustee.

(f) A court may reduce the amount of the property transferred if it determines that that amount substantially exceeds the amount required for the intended use. The amount of the reduction, if any, passes as unexpended trust property under subsection (3)(b).

(g) If no trustee is designated or no designated trustee is willing or able to serve, a court shall name a trustee. A court may order the transfer of the property to another trustee if

required to ensure that the intended use is carried out and if no successor trustee is designated in the trust instrument or if no designated successor trustee agrees to serve or is able to serve. A court may also make such other orders and determinations as are advisable to carry out the intent of the transferor and the purpose of this section.

Added by 1993 Montana Laws Ch. 494, § 72, eff 2003. Amended by 1995 Montana Laws Ch. 592, § 23, eff. 2005.

Nebraska

In brief

The Nebraska law adopts the language of Section 408 of the Uniform Trust Act and states that a trust may be created to provide for the care of an animal alive during the settlor's (trust maker's) lifetime. The trust terminates upon the death of the animal or, if the trust was created to provide for the care of more than one animal alive during the settlor's lifetime, upon the death of the last surviving animal.

In full

Revised Statutes of Nebraska § 30-3834 (UTC 408). Trust for care of animal.

(a) A trust may be created to provide for the care of an animal alive during the settlor's lifetime. The trust terminates upon the death of the animal or, if the trust was created to provide for the care of more than one animal alive during the settlor's lifetime, upon the death of the last surviving animal.

(b) A trust authorized by this section may be enforced by a person appointed in the terms of the trust or, if no person is so appointed, by a person appointed by the court. A person having an interest in the welfare of the animal may request the court to appoint a person to enforce the trust or to remove a person appointed.

(c) Property of a trust authorized by this section may be applied only to its intended use, except to the extent the court determines that the value of the trust property exceeds the amount required for the intended use. Except as otherwise provided in the terms of the trust, property not required for the intended use must be distributed to the settlor, if then living, otherwise to the settlor's successors in interest.

Added by 2003 Nebraska Laws L.B. 130, § 34, eff. Jan. 1, 2005.

Nevada

In brief

Nevada allows trusts to be created for the care of one or more animals alive at the time of the trust maker's death. The statute does not stipulate that the animals must be "domestic" or "pet" animals. According to this statute, a trust maker's intent must be liberally interpreted in favor of the creation of such a trust. Nevertheless, if the court determines that the amount provided in the trust exceeds what is required to care for the animal beneficiary, the excess amount will be distributed to the person who would have taken the trust property if the trust had ended on the date of the distribution. Such trusts end with the death of all animals covered.

In full

Nevada Revised Statutes
§ 163.0075. Validity of trust providing for care of one or more animals.

1. A trust created for the care of one or more animals that are alive at the time of the settlor's death is valid. Such a trust terminates upon the death of all animals covered by the terms of the trust. A settlor's expression of intent must be liberally construed in favor of the creation of such a trust.

2. Except as otherwise provided in this subsection, property of a trust described in subsection 1 may not be used in a manner inconsistent with its intended use. Except as otherwise directed by the terms of the trust, if a court determines that the value of a trust described in subsection 1 exceeds the amount required to care for the animal beneficiary, the excess amount must be distributed to the person who would have taken the trust property if the trust had terminated on the date of the distribution.

3. The intended use of a trust described in subsection 1 may be enforced by the trustee or, if a trustee was not designated, by a person appointed by the court to act as the trustee. A person having a demonstrated interest in the welfare of the animal beneficiary may petition the court for an order to appoint himself as trustee or to remove the trustee. The court shall give preference for appointment to a person who demonstrates such an interest.

Added by 2001 Nevada Laws Ch. 203 (A.B 33), § 1, eff. Oct. 1 2001.

New Hampshire

In brief

In New Hampshire, the law permits a person to create a trust to provide for the care of an animal or animals alive during the trust-maker's lifetime. The trust ends at the death of the last surviving animal.

In full

New Hampshire Uniform Trust Code
§ 564-B: 4-408. Trust for care of animal.

(a) A trust may be created to provide for the care of an animal alive during the settlor's lifetime. The trust terminates upon the death of the animal or, if the trust was created to provide for the care of more than one animal alive during the settlor's lifetime, upon the death of the last surviving animal.

(b) A trust authorized by this section may be enforced by a person appointed in the terms of the trust or, if no person is so appointed, by a person appointed by the court. A person having an interest in the welfare of the animal may request the court to appoint a person to enforce the trust or to remove a person appointed.

(c) Property of a trust authorized by this section may be applied only to its intended use, except to the extent the court determines that the value of the trust property exceeds the amount required for the intended use. Except as otherwise provided in the terms of the trust, property not required for the intended use must be distributed to the settlor, if then living, otherwise to the settlor's successors in interest.

Added by 2004 New Hampshire Laws Ch. 130 (H.B. 1224), § 130:1 eff. Oct. 1, 2004.

New Jersey

In brief

This statute provides that a trust for the care of a domesticated animal is valid. The trust terminates with the death of the animal or at the end of 21 years, whichever occurs earlier. The court may determine that the amount transferred substantially exceeds the amount required to satisfy the trust's intended purpose. Thereafter, the statute provides for the distribution of the excessive amount.

In full

New Jersey Statute § 3B:11-38. Trust for care of domesticated animals.

a. A trust for the care of a domesticated animal is valid. The intended use of the principal or income may be enforced by a person designated for that purpose in the trust instrument, a person appointed by the court, or a trustee. The trust shall terminate when no

living animal is covered by the trust, or at the end of 21 years, whichever occurs earlier.

b. Except as expressly provided otherwise in the trust instrument, no portion of the trust's principal or income may be converted to the use of the trustee or to any use other than for the benefit of the animal designated in the trust.

c. Upon termination of the trust, the trustee shall transfer the unexpended trust property as directed in the trust instrument. If no directions for such transfer exist, the property shall pass to the estate of the creator of the trust.

d. The court may reduce the amount of the property transferred if it determines that the amount substantially exceeds the amount required for the intended use. The amount of any reduction shall be transferred as directed in the trust instrument or, if no such directions are contained in the trust instrument, to the estate of the creator of the trust.

e. If no trustee is designated or if no designated trustee is willing or able to serve, a court shall appoint a trustee and may make such other orders and determinations as are advisable to carry out the intent of the creator of the trust and the purpose of this act.

Added by 2001 New Jersey Laws Ch. 144, § 1, eff. July 10, 2001.

New Mexico

In brief

Two statutes represent New Mexico's relevant pet trust laws. The first, Section 45-2-907, which was adopted in 1995, validates a trust for the care of a designated domestic or pet animal. Such a trust can run for no more than 21 years and ends when no living animal is covered by it. A court may reduce the amount of the property transferred, if it finds the amount is excessive in terms of its intended purpose.

The second statute, Section 46A-4-408, was adopted in 2003, but it did not repeal the previous pet trust law. This new section follows the language of the Uniform Trust Code and states that a trust for the care of an animal alive during the settlor's lifetime is valid. The trust ends when the last named animal dies and excess trust property is distributed to the settlor, if alive, or the settlor's heirs.

In full

New Mexico Statute § 45-2-907
Honorary trusts; trusts for pets.

A. Subject to Subsection C of this section, if (i) a trust is for a specific lawful noncharitable purpose or for lawful noncharitable purposes to be selected by the trustee and (ii) there is no definite or definitely ascertainable beneficiary designated, the trust may be performed by the trustee for twenty-one years but no longer, whether or not the terms of the trust contemplate a longer duration.

B. Subject to this subsection and Subsection C of this section, a trust for the care of a designated domestic or pet animal is valid. The trust terminates when no living animal is covered by the trust. A governing instrument shall be liberally construed to bring the transfer within this subsection, to presume against the merely precatory or honorary nature of the disposition, and to carry out the general intent of the transferor. Extrinsic evidence is admissible in determining the transferor's intent.

C. In addition to the provisions of Subsection A or B of this section, a trust covered by either of those subsections is subject to the following provisions:

(1) except as expressly provided otherwise in the trust instrument, no portion of the principal or income may be converted to the use of the trustee or to any use other than for the trust's purposes or for the benefit of a covered animal;

(2) upon termination, the trustee shall transfer the unexpended trust property in the following order:

(a) as directed in the trust instrument;

(b) if the trust was created in a nonresiduary clause in the transferor's will or in a codicil to the transferor's will, under the residuary clause in the transferor's will; and

(c) if no taker is produced by the application of Subparagraph (a) or (b), to the transferor's heirs under the provisions of Section 45-2-711 NMSA 1978;

(3) for the purposes of Section 45-2-707 NMSA 1978, the residuary clause is treated as creating a future interest under the terms of a trust;

(4) the intended use of the principal or income can be enforced by an individual designated for that purpose in the trust instrument or, if none, by an individual appointed by a court upon application to it by an individual;

(5) except as ordered by the court or required by the trust instrument, no filing, report, registration, periodic accounting, separate maintenance of funds, appointment or fee is required by reason of the existence of the fiduciary relationship of the trustee;

(6) a court may reduce the amount of the property transferred, if it determines that amount substantially exceeds the amount required for the intended use. The amount of the reduction, if any, passes as unexpended trust property under the provisions of Paragraph (2) of Subsection C of this section; and

(7) if no trustee is designated or no designated trustee is willing or able to serve, a court shall name a trustee. A court may order the transfer of the property to another trustee, if required to assure that the intended use is carried out and if no successor trustee is

designated in the trust instrument or if no designated successor trustee agrees to serve or is able to serve. A court may also make such other orders and determinations as shall be advisable to carry out the intent of the transferor and the purpose of this section.

Added by 1995 New Mexico Laws Ch. 210 (H.B.517), § 30, eff. July1,1995.

New Mexico Statute
§ 46A-4-408. *Trust for care of animal.*

A. A trust may be created to provide for the care of an animal alive during the settlor's lifetime. The trust terminates upon the death of the animal or, if the trust was created to provide for the care of more than one animal alive during the settlor's lifetime, upon the death of the last surviving animal.

B. A trust authorized by this section may be enforced by a person appointed in the terms of the trust or, if no person is so appointed, by a person appointed by the court. A person having an interest in the welfare of the animal may request the court to appoint a person to enforce the trust or to remove a person appointed.

C. Property of a trust authorized by this section may be applied only to its intended use, except to the extent the court determines that the value of the trust property exceeds the amount required for the intended use. Except as otherwise provided in the terms of the trust, property not required for the intended use must be distributed to the settlor, if then living, otherwise to the settlor's successors in interest.

Added by 2003 New Mexico Laws Ch. 122 (H.B.48), § 4-408, eff. July 1, 2003.

New York

In brief

The New York statute validates trusts for the care of designated domestic or pet animals. Any such trusts end when no living animal is covered by the trust, or at the end of 21 years, whichever occurs earlier. When a trust ends, the trustee must transfer the unused trust property as directed by the trust or, if the trust instrument contains no directions, the property shall pass to the estate of the grantor. A court may reduce the amount of the property allocated to the care of a pet by the trust if it believes that amount is excessive in terms of the amount required.

In full

Consolidated Laws of New York
§ 7-8.1. *Honorary trusts for pets.*

(a) A trust for the care of a designated domestic or pet animal is valid. The intended use of the principal or income may be enforced by an individual designated for that purpose in the trust instrument or, if none, by an individual appointed by a court upon application to it by an individual, or by a trustee. Such trust shall terminate when no living animal is covered by the trust, or at the end of twenty-one years, whichever occurs earlier.

(b) Except as expressly provided otherwise in the trust instrument, no portion of the principal or income may be converted to the use of the trustee or to any use other than for the benefit of a covered animal.

(c) Upon termination, the trustee shall transfer the unexpended trust property as directed in the trust instrument or, if there are no such directions in the trust instrument, the property shall pass to the estate of the grantor.

(d) A court may reduce the amount of the property transferred if it determines that amount substantially exceeds the amount required for the intended use. The amount of the reduction, if any, passes as unexpended trust property pursuant to paragraph (c) of this section.

(e) If no trustee is designated or no designated trustee is willing or able to serve, a court shall appoint a trustee and may make such other orders and determinations as are advisable to carry out the intent of the transferor and the purpose of this section.

Added by 1996 New York Laws Ch. 159 (S. 5207-A), § 1, eff. June 18, 1996. Renumberd by 2003 New York Laws Ch. 630 (A. 7510-B), § 3, eff. Mar. 28, 2004.

North Carolina

In brief

This North Carolina statute validates a trust for the care of one or more designated domestic or pet animals alive when the trust was created. The trustee cannot use any of the income or principal for anything but the care of the animal or animals, unless the trust provides otherwise. The trust ends when the last surviving animal mentioned in the trust dies. The trust is liberally applied as a legally enforceable instrument rather than an honorary trust, and extrinsic evidence is admissible to this purpose. The court can reduce the amount of the trust if it decides it significantly exceeds the amount needed to care for the animal or animals.

In full

North Carolina Uniform Trust Code § 36C-4-408. Trust for care of animal.

(a) Subject to this section, a trust for the care of one or more designated domestic or pet animals alive at the time of creation of the trust is valid.

(b) Except as expressly provided otherwise in the trust instrument, no portion of the principal or income may be converted to the use of the trustee or to any use other than for the benefit of the designated animal or animals.

(c) The trust terminates at the death of the animal or last surviving animal. Upon termination, the trustee shall transfer the unexpended trust property in the following order:

(1) As directed in the trust instrument.

(2) If the trust was created in a preresiduary clause in the settlor's will or in a codicil to the settlor's will, under the residuary clause in the settlor's will.

(3) If no taker is produced by the application of subdivision (1) or (2) of this subsection, to the settlor, if then living, otherwise to the settlor's heirs determined as of the date of the settlor's death under Chapter 29 of the General Statutes.

(d) The intended use of the principal or income can be enforced by a person designated for that purpose in the trust instrument or, if none, by a person appointed by the clerk of superior court having jurisdiction over the trust upon application to the clerk of superior court by a person.

(e) Except as ordered by the clerk of superior court or required by the trust instrument, no filing, report, registration, periodic accounting, separate maintenance of funds, appointment, bond, or fee is required by reason of the existence of the fiduciary relationship of the trustee.

(f) A governing instrument shall be liberally construed to bring the transfer within this section, to presume against the merely precatory or honorary nature of the disposition, and to carry out the general intent of the settlor. Extrinsic evidence is admissible in determining the settlor's intent.

(g) The clerk of superior court may reduce the amount of the property transferred, if the clerk of superior court determines that the amount substantially exceeds the amount required for the intended use. The amount of the reduction, if any, passes as unexpended trust property under subsection (c) of this section.

(h) If no trustee is designated or if no designated trustee agrees to serve or is able to serve, the clerk of superior court must name a trustee. The clerk of superior court may order the transfer of the property to another trustee, if required to assure that the intended use is carried out and if no successor trustee is designated in the trust instrument or if no designated successor trustee agrees to serve or is able to serve. The clerk of superior court may also make other orders and determinations as are advisable to carry out the intent of the settlor and the purpose of this section.

Added by 2005 North Carolina Laws S.L. 2005-192 (S.B. 679), § 2, eff. Jan. 1, 2006. Amended by 2006 North Carolina Laws S.L. 2006-259 (S.B. 1523), § 13(b), eff. Oct. 1, 2006.

North Dakota

In brief

This section allows a settlor to create a trust for an animal alive during the settlor's lifetime. The trust terminates upon the death of the last surviving animal covered by the trust. Property of a trust may only be applied to the trusts intended use. Property that the court determines exceeds the intended use must be distributed to the settlor, if living, otherwise to the settlor's successors in interest.

In full

North Dakota Century Code § 59-12-08. (408) Trust for care of animal.

1. A trust may be created to provide for the care of an animal alive during the settlor's

lifetime. The trust terminates upon the death of the animal or, if the trust was created to provide for the care of more than one animal alive during the settlor's lifetime, upon the death of the last surviving animal.

2. A trust authorized by this section may be enforced by a person appointed in the terms of the trust or, if no person is so appointed, by a person appointed by the court. A person having an interest in the welfare of the animal may request the court to appoint a person to enforce the trust or to remove a person appointed.

3. Property of a trust authorized by this section may be applied only to its intended use, except to the extent the court determines that the value of the trust property exceeds the amount required for the intended use. Except as otherwise provided in the terms of the trust, property not required for the intended use must be distributed to the settlor, if then living, otherwise to the settlor's successors in interest.

Added by 2007 North Dakota Laws Ch. 549 (H.B. 1034), § 18, eff. Aug. 1, 2007.

Ohio

In brief

This Ohio statute permits a person to create a trust to provide care for an animal or animals alive during the trust maker's lifetime. The trust terminates upon the death of the animal or upon the death of the last surviving animal covered by the trust. A person named in the trust or by the court may enforce the terms of the trust. The property in the trust can be used for no purpose other than for the care of the animal or animals named. The court can reduce the amount of the property if it feels it is excessive to the needs of trust's purpose.

In full

Ohio Revised Code § 5804.08. Trust for care of animal.

(A) A trust may be created to provide for the care of an animal alive during the settlor's lifetime. The trust terminates upon the death of the animal or, if the trust was created to provide for the care of more than one animal, upon the death of the last surviving animal.

(B) A person appointed in the terms of a trust or, if no person is so appointed, a person appointed by the court may enforce a trust authorized by this section. A person having an interest in the welfare of an animal that is provided care by a trust authorized by this section may request the court to appoint a person to enforce the trust or to remove a person appointed.

(C) The property of a trust authorized by this section may be applied only to its intended us, except to the extent the court determines that the value of the trust property exceeds the amount required for the intended use. Except as otherwise provided in the terms of the trust, property not required for the intended use must be distributed to the settlor if then living or to the settlor's successors in interest.

Added by 2006 Ohio Laws File 128 (Sub. H.B. 416), § 1, eff. Jan. 1, 2007.

Oklahoma

No specific statute located.

Oregon

In brief

Oregon's Pet Trust law is based on the Uniform Trust Code. Under this law, a trust may be established to provide care for one or more animals alive during the settlor's lifetime. The trust ends when the last surviving animal covered by the trust dies. An oral or written declaration shall be liberally construed in favor of finding the creation of a trust under this section.

In full

Oregon Revised Statutes § 130.185. Pet trust.

(1) A trust may be created to provide for the care of one or more animals that are alive during the settlor's lifetime. The trust terminates upon the death of the animal or, if the trust was created to provide for the care of one or more animal, upon the death of the last surviving animal. An oral or written declaration shall be liberally construed in favor of finding the creation of a trust under this section. There is a presumption against merely precatory or honorary disposition on behalf of an animal.

(2) A trust authorized by this section may be enforced by a person appointed in the terms of the trust or, if a person is not appointed in the terms of the trust, by a person appointed by the court. A person having an interest in the welfare of the animal may request the court to appoint a person to enforce the trust or to remove a person appointed. Reasonable compensation for a person appointed by the court may be paid from the assets of the trust.

(3) Property of a trust authorized by this section may be applied only to its intended use. Upon termination of the trust, property of the trust must be distributed to those persons designated in the trust. In the absence of a designation, the property shall be distributed to the settlor if the settlor is living when the distribution is made, or to the settlor's successors in interest if the settlor is not living when the distribution is made.

(4) Except as ordered by a circuit court or required by the trust instrument, a trustee for a trust authorized under this section need not pay any fee or make any filing, report, registration, periodic accounting, separate

maintenance of funds or appointment by reason of the existence of the fiduciary relationship of the trustee. A person appointed to enforce the trust may request a report under ORS 130.710(3).

Added by 2005 Oregon Laws Ch. 348 (S.B. 275), § 28, eff. Jan. 1, 2006.

Pennsylvania

In brief

Under this statute, which became law in 2006, a trust can be created to provide for the care of an animal alive during the trust maker's lifetime, and ends on the death of the animal or the last surviving animal, if the trust was created to cover more than one animal. Such a trust may be enforced by someone named in the trust or by the court. The amount of the trust can be reduced by the court if it significantly exceeds what is needed to care for the animal(s).

In full

Pennsylvania Statutes and Consolidated Statutes § 7738. Trust for care of animal- UTC 408.

(a) Creation and termination. – A trust may be created to provide for the care of an animal alive during the settlor's lifetime. The trust terminates upon the death of the animal or, if the trust was created to provide for the care of more than one animal alive during the settlor's lifetime, upon the death of the last surviving animal.

(b) Enforcement. – A trust authorized by this section may be enforced by a person appointed in the trust instrument or, if no person is so appointed, by a person appointed by the court. A person having an interest in the welfare of the animal may request the court to appoint a person to enforce the trust or remove a person appointed.

(c) Limitation. – Property of a trust authorized by this section may be applied only for its

intended use, except to the extent the court determines that the value of the trust property exceeds the amount required for the intended use. Except as otherwise provided in the trust instrument, property not required for the intended use must be distributed to the settlor if then living, otherwise to the settlor's successors in interest.

Added by 2006 Pennsylvania Laws Act 2006-98 (S.B. 660), § 9, eff. Nov. 6, 2006.

Rhode Island

In brief

The Rhode Island law states that a trust may be created to provide for the care of an animal or animals alive during the trust-maker's lifetime. The trust ends when the last animal covered by the trust dies. The statute lists a distribution schedule for trust property that remains after the animal had died and also states that such trusts must be liberally interpreted to carry out the transferor's intent.

In full

General Laws of Rhode Island §4-23-1. Trust for care of animals.

(a) A trust may be created to provide for the care of an animal alive during the settlor's lifetime. The trust terminates upon the death of the animal, or if the trust was created to provided [sic] for the care of more than one animal alive during the settlor's lifetime upon the death of the last surviving animal.

(b) Except as provided in this section, the provisions of the general laws which govern the creation and administration of express trusts applies to the trust for the care of an animal.

(c) A trust authorized by this section may be enforced by a person appointed in the terms of the trust or, if no person is so appointed, by a person appointed by the court. A person having interest in the welfare of the animal may request the court to appoint a person to enforce the trust or to remove the appointed person. The appointed person shall have the rights of a trust beneficiary for the purpose of enforcing the trust, including receiving accountings, notices, and other information from the trustee and providing consents.

(d) Property of a trust appointed by this person may be applied only to its intended use, except to the extent the court determines that the value of the property exceeds the amount required for the intended use. Property not required for the intended use, including the trust property remaining upon termination, shall be distributed in the following order of priority:

(1) As directed by the terms of the trust;

(2) To the settlor, if then living;

(3) Pursuant to the residuary clause of the settlor's will;

(4) To the settlor's heirs in accordance with the Rhode Island general laws on decent and distribution.

(e) The governing instrument shall be liberally construed in order to presume against the merely precatory or honorary nature of the disposition and to carry out the general intent of the transferor. Extrinsic evidence is admissible in determining the transferor's intent.

(f) If a trustee is not designated or designated trustee is not willing or able to serve, the probate court shall name a trustee; a court may order the transfer of the property to another trustee, if the court makes a factual finding that it is necessary to assure the intended use is carried out and if a successor trustee is not designated in the trust instrument or if a designated trustee does not agree to serve or is unable to serve.

Added by 2005 Rhode Island Laws Ch. 05-388 (05-H 5430), § 1, eff. July 19, 2005.

South Carolina

In brief

A trust may be created to provide for the care of an animal alive or in gestation during the trust maker's lifetime, whether or not the animal is alive at the time the trust is created. The trust ends upon the death of the last surviving animal. Such a trust may be enforced by a person named in the trust (or by the court, if no one is named in the trust). Property in the trust can only be used for its intended purpose of caring for the named animal(s). The court can reduce the amount of the property if it determines that it exceeds the amount needed for the care of the named animal(s).

In full

South Carolina Trust Code
§ 62-7-408. Trust for care of animal.

(a) A trust may be created to provide for the care of an animal alive or in gestation during the settlor's lifetime, whether or not alive at the time the trust is created. The trust terminates upon the death of the last surviving animal.

(b) A trust authorized by this section may be enforced by a person appointed in the terms of the trust or, if no person is so appointed, by a person appointed by the court. A person concerned for the welfare of the animal may request the court to appoint a person to enforce the trust or remove a person appointed.

(c) Property of a trust authorized by this section may be applied only for its intended use, except to the extent the court determines that the value of the trust property exceeds the amount required for the intended use. Except as otherwise provided in the terms of the trust, property not required for the intended use must be distributed to the settlor, if then living, otherwise to the settlor's successors in interest.

Added by South Carolina Laws Act 66 (S.B. 422), § 1, eff. Jan. 1, 2006.

South Dakota

In brief

South Dakota has two statutes that apply to animal trusts. Statute 55-1-21 states that a trust for a designated animal is valid, it terminates when no living animal is covered by the trust, the governing instrument shall be liberally construed, and extrinsic evidence is admissible to determine the transferor's intent.

Statute 55-1-22 provides that no principal or income may be converted for any use other than the intended use, unless the trust provides otherwise. The court may reduce the trust if it determines that the amount substantially exceeds the amount required for the trust's intended use. The statute also provides for the distribution of unexpended trust property when the trust terminates, and when the court determines the amount in the trust substantially exceeds the amount required.

In full

South Dakota Codified Laws § 55-1-21. Trust for care of designated animal.

Subject to the provisions of § 55-1-22, a trust for the care of a designated animal is valid. The trust terminates when no living animal is covered by the trust. A governing instrument shall be liberally construed to bring the transfer within this section, to presume against the merely precatory or honorary nature of the disposition, and to carry out the general intent of the transferor. Extrinsic evidence is admissible in determining the transferor's intent.

South Dakota Codified Laws § 55-1-22. Provisions governing trusts for specific purposes selected by trustee and for care of animals.

Any trust provided for by §§ 55-1-20 and 55-1-21 is subject to the following provisions:

(1) Except as expressly provided otherwise in the trust instrument, no portion of the principal or income may be converted to the use of the trustee or to any use other than for the trust's purposes or for the benefit of a covered animal;

(2) Upon termination, the trustee shall transfer the unexpended trust property in the following order:

(a) As directed in the trust instrument;

(b) If the trust was created in a nonresiduary clause in the transferor's will or in a codicil to the transferor's will, then under the residuary clause in the transferor's will; and

(c) If no beneficiary results from the application of subsection (a) or (b) of this subdivision, then to the transferor's heirs under § 29A-2-711;

(3) For the purposes of § 29A-2-707, the residuary clause is treated as creating a future interest under the terms of a trust;

(4) The intended use of the principal or income may be enforced by a person designated for that purpose in the trust instrument or, if none, by an individual appointed by a court upon application to it by that person;

(5) Except as ordered by the court or required by the trust instrument, no filing, report, registration, periodic accounting, separate maintenance of funds, appointment, or fee is required by reason of the existence of the fiduciary relationship of the trustee;

(6) A court may reasonably reduce the amount of the property transferred if it determines that that amount substantially exceeds the amount required for the intended use. The amount of the reduction, if any, passes as unexpended trust property under subdivision (2) of this section;

(7) If no trustee is designated or no designated trustee is willing or able to serve, a court shall name a trustee. A court may order the

transfer of the property to another trustee if required to ensure that the intended use is carried out and if no successor trustee is designated in the trust instrument or if no designated successor trustee agrees to serve or is able to serve. A court may also make such other orders and determinations as are advisable to carry out the intent of the transferor and the purpose of §§ 55-1-20 to 55-1-23, inclusive.

Added by 2006 South Dakota Laws Ch. 247 (H.B. 1178), § 3, approved Feb. 22, 2006.

Tennessee

In brief

The Tennessee trust law, which was amended in 2007, validates a trust created to provide for the care of an animal, or animals, alive during the settlor's lifetime. The trust ends upon the death of the last surviving animals covered under the trust. The trust may not run for more than 90 years.

In full

Tennessee Uniform Trust Code § 35-15-408. Trusts for care of animals.

(a) A trust may be created to provide for the care of an animal alive during the settlor's lifetime. The trust terminates upon the death of the animal or, if the trust was created to provide for the care of more than one (1) animal alive during the settlor's lifetime, upon the death of the last surviving animal. The trust may not be enforced for more than ninety (90) years.

(b) A trust authorized by this section may be enforced by a person appointed in the terms of the trust or, if no person is so appointed, by a person appointed by the court. A person having an interest in the welfare of the animal may request the court to appoint a person to enforce the trust or to remove a person appointed.

(c) Property of a trust authorized by this section may be applied only to its intended use, except to the extent the court determines that the value of the trust property exceeds the amount required for the intended use. Except as otherwise provided in the terms of the trust, property not required for the intended use must be distributed to the settlor, if then living, otherwise to the settlor's successors in interest.

Added by 2004 Tennessee Laws Ch. 537 (S.B. 560), § 30, eff. July 1, 2004. Amended by 2007 Tennessee Laws Ch. 24 (S.B. 1046), § 13, eff. Apr. 12, 2007.

Texas

In brief

This statute comprises the pet trust law of Texas. It states that a trust may be established to provide for the care of animals alive during the trust-maker's lifetime. The trust ends with the death of the last surviving animal covered by the trust. Such a trust may be enforced by someone named in the trust or, if no one has been named, by a person appointed by the court. The law also provides a distribution schedule for any assets remaining in the trust.

In full

Texas Property Code §112.037. Trust for care of animal.

(a) A trust may be created to provide for the care of an animal alive during the settlor's lifetime. The trust terminates on the death of the animal or, if the trust is created to provide for the care of more than one animal alive during the settlor's lifetime, on the death of the last surviving animal.

(b) A trust authorized by this section may be enforced by a person appointed in the terms of the trust or, if a person is not appointed in the terms of the trust, by a person appointed by the court. A person having an interest in the welfare of an animal that is the subject of a trust authorized by this section may request the court to appoint a person to enforce the trust or to remove a person appointed to enforce the trust.

(c) Except as provided by Subsections (d) and (e), property of a trust authorized by this section may be applied only to the property's intended use under the trust.

(d) Property of a trust authorized by this section may be applied to a use other than the property's intended use under the trust to the extent the court determines that the value of the trust property exceeds the amount required for the intended use.

(e) Except as otherwise provided by the terms of the trust, property not required for the trust's intended use must be distributed to:

(1) if the settlor is living at the time the trust property is distributed, the

settlor; or

(2) if the settlor is not living at the time the trust property is distributed:

(A) if the settlor has a will, beneficiaries under the settlor's will; or

(B) in the absence of an effective provision in a will, the settlor's heirs.

(f) For purposes of Section 112.036, the lives in being used to determine the maximum duration of a trust authorized by this section are:

(1) the individual beneficiaries of the trust;

(2) the individuals named in the instrument creating the trust; and

(3) if the settlor or settlors are living at the time the trust becomes irrevocable, the settlor or settlors of the trust or, if the settlor or settlors are not living at the time the trust becomes irrevocable, the individuals who would inherit the settlor or settlors' property under the law of this state had the settlor

or settlors died intestate at the time the trust becomes irrevocable.

Added by 2005 Texas Laws Ch. 148 (H.B. 1190), § 6, eff. Jan. 1, 2006.

Utah

In brief

This Utah statute states that a valid trust can be created for the care of a designated domestic or pet animal. The trust ends when no living animal is covered by the trust. Trusts under this section shall be liberally interpreted in favor of the creation of a legally enforceable trust, rather than an honorary one. Evidence outside the actual trust document will be admissible by the court in determining the transferor's intent. No part of the principal or income may be used for any purposes other than the trust's original purpose. The court can reduce the amount of the trust if it decides it significantly exceeds the amount needed to care for the animal or animals.

In full

Utah Uniform Probate Code § 75-2-1001. Honorary trusts – Trusts for pets.

(1) Subject to Subsection (3), if a trust is for a specific lawful noncharitable purpose or for a lawful noncharitable purpose to be selected by the trustee and there is no definite or definitely ascertainable beneficiary designated, the trust may be performed by the trustee for 21 years but no longer whether or not the terms of the trust contemplate a longer duration.

(2) Subject to this Subsection (2) and Subsection (3), a trust for the care of a designated domestic or pet animal is valid. The trust terminates when no living animal is covered by the trust. A governing instrument shall be liberally construed to bring the transfer within this subsection, to presume against the merely precatory or honorary nature of the disposition, and to carry out the general intent of the

transferor. Extrinsic evidence is admissible in determining the transferor's intent.

(3) In addition to the provisions of Subsection (1) or (2), a trust covered by either of those subsections is subject to the following provisions:

(a) Except as expressly provided otherwise in the trust instrument, no portion of the principal or income may be converted to the use of the trustee or to any use other than for the trust's purposes or for the benefit of a covered animal.

(b) Upon termination, the trustee shall transfer the unexpended trust property in the following order:

(i) as directed in the trust instrument;

(ii) if the trust was created in a nonresiduary clause in the transferor's will or in a codicil to the transferor's will, under the residuary clause in the transferor's will; and

(iii) if no taker is produced by the application of Subsection (3)(b)(i) or (ii), to the transferor's heirs under Section 75-2-711.

(c) For the purposes of Section 75-2-707, the residuary clause is treated as creating a future interest under the terms of a trust.

(d) The intended use of the principal or income can be enforced by an individual designated for that purpose in the trust instrument or, if none, by an individual appointed by a court upon application to it by an individual.

(e) Except as ordered by the court or required by the trust instrument, no filing, report, registration, periodic accounting, separate maintenance of funds, appointment, or fee is required by reason of the existence of the fiduciary relationship of the trustee.

(f) A court may reduce the amount of the property transferred, if it determines that that amount substantially exceeds the amount required for the intended use. The amount of the reduction, if any, passes as unexpended trust property under Subsection (3)(b).

(g) If no trustee is designated or no designated trustee is willing or able to serve, a court shall name a trustee. A court may order the transfer of the property to another trustee, if required to assure that the intended use is carried out and if no successor trustee is designated in the trust instrument or if no designated successor trustee agrees to serve or is able to serve. A court may also make such other orders and determinations as shall be advisable to carry out the intent of the transferor and the purpose of this section.

Added by 1998 Utah Laws Ch, 39 (S.B. 75), § 87, eff. July 1, 1998. Amended by 2003 Utah Laws Ch. 131 (H.B. 165), § 66, eff. May 5, 2003.

Vermont

In brief

The Vermont statute was enrolled in 2009, and permits a person to create a trust to provide care for an animal or animals alive during the trust maker's lifetime. The trust terminates upon the death of the animal or, upon the death of the last surviving animal covered by the trust. A person named in the trust or by the court may enforce the terms of the trust. The property in the trust can be used for no purpose other than for the care of the animal or animals named. The court can reduce the amount of the property if it feels it is excessive to the needs of trust's purpose.

In full

Vermont Trust Code, Title 14A § 408.
Trust for care of animal.

(a) A trust may be created to provide for the care of an animal alive during the settlor's lifetime. The trust terminates upon the death of the animal or, if the trust was created to provide for the care of more than one animal alive during the settlor's lifetime, upon the death of the last surviving animal.

(b) A trust authorized by this section may be enforced by a person appointed in the terms of the trust or, if no person is so appointed, by a person appointed by the probate court. A person having an interest in the welfare of the animal may request the probate court to appoint a person to enforce the trust or to remove a person appointed.

(c) Property of a trust authorized by this section may be applied only to its intended use, except to the extent the probate court determines that the value of the trust property exceeds the amount required for the intended use. Except as otherwise provided in the terms of the trust, property not required for the intended use must be distributed to the settlor, if then living, otherwise to the settlor's successors in interest.

Added by 2009 Vermont Laws Act 20 (S. 86), § 1, eff. July 1, 2009.

Virginia

In brief

The Virginia pet trust law provides that a trust may be created for the care of an animal or animals alive during the trust maker's lifetime. The trust ends upon the death of the last surviving animal. The trust instrument shall be liberally construed, and extrinsic evidence is admissible to determine the trust maker's intent. The provisions of the trust may be enforced by someone named in the trust or, if no one is named, by a court appointee. If the court determines that the assets in the trust significantly exceed the requirements of caring for the named animals, it (the court) can distribute the excess to the trust maker, if still alive, or to the trust maker's heirs.

In full

Virginia's Uniform Trust Code § 55-544.08. Trust for care of animal.

A. A trust may be created to provide for the care of an animal alive during the settlor's lifetime. The trust terminates upon the death of the animal or, if the trust was created to provide for the care of more than one animal alive during the settlor's lifetime, upon the death of the last surviving animal. Funds from the trust may be applied to any outstanding expenses of the trust and for burial or other postdeath expenditures for animal beneficiaries as provided for in the instrument creating the trust.

B. The instrument creating the trust shall be liberally construed to bring the transfer within the scope of trusts governed by this section, to presume against the merely precatory or honorary nature of the disposition, and to carry out the general intent of the transferor. Extrinsic evidence is admissible in determining the transferor's intent.

C. A trust authorized by this section may be enforced by a person appointed in the terms of the trust or, if no person is so appointed, by a person appointed by the court. A person having an interest in the welfare of the animal may request the court to appoint a person to enforce the trust or to remove a person appointed. The appointed person shall have the rights of a trust beneficiary for the purpose of enforcing the trust, including receiving accountings, notices, and other information from the trustee and providing consents. Reasonable compensation for a person appointed by the court may be paid from the assets of the trust.

D. Except as ordered by a court or required by the trust instrument, no filing, report, registration, periodic accounting, separate maintenance of funds, appointment, or surety bond shall be required by reason of the existence of the fiduciary relationship of the trustee.

E. Property of a trust authorized by this section may be applied only to its intended use, except to the extent the court determines that the value of the trust property exceeds the amount required for the intended use. Except as otherwise provided in the terms of the trust, property not required for the intended use shall be distributed to the settlor, if then living. If the settlor is deceased, such property shall be distributed pursuant to the residuary clause of the settlor's will if the trust for the animal was created in a preresiduary clause in the will or pursuant to the residuary provisions of the inter vivos trust if the trust for the animal was created in a preresiduary clause in the trust instrument; otherwise, such property shall be distributed to the settlor's successors in interest.

Added by 2005 Virginia Laws Ch. 935 (S.B. 891), § 1, eff. July 1, 2006. Amended by 2006 Virginia Laws Ch. 666 (H.B. 906), § 1, eff. July 1, 2006.

Washington

In brief

This chapter recognizes and validates certain trusts established for the benefit of animals, specifically nonhuman animal with vertebrae. The trust can cover one or more animals, provided they are individually identified or labeled in the trust. Such a trust terminates when no animal beneficiary remains living. Evidence outside the trust document will be allowed by the court to help determine the trustor's intent. This chapter applies to trusts that are created on or after July 22, 2001, and to trusts in existence on July 22, 2001, but that are revocable by the trustor on July 22, 2001.

In full

Revised Code of Washington – Chapter 11.118 – Trust – Animals.

11.118.005. Purpose – Intent. The purpose of this chapter is to recognize and validate certain trusts that are established for the benefit of animals. Under the common law such trusts were unenforceable at law. The legislature intends that such trusts be recognized as valid, and that such trusts be enforceable in accordance with their terms.

Added by 2001 Washington Laws Ch. 327 (S.H.B. 2046), § 1, eff. July 22, 2001.

11.118.010. Definition. As used in this chapter, "animal" means a nonhuman animal with vertebrae.

Added by 2001 Washington Laws Ch. 327 (S.H.B. 2046), § 2, eff. July 22, 2001.

11.118.020. Validity of animal trust. A trust for the care of one or more animals is valid. The animals that are to be benefited by the trust may be individually identified, or may be identified in such other manner that they can be readily identified. Unless otherwise provided in the trust instrument or in this chapter, the trust will terminate when no animal that is designated as a beneficiary of the trust remains living.

Added by 2001 Washington Laws Ch. 327 (S.H.B. 2046), § 3, eff. July 22, 2001.

11.118.030. Use of trust principal or income. Except as expressly provided otherwise in the trust instrument or in RCW 11.118.070, and except as may be necessary to pay the trustee reasonable compensation and to reimburse the trustee for reasonable costs incurred on behalf of the trust, no portion of the principal or income of the trust may be converted to the use of the trustee or to any use other than for the trust's purpose or for the benefit of the designated animal or animals.

Added by 2001 Washington Laws Ch. 327 (S.H.B. 2046), § 4, eff. July 22, 2001.

11.118.040. Termination of trust. Upon termination of the trust, the trustee shall transfer the unexpended trust property in the following order:

(1) As directed in the instrument;

(2) If the trust was created in a nonresiduary clause in the trustor's will or in a codicil to the trustor's will and the will or codicil does not direct otherwise, under the residuary clause in the trustor's will, which shall read as though the testator died on the date the trust terminated; and

(3) If no taker is produced by the application of subsection (1) or (2) of this section, to the trustor's heirs under RCW 11.04.015, as it exists at the time of the trust's termination.

Added by 2001 Washington Laws Ch. 327 (S.H.B. 2046), § 5, eff. July 22, 2001.

11.118.050. Enforcement of trust provisions. The intended use of the principal or income can be enforced by a person designated for that purpose in the trust instrument, by the person having custody of an animal that is a beneficiary of the trust, or by a person appointed by a court upon application to it by any person. A person with an interest in the welfare of the animal may petition for an order appointing or removing a person designated or appointed to enforce the trust.

Added by 2001 Washington Laws Ch. 327 (S.H.B. 2046), § 6, eff. July 22, 2001.

11.118.060. Accounting requirements. Except as ordered by the court or required by the trust instrument, no filing, reporting, registration, or periodic accounting shall be required of the trust or the trustee.

Added by 2001 Washington Laws Ch. 327 (S.H.B. 2046), § 7, eff. July 22, 2001.

11.118.070. Appointment and removal of trustee. If no trustee is designated or no designated trustee is willing or able to serve, the court shall name a trustee. The court may order the removal of an acting trustee and the transfer of the property to another trustee if it is necessary or appropriate in order to assure that the intended use is carried out. A court may also make such other orders and determinations as shall be advisable to carry out the intent of the trustor and the purpose of this chapter.

Added by 2001 Washington Laws Ch. 327 (S.H.B. 2046), § 8, eff. July 22, 2001.

11.118.080. Construction of trust language. In construing the language of a trust for an animal, the governing instrument shall be liberally construed to provide the protections of this chapter. It is presume that language contained in a trust for an animal is not merely precatory or honorary in nature unless it can be shown by clear and cogent evidence that such as the trustor's intent. Extrinsic evidence is admissible in determining the trustor's intent.

Added by 2001 Washington Laws Ch. 327 (S.H.B. 2046), § 9, eff. July 22, 2001.

11.118.090. Application of rule against perpetuities – Effective date of trust. RCW 11.98.130 through 11.98.160 apply to trusts that are subject to this chapter.

Added by 2001 Washington Laws Ch. 327 (S.H.B. 2046), § 11, eff. July 22, 2001.

11.118.100. Trustee powers. Except as otherwise provided in the trust instrument or in this chapter, all powers and duties conferred on a trustee under Washington law also apply to the trustee of a trust for animals.

Added by 2001 Washington Laws Ch. 327 (S.H.B. 2046), § 12, eff. July 22, 2001.

11.118.110. Application of chapter. This chapter applies to trusts that are created on or after July 22, 2001, and to trusts that are in existence on July 22, 2002, but that are revocable by the trustor on July 22, 2001. If a trustor is incompetent to exercise a power of revocation on July 22, 2002, this chapter does not apply to such trust unless the trustor later becomes competent to exercise such power of revocation, in which case this chapter applies to such trust.

Added by 2001 Washington Laws Ch. 327 (S.H.B. 2046), § 13, eff. July 22, 2001.

West Virginia

No specific statute located.

Wisconsin

In brief

While not specifically a pet trust law, Wisconsin's statute states that a person may establish a general honorary trust with no human beneficiary, provided it is not for a "capricious purpose."

In full

Wisconsin Statutes Annotated § 701.11. Honorary trusts; cemetery trusts.

(1) Except under sub. (2), where the owner of property makes a testamentary transfer in trust for a specific noncharitable purpose, and there is no definite or definitely ascertainable human beneficiary designated, no enforceable trust is created; but the transferee has power to apply the property to the designated purpose, unless the purpose is capricious. If the transferee refuses or neglects to apply the property to the designated purpose within a reasonable time and the transferor has not manifested an intention to make a beneficial gift to the transferee, a resulting trust arises in favor of the transferor's estate and the court is authorized to order the transferee to retransfer the property.

(2) A trust may be created for maintaining, keeping in repair and preserving any grave, tomb, monument, gravestone or any cemetery. Any cemetery company, association or corporation may receive property in trust for any of those purposes and apply the income from the trust to the purpose stated in the creating instrument.

(3) (a) A trust described in sub. (2) is invalid to the extent it was created for a capricious purpose or the purpose becomes capricious.

(b) If the assets of any trust described in sub. (2) are valued at less than $5,000 and the court finds that the cost of operating the trust will probably defeat the intent of the settlor or if the trustee, including a cemetery company, association or corporation, named in the creating instrument is improperly described, the court may order distribution of the assets on terms which will as nearly as possible carry out the settlor's intention.

Added by 1969 Wisconsin Laws Ch. 283, § 17, eff. July 1, 1971.

Wyoming

In brief

This statute, representing Wyoming's pet trust law, states that a trust may be created to provide for the care of an animal alive during the settlor's lifetime. The trust terminates upon the death of the last animal named in the trust. The provisions of the trust may be enforced by someone named in the trust or, if no one is named, by a court appointee. If the court determines that the assets in the trust significantly exceed the requirements of caring for the named animals, it can distribute the excess to the trust maker, if still alive, or to the trust maker's heirs.

In full

Wyoming's Uniform Trust Code
§ 4-10-409. Trust for care of animal.

(a) A trust may be created to provide for the care of an animal alive during the settlor's lifetime. The trust terminates upon the death of the animal or, if the trust was created to provide for the care of more than one (1) animal alive during the settlor's lifetime, upon the death of the last surviving animal.

(b) A trust authorized by this section may be enforced by a person appointed in the terms of the trust, trust advisor, trust protector or, if no person is so appointed, by a person appointed by the court. A person having an interest in the welfare of the animal may request the court to appoint a person to enforce the trust or to remove a person appointed.

(c) Property of a trust authorized by this section may be applied only to its intended use, except to the extent the court determines that the value of the trust property exceeds the amount required for the intended use. Except as otherwise provided in the terms of the trust, property not required for the intended use shall be distributed to the settlor, if then living, otherwise to the settlor's successors in interest.

Added by 2003 Wyoming Laws Ch. 124 (H.B. 77), § 1, eff. July 1, 2003.

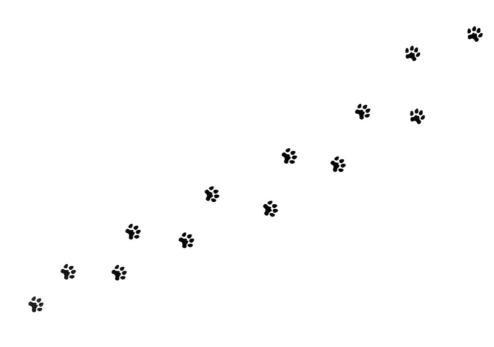

Sample pet trust (applicable in those U.S. states that permit such trusts)

Most people are unlikely to draft their own pet trust document, wisely opting instead to seek professional legal help. Therefore, you should read this sample document for general interest only. Do not construe it as legal advice.

(Lawyers who are unfamiliar with drafting pet trusts, however, may wish to use it as a reference point, with due consideration to local state requirements. They may also want to consider the List of Additional Potential Trust Clause Considerations that follow the Ginger Pet Trust sample document).

Let's decide to set up a pet trust for your dog, *Ginger*, and perhaps *Ginger's* offspring if she is pregnant when you die.

In this case, we will name the trust the *Ginger* Pet Trust and we will refer to *Ginger* throughout the document. You, of course, would use your own pet's name. If you have several animals, you might call the trust by a collective name, such as the John G. Doe Pet Animals Trust and you would refer to *my pet animals* throughout the text of the document.

The term "custodian" in the form below refers to the person you want to posess your pet and serve as its caregiver.

The *Ginger* Pet Trust

The *Ginger* Pet Trust shall be held and administered as follows:

1.1 Mortgages and encumbrances on home:

My trustee shall first apply trust assets to pay off all mortgages and other encumbrances on my home, located at (**address**) legally described as (**legal description**) hereafter, *my home.*

1.2 Establishment of gift fund:

My trustee shall next set aside as a gift fund an amount of property (**which can be at the trustee's discretion or a defined amount of money**) sufficient to generate income for the purposes set forth in paragraph 1.4

below, for the lifetime of *Ginger*, my pet dog (**or, if you have more than one pet you can name them or word this as** *all pet animals I owned or cared for at the time of my death*), and the life or lives of any offspring of *Ginger* (**or other pet animals**) conceived, but not born, at the time of my death.

My trustee shall fix the amount of this fund within a reasonable period of time after my death, at my trustee's sole discretion (**or you can set a specific time frame**) based upon the trustee's experience carrying out the purposes of this trust; provided, however, that if my pet animal's (**or animals'**) custodian (**if you have named one**) or trustee incurs legal expenses to enforce the *Ginger* Pet Trust, my trustee shall set the amount

181

of the trust fund after such expenses are determined and settled and repaid from the remaining estate funds.

My trustee may add amounts to the trust fund as the trustee determines to provide a reasonable buffer against unforeseeable situations incidental to carrying out the terms and intent of this trust, not to exceed (**XX %**) of the amount the trustee deems necessary to fulfill the purpose of the trust.

This pet trust fund shall be designated and hereafter referred to as the *Ginger* Pet Trust.

1.3 Excess trust funds:

My trustee shall distribute any trust funds above the amount necessary to establish the *Ginger* Pet Trust to the following beneficiaries (**list of beneficiaries**). (**You can also leave these funds in the trust and gift them over to named beneficiaries after the death of** *Ginger*). Before making such distributions, however, my trustee shall obtain from each beneficiary a standard written release in a form acceptable to my trustee at my trustee's sole discretion, of any claims or challenges to the legitimacy of the *Ginger* Pet Trust.

My trustee shall distribute any trust funds above the amount necessary to establish the *Ginger* Pet Trust and any trust funds then remaining in the *Ginger* Pet Trust after the death of *Ginger* (or other named pets if there are any named initial in a pet trust) into (X) equal parts and dispose of such parts as follows:

1. My trustee shall pay or transfer two (2) of such parts to (name charity here). The receipt of the treasurer or other proper officer of this entity shall be a sufficient discharge to my trustee.

2. My trustee shall pay or transfer one (1) of such parts to (name charity here). The receipt of the treasurer or other proper officer of this entity shall be a sufficient discharge to my trustee.

1.4 Administration of the *Ginger* Pet Trust:

(A) APPOINTMENT OF CUSTODIAN: I appoint (name and address of the person you have chosen as custodian of your pet or pets) as the custodian of my home and my dog, *Ginger*.

I designate my custodian as the person entitled to enforce the intended use of the principal or income of the *Ginger* Pet Trust pursuant to (the local legislation should be identified). If (party named above) fails or stops acting as custodian for any reason, I appoint (name and address of your alternative custodian) as successor custodian.

(B) RIGHTS OF CUSTODIAN: My custodian shall own my dog, *Ginger*, which I leave to his (**or her**) care and consideration, (**The following is an elective and may or may not be included.**) And he (**or she**) shall live in my home rent-free for as long as he (or she) serves as custodian of *Ginger*. (**This next item is also all optional and may or may not be included.**) My custodian shall pay all his or her own personal living expenses, including but not limited to all utilities, propane, phone, and other services not exclusively required by *Ginger*.

My custodian also shall be responsible for repairs to my home, reasonable wear and tear excepted. My trustee's determination as to whether an expense is personal to the custodian or a trust expense shall be conclusive on all persons.

My custodian shall maintain reasonable communications with my trustee and vice versa, so my trustee is informed in a timely manner of the state of the affairs of both *Ginger* and my home (as the case may be).

(C) DISTRIBUTION OF FUNDS: My trustee may, at his (**or her**) sole discretion (**or this can be mandatory, as in shall**) distribute to my custodian, or apply for the benfit of *Ginger* (**directly or indirectly**), such amounts of the net income or principal, or both, as my trustee determines, at his (**or her**) sole discretion, to be necessary or advisable for care of *Ginger*. Such care may (**or shall**) take into account *Ginger's* living standard at my death, including, but not limited to, costs for food, medical care, and burial of *Ginger's* remains and other matters as relevant regarding *Ginger* and determined by my trustee.

My trustee also may (**or shall**) apply trust income and principal for any legal expenses incurred by my trustee or my custodian which are necessary to enforce the purposes of the *Ginger* Pet Trust.

I authorize my trustee to periodically add to the principal any income not distributed. I further authorize my trustee to use the principal, where necessary, to carry out the objectives of the trust, bearing in mind the likely future expenses of the trust and the size of the buffer established for the fund. My trustee is not authorized to borrow money or mortgage my home to provide income for the purposes of the trust.

(**D**) TERMINATION OF TRUST: The *Ginger* Pet Trust shall terminate with the occurrence of any of the following events:

(1) My last appointed custodian fails to carry out his (**or her**) custodial responsibilities for any reason.

(2) *Ginger* dies.

(3) My last appointed custodian notifies my trustee in writing of his (**or her**) intention to vacate my home.

Upon any of these events, my trustee shall, within 60 (**or some other specified but reasonable number**) days, notify my then-serving custodian in writing that the trust has been terminated.

(**You may want to include the following – or something like it – in your trust agreement if your pet's custodian is to live in your home while taking care of your pet.**)

If *Ginger's* custodian has served until *Ginger's* death, (**regardless of when this person began serving**), my trustee shall notify this custodian that he (**or she**) may purchase my home at seventy-five percent (75 %) of its fair market value. My trustee shall select a qualified appraiser to determine this fair market value and shall include this appraised value in the termination notice.

Ginger's custodian may exercise the option to purchase mentioned above by notifying my trustee, in writing, within sixty (60) days (or some other reasonable number of days) of the date that notice of termination was posted. The custodian will provide evidence with this notification of his (or her) ability to finance this purchase.

Should my custodian terminate the trust before *Ginger* has died, or fails to exercise this option as I have specified, my trustee shall sell my home on the open market, giving preference to offers made by my relatives or friends in the order received. My trustee shall add the proceeds of the sale of my home to assets remaining in the *Ginger* Pet Trust and shall distribute the balance as follows:

(This list will likely be the same as the list in para. 1.3)

If *Ginger* (or any of my pet animals) is alive the time of termination, I give him to my last serving custodian.

(**Note:** A clause can be inserted in this section permitting the estate trustee/executor to appoint a substitute custodian if the last appointed custodian fails to carry out his or her duties.)

Generic Pet Trust Sample

[Include in section of will devoted to specific gifts and legacies.]

I leave [description of pet animal] and [amount of money adequate for animal's care and trust administration expenses] to [name of trustee], in trust, under the terms of the [name of trust] created under Article [X] of this will. If [animal] does not survive me by [survival period], this provision of my will is of no effect.

List of Additional Potential Trust Clause Considerations

Article [x] – Trust for [animal]

A. Conditions of Creation

This trust is to be created upon the conditions stated in Article [x].

B. Governing Law

This trust is to be governed by [name of state] law unless this article provides to the contrary.

C. Trustees

I appoint [primary trustee] as the trustee of this trust. If [primary trustee] is unwilling or unable to serve, I appoint [alternate trustee] as trustee.

D. Bond

No bond shall be required of any trustee named in this article.

E. Trustee Compensation

The trustee shall be entitled to reasonable compensation from the trust for serving as trustee. [or]

No trustee shall be entitled to compensation for serving as trustee.

F. Beneficiaries of Trust

[Caregiver] is the beneficiary of this trust provided [Caregiver] receives [name of animal] into [his] [her] home and provides [animal] with proper care as defined in Section G of this Article. The trustee shall deliver [animal] into [Caregiver's] possession after securing a written promise from [Caregiver] to provide [animal] with proper care. If [Caregiver] (1) dies, (2) is unable to provide [animal] with proper care, or (3) is not providing [animal]

with proper care, [alternate beneficiary] will then become the beneficiary of this trust provided [alternate beneficiary] provides [animal] with proper care. [continue in like manner for additional alternates]

If there is no qualified alternate beneficiary, [allow the trustee to select caregiver, other than the trustee] [create animal care panel to select caregiver] [donate animal].

G. Proper Care

Proper care means [description of care including, for example, requirement of regular visits to a veterinarian].

The trustee shall visit [caregiver]'s home at least [monthly] [quarterly] [annually] to make certain [animal] is receiving proper care. If in the trustee's sole discretion [animal] is not receiving proper care as defined above, trustee shall immediately remove [animal] from the beneficiary's possession and deliver the animal to the alternate beneficiary.

H. Distribution of Trust Property While [Animal] is Alive

1. Care of [Animal]

The trustee shall distribute [amount] to the beneficiary each [month] [year] provided the beneficiary is taking proper care of [animal] as defined in Section G of this Article. [or]

The trustee shall reimburse [caregiver] for all reasonable expenses [caregiver] incurs in the proper care of [animal] as defined in Section G of this Article. Reasonable expenses include, but are not limited to, [food, housing, grooming, medical care, and burial or cremation fees.]

[2. Caregiver Compensation]

The trustee [shall] [may] pay [dollar amount] to trustee on a [monthly] [annual] basis provided [caregiver] is taking proper care of [animal] as defined in Section G of this Article.

[3. Liability Insurance]

The trustee [shall] [may] use trust property to purchase liability insurance to protect the trust, the trustee, and [caregiver] from damage [animal] causes to property or persons.]

[4. Offspring of [Animal]]

The trustee [shall] [may] [shall not] use trust property to reimburse [caregiver] for expenses associated with any offspring of [animal].

[5. Excess Principal]

If a court determines that this trust contains excess property and orders the trustee to distribute that property other than as described above, then that excess shall be distributed under Subsection (I) as if this trust were terminating] [to [name of beneficiary]].

I. Termination of Trust

This trust terminates on the earlier of (a) 21 years after [testator's] death, or (b) upon the death of [animal].

[consider including how death of animal is to be proved, e.g., death certificate from a vet]

[consider having trust also terminate when animal is deemed "lost" – require evidence to prove loss of pet, e.g., copies of police reports, ads in newspapers seeking the pet's return, copies of posters placed in the community, etc.]

J. Distribution of Property Upon Trust Termination

Upon the termination of this trust all remaining trust property shall pass to [remainder beneficiary] if [he] [she] is alive at the time of trust termination. If [remainder beneficiary] is not alive at the time of trust termination, all remaining trust property shall pass to [alternate remainder beneficiary] if [he] [she] is alive at the time of trust termination. [continue in like manner for additional alternates]

K. Spendthrift Provision

This is a spendthrift trust, that is, to the fullest extent permitted by law, no interest in the income or principal of this trust may be voluntarily or involuntarily transferred by any beneficiary before payment or delivery of the interest by the trustee.

L. Principal and Income

The trustee shall have the discretion to credit a receipt or charge an expenditure to income or principal or partly to each in any manner which the trustee determines to be reasonable and equitable.

M. Trustee Powers

The trustee shall have [all powers granted to trustees under [name of state] law. [or] The trustee shall have the following powers: [enumerate trustee powers]

N. Exculpatory Clause

The trustee shall not be liable for any loss, cost, damage, or expense sustained through any error of judgment or in any other manner except for and as a result of a trustee's own bad faith or gross negligence.

(**Note:** Additional provisions will be necessary if the animal and its offspring are valuable from a monetary standpoint.)

After death services for pets

Disclaimer

The fact that various suppliers are listed in this or other sections of the book in no way indicates that the authors, editor, or publisher endorse such suppliers. Listings are meant to give readers an indication of the types of services that are available, the range of products and services they provide, and approximate costs. Readers who make purchases from these suppliers do so entirely at their own risk.

Pet cemeteries and crematories

U.S.A.

If you want to bury your pet in a pet cemetery, look for one that is a member of the International Association of Pet Cemeteries & Crematories (IAOPCC) or the Accredited Pet Cemetery Society (APCS). Members are expected to adhere to guidelines and business practices that are in the interest of customers.

With Internet access, you can reach these organizations at:

IAOPCC www.iaopc.com and,
APCS www.visitrollingacres.com/apcs.html

If you wish to write or telephone, the contact information is:

International Association of Pet Cemeteries & Crematories
5055 Route 11
Ellenburg Depot, NY 12935
Tel: (518) 594-3000
Fax: (518) 594-8801

Accredited Pet Cemetery Society
Angie Pavone, President
Paws Awhile Pet Memorial Park
3426 Brush Road
Richfield, OH 44286
Tel: (330) 659-4270
Fax: (330) 659-4254

The services provided by pet cemeteries vary, but may include picking up your pet's body, cremation, building a burial box or providing a casket, and preparing a grave. Some cemeteries have a chapel and provision for viewing.

Many cemeteries will also provide grave markers or let you supply your own.

Prices for a spot in a cemetery range widely but, in the United States, you may pay from $500 for a small pet to $700 for a plot that will accommodate an extra-large animal. Pine boxes or caskets will range anywhere from $100 (pine box for a small pet) to $500 plus (custom casket for a large animal).

Australia

There appears to be no Australian association of pet cemeteries and no single Internet site dedicated to listing pet cemeteries and crematories. Furthermore, at the time of writing, only one Australian pet cemetery was listed with the International Association of Pet Cemetaries and Crematories (IAOPCC).

There are, however, a number of pet cemeteries in Australia, and the following list, while not comprehensive, may provide a starting point for Australian pet owners who are looking at pet cemeteries. Veterinarians are another good source of information.

The single Australian pet cemetery that is listed with the IAOPCC is:

Compass Pet Heritage Cemetery & Crematory. PO Box 810, Goulburn, NSW, AUS 2580, Tel: 61-2-48445588.

Other pet cemeteries in Australia include:

Australian Pet Cremation Burial Services. Located in Melbourne, Victoria. Contact:

Randall and Bernadette Silva
Tel: 1300-302-575, Mobile: 0418-359-009, postcode 3000. You can access information through the Ozdoggy Internet site at www.ozdoggy.com.au/index.html Ozdoggy is a web portal to a variety of pet services in Australia.

Pets in Peace
1/10 Kenrose St, Carina, QLD 4152,
www.petsinpeace.com.au

Locations in:

- Brisbane (Tel: (07) 3801-2144)
- Gold Coast (Tel: 1-800-100-909)
- Sunshine Coast (Tel: 1-800-100-909)
- Toowoomba (Tel: 0417 365 437);
- Ipswich (Tel: 1-800-100-909)
- Hervey Bay (Tel: 1-800-100-909)
- Beaudesert Area (Tel: 1-800-100-909)
- South Burnett (Tel: 1-800-100-909)

Pets at Peace
PO Box 665,
Camden
NSW 2570
Tel: 1-800-636-797
Fax: (02) 4648 0245
www.petsatpeace.com.au

This is a family operated company and has branches located at:

- Sydney Metropolitan
  Freecall 1-800-636-797
- Newcastle/Central Coast
  Freecall 1-800-636-798
- Illawarra
  Freecall 1-800-819-279
- Canberra (02) 6291-6974
- The Hills District Sydney
  0417-406-730
- Orange/Dubbo / Bathurst
  (02) 6365-9194

Keffanella Park. The Sunshine Coast Pet Cemetery
Tunnel Ridge Rd.,
Mooloolah
QLD 4553
Tel: 0407 94 8293

Pet Rest Cremations
Lot 64, Sippy Downs,
Sippy Downs
QLD 4556
Tel: (07) 5450183

Atkinson's Pet Crematorium & Cemetery
Walkerville, SA
Tel: 61 8 8342 9477

Pets at Rest Memorial Garden
2964 Tasman Highway
Orielton 7172
Tasmania
Tel: 0417-147-331
E-mail: memorialgardens@bigpond.com

Pet Heaven NQ
Two Mile Creek, Bruce Highway
Blue Water QLD
PO Box 7614 BC., Garbutt, QLD 4814
Tel: 07 47 513 220
Mobile: 0417 614 551
Fax: 07 47 513 221
E-mail: info@petheaven.com.au

Possum Ridge Pet Cremations
PO Box 114, Earlville
QLD 4870
Tel: 07-4036-1888
Fax: 07-4036-2619
www.yaps.org.au/cremation.html

Note: Many cemeteries offer cremation services as well as burial services.

Canada

Several Canadian pet cemeteries are also members of the International Association of Pet Cemeteries & Crematories (IAOPCC) and are listed in the Canada section. If there is nothing in your area check your local business telephone directory.

Remember, however, that not all of the cemeteries listed will be members of an organization that asks its members to adhere to specific standards. It will be up to you to investigate those in which you are interested.

United Kingdom

The Association of Private Pet Cemeteries and Crematoria is an organization that has created a code of practice to ensure its members adhere to a high professional standard. Their website provides a list of its members that are located throughout the United Kingdom.

Contact information for the Association of Private Pet Cemeteries and Crematoria is:
Nunclose
Armathwaite
Carlisle
CA4 9JT
Tel: 01252 844478
www.appcc.org.uk/
General Enquiries/comments
contact@appcc.org.uk

New Zealand

New Zealand Pet Crematorium Association Incorporated was registered in July 2000. According to its website: "The founding members of this association, numbering six, cover New Zealand from Whangarei to Mosgiel. As members they are committed and accountable for the services they provide. NZPCA will provide education, information, products, programs and services to help members enhance the quality of the service to pet owners."

A current list of members may be found at:
www.petsatrest.co.nz/NZPCA/location.html

Here is a short list compiled by researching the Internet. This list is not comprehensive, but it will provide a starting point for pet owners in New Zealand. Alternatively, consult your local business directory or veterinarian for the names and locations of pet cemeteries and crematories in your area.

Animal Cremation Services Ltd.
17 Kingsford Smith Street
Rongotai
Wellington City
Wellington 6022
Tel: (04) 3879009
Fax: (04) 3879019

Fond Farewells
PO Box 195
Hamilton City 3214
Tel (07) 8563111
Fax (07) 8563119
Freephone 0508 366332

Bay of Plenty Pet Cremations
Mt Maunganui
Tel: (07) 5745544

Pet Cremations Ltd
PO Box 97-467
South Auckland Mail Centre
Auckland
Tel: + 64 9 263 8782
Fax: + 64 9 263 8783
www.petcremations.co.nz

Pets at Rest Ltd
6/110 Mays Road, PO Box 12708
Penrose, Auckland 1030
Tel: + 64 9 6330203,
Fax: + 64 9 6330206
www.petsatrest.co.nz

Urns and caskets

Keep in mind that many pet cemeteries/crematories will also provide urns, caskets, and other after-death products. The following is a list of some of the hundreds of small businesses that supply these items. Many will ship their products anywhere in the world.

The suppliers listed here should give you an idea of the range of available products and prices. If you have Internet access, you should check the IAOPCC site, because it lists several suppliers.

You will find a large variety of urn sizes, styles, materials and prices. For example, urns may be manufactured from wood, ceramic or stone. Styles include traditional, garden, vase, figurine and others. Sizes run from tiny to huge. Prices will depend on all of these factors.

Similarly, caskets are made from a variety of materials and range greatly in size and price.

Remember, if you do not find a supplier in your own area among those in this starter list, check the Internet yourself, or ask your veterinarian or a representative of a local pet cemetery/crematory.

If you want to make your own casket, try:
**Do-it-yourself coffins
for pets and people**
Woodcraft, PO Box 1686
Parkersburg
WV 26102-1686
800-225-1153
Check it out at:
www.funeralsohio.org/caskets.htm

Australia

Pets In Heaven
Tel: 0402 466 988
www.petsinheaven.com.au

This firm operates in Melbourne and its surrounding suburbs, and provides a variety of services and products.
It will dispatch special vehicles to pick up dead pets, hold funeral ceremonies, carry out cremations, and supply a variety of urns and caskets.

Ozdoggy is a portal to a variety of pet products and services in Australia, including caskets and urns.
www.ozdoggy.com.au/pet_cremation_services.html

Pet Heaven Memorials
Tel: 03-5986-3500
Fax: 03-5982-3055
www.petheavenmemorials.com.au

This is a family-owned and operated business that supplies three basic types of caskets, a range of cremation urns, and grave markers.

Canada

WoodruffForPets.com
123 Hillside Cres.
Cannington, Ontario
Canada, L0E 1E0
Tel: 1-705-432-2698
www.WoodruffForPets.com

These folks feature a line of handcrafted pine and cedar caskets with plush satin linings and pillows, starting at about CDN $215 and ending at CDN $285.
The cedar urns come in small, medium and large, with prices starting at CDN $65 to CDN $115. The firm has tons of other pet-related products and ships just about anywhere in the world.

United Kingdom

Poffins
Head office is at:
Poffins House
1 Walpole Close
Kings Meadow
Bicester, Oxon
OX26 2YF, UK
Tel: 01869 244010
Fax: 01869 601123

Day-to-day operations are at:
77 Heyford Park, Upper Heyford
Bicester, OX25 5HD
www.poffins.co.uk/caskets.html

This firm offers a line of oak or mahogany veneer ashes caskets with figurine tributes or brass plaques £14.90 to £22.50, depending on size and type of wood. It also sells marble ashes caskets (£31.39); high-quality pine or rosewood photo frames, with fitted ash box on the rear (£33.33); large marble urns (£150.53); a book urn (£70.48); rock urns; and many other styles, including pottery urns. The firm also carries caskets for the ashes of horses and ponies.

Cranmore Irish Pet Crematoria

Northern Ireland:
45 Tullyrusk Road
Dundrod
Co. Antrim BT27 4JH
Tel: 028 9082 5713
Fax: 028 9082 5723
www.petcrematoriumireland.com/ni/index.htm

The Republic of Ireland:
Tel: 01-281 9744
Fax: 01 281 1884

The firm serves both the Republic of Ireland and Northern Ireland,

and offers a variety of standard and discreet casket for customers of its cremation service. The standard caskets include a pottery urn and wooden casket, while the discreet caskets include a sleeping cat and carved dog.

United States

T&S Pet Memorials
PO Box 5173
Ocean Isle
NC 28469
www.tspetmemorials.com

This website offers a wide variety of pet memorials, but not all of its products are after-death items. Urns and caskets top its product list, followed by headstones, sympathy gifts and garden stones. There is an extensive list of other items as well.

The urn and casket lines are comprehensive. Small wooden urns start at about $50 and become more expensive for larger pets. Caskets for a small dog or cat start at about $125. T&S accepts certified checks, money orders and personal checks. If you want to pay online with a credit card, you have to use PayPal.com.

Forever Pets, Inc.
Jamie Minea, Owner
Forever Pets, Inc.
1848 50th St. E.
Ste 103, Inver Grove Heights
MN 55077
Tel: (888) 450-7727
E-mail: minea@foreverpets.com
www.foreverpets.com

Forever Pets, Inc. started as a wholesale supplier of pet cremation urns and burial markers in 1996. It is located in St. Paul, Minnesota. Forever Pets, Inc. developed its first website in 1997 so it could sell directly to the public. Owner Jamie Minea says on the website:

"We attempt to ship all urn orders the same business day as received if placed by 11 a.m. Central Time, otherwise we will ship out the next business day from St. Paul, Minnesota. Only burial markers take longer to ship."

All About Pet Urns
PO Box 85, Sharon
PA 16146
Tel: 330-219-8628
https://www.storesonline.com/site/75983 7/page/45029

This firm has an extensive line of urns for cats and dogs, including custom pet memorial planters that will house both your pet's ashes and a favorite plant in separate compartments. They also provide biodegradable urns.

The promotional material on the website states:

"We love our pets and they deserve the very best from us. Here you will find something perfect for preserving your pet's memory. We offer memorial products for every budget. We specialize in unique urns for pets, and offer you free standard shipping on our urns, caskets, and memorial products. Quality counts in extending our love to our best friends so that is why we offer a huge selection of the top pet memorial products available today."

**Faithful Friend Pet Caskets
and Urns**
1135 North Main Street
PO Box 646
Bowling Green
OH 43402

Tel: (419) 353-2007
1-800-567-PETS (7387)
Fax: (419) 354-8075
E-mail: FaithfulFriend@wcnet.org
www.faithfulfriendpet.com

This firm sells urns shaped like a
sleeping cat or a dog bone ($58), and
octagonal and rectangular (6 different
sizes) caskets at prices ranging from
$141 to $336.

Pet Memories
1012 Acapulco LN
Arlington
Texas 76017

Tel: 1-800-756-6492
Fax: (817) 468-4675
www.petmemory.com

Pet Memories offers rigid polyurethane
caskets with a natural grain finish and
a soft flocked lining. The casket is
airtight, water resistant, and able to
withstand pressure exceeding 360
pounds per square inch. A variety of
sizes are available at costs ranging
from $115 to $430. The urn selection
includes hollow cat urns, doghouse
urns, figurine urns, photo urns, tower
urns, wooden box urns, garden granite
urns and horse cremation urns. There
is also a selection of flat market urns
in circular, paw print and bone shapes.
Prices begin at under $70 for one of
the flat marker urns and run up to
$250 for a horse cremation urn with
a figurine.

New Zealand

Loving Tributes
River Road RD2
Christchurch

Tel: (03) 325-7326
Fax: (03) 325-7037
www.lovingtributes.co.nz

This firm provides caskets, urns, and
a variety of other products and services.
These products and services include
cremation arrangements, funeral and
memorial services, grief counseling,
euthanasia support, headstones, garden
rocks and crosses.

Monuments/memorials

It would be impossible to list all of the
companies that provide monuments and
memorials of various types for bereaved
pet owners. A few are included here to
get you started and to show the range of
products and services available, but we
suggest you use the Internet for a more
comprehensive listing.

If you do not have access to the
Internet, consult your vet, local business directory, pet cemetery, or other
pet services provider.

Should you wish to mark your pet's
grave with a stone monument or marker and there are no firms in your area
that specialize in these items, there are
businesses in other parts of the state or
country that will engrave a monument
to your specifications and ship it to you.

Alternatively, you might approach a
local monument maker for human
grave sites and ask whether they
would consider making a stone for
Fido or *Fifi*. Engraved stones for pets

are usually smaller than engraved stones for humans.

Below are some of the companies and products available for marking the graves of your pets.

Australia

Memorystone.com.au
Factory 2
104-106 Killara Road
Campbellfield
Vic 3061

Tel: (03) 9357-6234
Fax: (03) 9357-6236
https://memorystone.com.au/
index1.htm

These folks make memorial stones to mark a variety of events, one of them being the death of a pet. In their pet-stones section, they state:

"Petstones are designed to serve as an attractive, permanent grave marker for you or your family to treasure in memory of the love and devotion given by your pet. They give so much – they deserve to be remembered!

"And Petstones are fashioned from natural slate and permanently engraved with your own personal message of remembrance. They are impervious to the elements and will look beautiful either inside or outside for generations to come."

Canada

Canadian supplier of gravestones and monuments for pets appear to be limited, perhaps because the proximity to the United States makes it easy for Canadians to order these products

online and have them shipped at relatively little cost. Canadians who want a domestic product might check with local gravestone makers for humans.

United Kingdom

Stone Essentials
Mount Spring Works
Off Burnley Road East
Waterfoot. Rossendale
Lancashire, BB4 9LA

Workshop: 01706 210605
Tel: 01254 888624
Fax: 01706 228707
www.stone-essentials.co.uk

This is a family stonemasonry business that cuts and engraves pet headstones and memorials as part of a more comprehensive line of stonework products and services. Dog grave markers and cat gravestones are just a few of the options this business provides.

United States

4everinmyheart.com
Specialty Pet Products
PO Box 215
Narberth, PA 19072

Tel: 1-800-873-7387
Fax: (610) 649-2935
www.4everinmyheart.com

This company will engrave monuments from river rock (in the $40 range for a 4" to 6" rock all the way up to about $260 for the 10" to 16" extra large rock) with a ceramic color photograph tile. An engraved slice of granite ranges from about $70 to $210, depending on size and engraving. Slate memorials are less expensive and the bronze photographic memorials range from $350 to $650. It also sells a quality line of garden memorials, urns and plaques. Products are shipped directly to your door.

Memorable Images
PO Box 210766
Nashville
TN 37221-0766

Tel: (615) 216-7587
1-866-374-6758 (toll free)
www.memorable-images.co.

This firm makes photo tiles. In other words, you can have a photograph of your pet digitally produced on white ceramic for use as a grave marker or to sit on your mantle or coffee table. If your photo is not perfect, they can add or remove objects from it to produce the image you want.

The firm does not sell directly to the public, and you must contact it for the name of a dealer in your area.

Forever Pets, Inc
(See *Urns and caskets section page 189.*)

New Zealand

Pets at Rest
(See *Pet cemeteries and crematories section page 188.*)

This firm provides a variety of other services. If you are looking for a firm that deals exclusively with grave markers for pets, you should look for such firms in local printed directories or query companies that make headstones and grave markers for humans. Some may be willing to take special orders for pet markers.

Virtual pet cemeteries and memorial sites

Virtual pet cemeteries are essentially Internet websites that have been established by individuals or organizations so that pet owners can post an epitaph to a deceased pet. Some people write anecdotes about their pet, or discuss how much they miss it. Some write poems. Many accompany their writing with a picture of the animal. The following sample sites will give you a little taste of the virtual pet cemetery sites that are out there and how people use them. Many are free, some charge a small fee, and others ask for a donation. Please note that any prices given are subject to change.

The Virtual Pet Cemetery
www.virtualpetcemetery.org/pet/index.html

Free, but will process your epitaph more quickly with a small donation. Includes space for a photo and your written epitaph. VirtualPetCemetery.org claims that over the past decade it has become the "best-known pet cemetery in the world."

pets.ca Virtual Pet Cemetery
www.pets.ca/petsites/index_cemetery.php

Free. Space for a photo and your written epitaph.

Wild Rose Virtual Pet Cemetery
www.wildrosecemeteries.com

Free, but asks for donations to continue services. Includes the choice of headstones, backgrounds, photo placement, and space for your written epitaph.

Gone to Dogstar
www.gonetodogstar.com

Text only Dogstar is free, while a premium Dogstar memorial is USD$25. This is a creative approach, with dogs being buried in constellations. The premium Dogstar memorial provides space for photos and tributes.

Eternal Pet.com
www.eternalpet.com/index.htm

Professional online tributes available for USD$10. Space for a photo and tribute. Separate pages available for cats, dogs, birds, fish, amphibians, horses, reptiles, rabbits and hamsters.

In Memory of Pets

www.in-memory-of-pets.com

Free, but accepts donations. Space for a photo and a story.

Rainbow Bridge Pet Memorial Website

www.petloss.com

Free. Space for a photo and a tribute. This is an extensive site that was founded by an individual in 1995 and features pet loss support, chat room, and special weekly memorial ceremonies. As of August 2008, the names of more than 163,000 pets appeared on the *Bridgelist,* which is essentially a list of pets that have died and whose owners commemorated them by adding their names to the list. Where does the name come from? You better read that for yourself online in any of 11 languages, including English.

Angel Hearts

www.angel-hearts.org

Free. A beautiful site with poems and the ability to post several pictures of your departed pet for others to view.

Pet loss support resources

A surprising number of organizations provide counseling to people who are grieving the loss of a companion animal. In the United States, many university veterinary schools offer such services. Some organizations staff their services and hotlines with professional grief counselors; many use veterinary student volunteers. If you would like this type of counseling, contact your veterinarian or nearest veterinary school; if you have access to the Internet, check out the Pet Loss Support Page www.pet-loss.net/index.html and/or search pet loss counseling to find out where you can get help in your area.

Where to get help

In Australia

There are a number of courses offered to educate people to become pet loss grief counselors, so there must be grief counselors available. To find them, however, you may have to consult with your veterinarian. Nevertheless, one who is listed on the Internet is:

Jean Griffin
Registered Psychologist
Strathfield
Sydney NSW
Australia
Telephone (02) 9763-1104

In Canada

We were unable to find any national Canadian organizations that provide pet loss support through the use of a 1-800 number. Instead, here is a list of support organizations and counselors on a province-by-province basis. Note that not all provinces are represented.

Alberta

NORTH

Pet Therapy Society of Northern Alberta
www.pettherapysociety.com
/pawstoremember.html

Tel: (780) 413-4682

SOUTH

Straja Linder King
www.spiritualdirections.com
Tel: (403) 210-2802

British Columbia

VANCOUVER

Monica Franz, BA, RCAT, BCATR
www.monicafranz.ca

Tel: (604) 732-3220
#410–943
West Broadway
Vancouver, B.C.
V5Z 1K1

Vancouver continues on the next page

**Ruth Shell, MA, RCC, and
Lucy the comfort spaniel**
www.ruthshell.com
Tel: (604) 681-7175
671F Market Hill (False Creek)
Vancouver, BC V5Z 4B5

Shiri Joshua, M.A.
www.shirijoshua.com
Tel: 1-778-319-PETS (7387)

VICTORIA

Pacific Animal Therapy Society
http://members.shaw.ca/patspets
Tel: (250) 389-8047
8 a.m. to 9 p.m. daily Pacific Time

This organization operates a pet loss
support line, partly funded by donations from veterinary clinics in the
Greater Victoria area. The pet loss support line offers emotional comfort to
anyone who has experienced or antici-
pates losing a companion.

SURREY

Daybreak Counselling Services
www.daybreakcounselling.com
Tel: (604) 802-6959

Support, counseling and seminars
offered, based in Surrey, B.C.

Manitoba
WINNIPEG

**Winnipeg Humane Society
Pet Loss Support Group**
www.winnipeghumanesociety.ca/your
_Pet/pet_Loss_Support.php
Tel: (204) 988-8804

Anne Papadopoulos Mulders
www.members.shaw.ca/pet-loss

Nova Scotia
DARTMOUTH

Bide Awhile Animal Shelter
www.bideawhile.org
67 Neptune Crescent, PO Box 50029
RPO Southdale, Dartmouth
NS B2Y4S2
Tel: (902) 469-9578

Ontario
MISSISSAUGA

Halton/Peel Pet Loss Support Group
(905) 272-4040 (Mississauga area)
(905) 842-2252 (Oakville area)
(905) 637-5233 (Burlington area)

Note: These numbers courtesy of three
funeral homes. Ask to leave a message
for the Pet Loss Support Group, and
your message will be forwarded by the
funeral home staff.
www.mississaugapets.com/petloss.html
E-mail: petloss@sympatico.ca

OTTAWA

**Pet Loss Support Group
of Ottawa-Carleton**
www.lookmedia.ca/plsg

TORONTO

Bronwyn Dickson, M.S.W, R.S.W
www.grievingapet.com
Tel. (416) 999-7146

In United Kingdom

For an animal-loving nation, the U.K.
has surprisingly few pet loss support or
counseling facilities listed on the Internet.
Perhaps the British are able to cope under
these circumstances better than other
people. Here is one to begin with:

Blue Cross Pet Bereavement Service
www.bluecross.org.uk/web/site/AboutUs/
PetBereavement/PBSSIntro.asp
Tel: 0800 096 6606
E-mail: pbssmail@bluecross.org.uk

This service provides telephone and
e-mail support.

In the United States

The following organizations either
operate national telephone counseling
service through 1-800 numbers or can
point you to local services in your area.

**American Veterinary Medical
Association (AVMA)**
www.avma.org/careforanimals/animat-
edjourneys/animatedfl.asp
The American Veterinary Medical
Association website has a listing of grief
counseling resources in the *Goodbye
Good Friend* section of its website.

**Animal Love and Loss Network
(ALLN)**
www.alln.org
Tel: (410) 820-9575

The Animal Love and Loss Network
(ALLN) is based in Bozman, Maryland.
Its mission statement claims that it
"seeks to bring together those who are
mourning the injury, illness or loss
of an animal companion." The mission
statement further provides that it
"represent and support those who are
working to end the exploitation and
suffering of all animals." The website
provides weekly online forums to discuss
your loss with others.

Argus Institute
www.argusinstitute.colostate.edu/
find.htm
Tel: (970) 297-1242

This organization is associated with the
Colorado State College of Veterinary
Medicine. Argus counselors are trained
to deal with your grief due to the loss
of a pet. According to its website, Argus
Institute "can provide you with reading
resources, counseling, or support in
many situations, including how to talk to
children about pet loss, body-care issues,
or finding a support group."

In addition, "Argus counselors can provide support if your companion animal
has been injured or has been recently
diagnosed with a serious illness." Argus
Institute can assist you with treatment
or euthanasia decisions.

**Association for Pet Loss and
Bereavement**
www.aplb.org
Tel: (718) 382-0690

The APLB, headquartered in Brooklyn,
NY, operates a comprehensive website
offering information on various subjects
related to pet loss. It also provides telephone contact information to put you in
touch with counselors across the United
States and Canada. The APLB website
also provides contact information on
pet loss support groups on a state-by-
state basis.

The APLB is a non-profit association of
concerned people who are experienced
and knowledgeable about pet death.
Members are professional counselors as
well as pet-loving people from all other
walks of life. They are concerned with
helping pet lovers cope with pet loss.

This loose federation of individuals
and organizations from around the
world encompasses a collective core
of practical help and knowledge that

surpasses anything any single member could develop. Its aim is to develop and share the highest standards of professional excellence in pet bereavement counseling and public education.

The APLB will help you find appropriate counseling, personal supportiveness, and reading material. Its website offers chat rooms and individual e-mail assistance, as well as seminars and training sessions, a quarterly newsletter, a constantly updated listing of useful books on pet loss, and occasional national conferences.

Companion Animal Related Emotions (CARE) www.cvm.uiuc.edu/CARE
Tel: (877) 394-2273 (toll-free)
(217) 244-2273 in the Champaign, Illinois area

The University of Illinois, College of Veterinary Medicine, offers a confidential telephone service known as CARE. Its website states that those "who are either grieving the loss of a companion animal or are anticipating a loss are encouraged to call. If you need a compassionate, understanding person to talk to, we are here to listen and to support you." Their services are available Sunday, Tuesday, and Thursday evenings between 7-9 p.m. Central Time.

The Rainbow Bridge (See *Appendix K*)
www.petloss.com
This website provides extensive information on where to get pet loss support around the United States.

In New Zealand

Vicki Mathison. Counselor
251 Ranzau Road E.
Hope, Nelson 7001
New Zealand
Tel: 006 43 544 7255
E-mail: Timd@environment.cawthron.org.nz

Books to help with pet loss

Coping with Sorrow on the Loss of Your Pet
by Moira K. Anderson. 2nd Ed.
Loveland Co.
Alpine Publications 1996

Pet loss: A Thoughtful Guide for Adults and Children
by Herbert Nieberg, Ph.D.
& Arlene Fischer
New York, Harper & Row 1996

Loving and Losing a Pet: A Psychologist and a Veterinarian Share Their Wisdom
by Michael Stern Ph.D.
& Susan Cropper, D.V.M.
Northvale, NJ Jason Aronson Inc. 1998

The Loss of a Pet
by Wallace Sife, Ph.D. 3rd ed.
NY, Howell Book House 2005

When Only the Love Remains: The Pain of Pet Loss
by Emily Margaret Stuparyk
Hushion House 2000

Goodbye, Friend: Healing Wisdom for Anyone Who Has Ever Lost a Pet
by Gary Kowalski
New World Library 2006

Exotic pets prohibited vs. acceptable animals as pets

Pet Industry Joint Advisory Council (PIJAC)
While there may be considerable debate about what animals we should be prohibited from keeping as pets, the Pet Industry Joint Advisory Council (PIJAC) in Canada has drawn up a list of candidates it feels many people would consider reasonable.

Suggested list of animals that should *not* be kept as pets

- All *artiodactylous ungulates* (except domestic goats, sheep, pigs and cattle).

- All *canidae* (except the domestic dog).

- All *crocodilians* (such as alligators and crocodiles).

- All *edentates* (such as anteaters, sloths and armadillos).

- All *elephantidae* (elephants).

- All *erinacidae* (except the African pigmy hedgehog).

- All *felidae* (except the domestic cat).

- All *hyaenidae* (hyenas).

- All *marsupials* (except sugar gliders).

- All *mustelidae* (such as skunks, otters and weasels) except the domestic ferret.

- All *non-human primates* (such as gorillas and monkeys).

- All *pinnipeds* (such as seals, fur seals and walruses).

- All *perissodactylous ungulates* (except the domestic horse and ass).

- All *procyonidae* (such as raccoons, coatis and cacomistles).

- All *pteropodidae* (bats).

- All *raptors, diurnal and nocturnal* (such as eagles, hawks and owls).

- All *ratites* (such as ostriches, rheas and cassowaries).

- All *ursidae* (bears).

- All *venomous reptiles.*

- All *viverridae* (such as mongooses, civets and genets).

The PIJAC favors the prohibited species list approach because such lists are shorter and easier to enforce than lists of acceptable animals.

Canadian Federation of Humane Societies (CFHS)

The CFHS is opposed to the trade or keeping of wild animals as pets.

The CFHS defines a wild or exotic animal as any animal, native or non-native to Canada that has not been domesticated through many generations of selective and controlled breeding and thereby adapted to living in close association with humans.

Background/Rationale

- Domestic animal species have been selectively bred and managed for hundreds and thousands of years based on preferred attributes, such as temperament and behavior.

- Non-domestic animal species are often unpredictable, potentially dangerous, and by reason of these factors as well as by reason of their own needs, are unsuitable as pets.

- Wild or exotic animals are often acquired without full knowledge of the specific physiological, social, environmental, behavioral and exercise needs of the species. Many of these needs cannot be met when these animals are kept as pets.

- The trade or keeping of wild or exotic animals as pets causes suffering and death through capture, transport, abandonment and improper care.

- Escape, release or abandonment of wild or exotic animals may threaten animal and human health and the viability of native wildlife.

For urban areas, the following captive-born animals are considered acceptable by the CFHS:

- Dog
- Cat
- Guinea pig
- Rabbit
- Mouse
- Rat
- Gerbil
- Golden hamster
- Chinchilla
- Budgerigar
- Canary
- Other common cage birds
- Aquarium fish
- Finches
- Ferret

For rural areas with access to fields or paddocks, plus the appropriate shelter, the following captive-born species, in addition to the above, are appropriate as pets or companions:

- Horse
- Donkey
- Pig
- Sheep
- Goat
- Cattle
- Llama
- Domestic fowl
- Duck (Mallard or Muscovy types)
- Turkey
- Guinea fowl
- Peafowl
- Alpaca

Note: No amphibians (frogs, toads, newts, salamanders, etc.) or reptiles (turtles, lizards, iguanas, snakes, etc.) appear on either list.

Choosing an appropriate pet

Another Canadian agency, the Canadian Veterinary Medical Association (CVMA), is perhaps a little more flexible in terms of what animals should or should not be kept as pets, stating that the suitability of an animal species (domestic or non-domestic) as pets depends on the commitment of pet owners to:

- treat them humanely;
- provide for all of their physical, behavioral, and medical needs; and
- ensure that keeping the pet does not infringe on the rights and safety of members of the host community.

Background

Animal species selectively bred and managed over time for desirable traits make the best pets. Nevertheless, any animal may behave in ways that can be unpredictable and potentially dangerous.

Although members of certain wild species can be hand-raised and appear tame, they may be more likely to exhibit natural behaviors which could make them inappropriate to keep as pets.

When determining if an animal species is appropriate as a pet, ask yourself:

- Do I have, or can I get, adequate knowledge of the species regarding nutritional, health care, social and housing requirements? These needs should be easily met.
- Am I permitted by law to keep the animal on my premises?
- Is the animal likely to be a nuisance to neighbors on the basis of odor,

noise, messiness, unruliness, viciousness, or destructive behavior?

- Is the animal venomous or poisonous?
- Can the animal/species transmit diseases to humans, or to wild or domestic animals?
- Could the animal/species cause ecological damage if it escaped?
- Can the animal be transported in a humane manner?
- Can the animal be obtained from a captive breeding program?

As a footnote, very little has been said by most organizations about keeping insects as pets. Should you doubt that some people do keep insects, check out the Internet site www.amonline.net.au /insects/insects/pets.htm, which is dedicated to the keeping of insects as pets. Or try www.mantisuk.com, with its focus on pet mantids. There are actually many other sites dedicated to pet insects. Common sense would dictate that you should stick to domestic insects and spiders and read up on how to look after them.

Finding a qualified veterinarian for your exotic pet

The owner of an exotic pet must find a vet who knows how to deal with the type of animal he or she keeps, and who has the facilities, equipment, and materials to treat it. Many vets get only limited exposure to exotic animals during their training so, if possible, try to find a vet who specializes in exotics and has received specialized training – a residency in exotic animal medicine or board certified in an exotic animal specialty.

An exotic animal veterinarian is one who has taken additional training to treat exotic animals. For this purpose, exotic animals are defined as species other than farm animals or those most commonly kept as companions. Many animals, such as ferrets, rabbits, guinea pigs and small rodents, are anatomically and physiologically very different than dogs, cats and barnyard animals. To specialize in their care, a veterinary student must cover coursework and residencies that are beyond the scope of standard veterinary schools.

In the United States, exotic veterinarians are certified by the Association of Exotic Mammal Veterinarians.

If you cannot find a specialist, look for someone who has experience treating exotic pets. Ask whether the potential vet has taken special training or has memberships in specialty organizations such as the Association of Avian Veterinarians (AAV) or the Association of Reptile and Amphibian Veterinarians (ARAV).

If you cannot find someone who has experience with exotics, select a vet who has interest in exotic animals and is willing to learn about them and consult with specialists when necessary.

Whatever you do, do not wait until your pet gets sick to look for a vet, or you may be forced to take what you can get on short notice. Also, it is important for your pet to have an initial examination by its vet. This allows the vet to become familiar with you and your animal and allows you to become comfortable with the vet. You can also see whether the vet is a good match for you and your pet.

The ideal veterinarian for an exotic pet should be confident handling the animal and should spend some time during the initial examination discussing its care, diet, and any possible problems that may appear with that particular species.

The easiest way to get a lead on qualified veterinarians in your area is via the Internet. If you do not have access, go to a library or find someone who does. Here are some sites to check out:

www.altpet.net/vets. This site lists vets in the United States (state by state) and the U.K. who will treat exotic pets. About a dozen states are represented.

www.aav.org. This is the site of the Association of Avian Veterinarians. It will help anyone in the United States find qualified vets who specialize in birds.

www.arav.org/ECOMARAV/timssnet/ common/tnt_frontpage.cfm. This is the site of the Association of Reptilian and Amphibian Veterinarians. The members directory lists vets who are qualified, or specialize in, reptiles and amphibians in the U.S., and in more than two dozen foreign countries. Remember, not all of those listed are in private practice. Some are employed by zoos or other organizations.

www.aemv.org. This is the site of the Association of Exotic Mammal Veterinarians. It lists vets who specialize in exotics in the U.S. and internationally.

Animal retirement homes, temporary pet care providers and sanctuaries

In communities throughout the United States, there are retirement homes, temporary care providers, and sanctuaries that provide long and short-term homes for pets. Some of these facilities accept almost any type of creature, while others are dedicated to a single species or even a specific breed.

Pet owners who have no one else to consult when they become too old or too ill to continue looking after their animals can engage these homes for help. They can also arrange to have one of these establishments take their pet should they predecease it.

Some of these facilities are operated by individuals as either for-profit or not-for-profit businesses. Others are operated by veterinary schools, animal shelters or other animal welfare organizations.

What are the differences between these three types of facilities?

In general, animal retirement homes agree to look after a pet for the remainder of its life for a fee. A pet owner either turns his animal over to the home before he or she dies and pays for its upkeep, or makes arrangements to transfer the animals and a sum of money to the home after death. There are a variety of ways the fee can be paid upon the pet owner's death – a straight bequest from the will, an insurance policy, a trust fund, etc.

Temporary pet care providers also work on a fee basis, but agree to provide care for pets only as long as it takes to find them new homes. This is the type of service typically provided by veterinary schools or animal welfare organizations. Most claim to take great care in selecting homes for pets, including making follow-up visits to ensure the welfare of the animals. Some will provide care for life if they cannot find suitable homes for the animals.

Retirement homes and temporary pet care providers largely (but not exclusively) deal with dogs, cats, and sometimes birds. Most cannot accommodate larger animals, such as horses, donkeys, and larger birds, such as parrots and their kin. More exotic creatures, such as snakes, reptiles and wild animals, should be kept away from shelter-run organizations because they tend to feel these species should be euthanized.

Larger animals and the exotics may find a more welcoming home at a sanctuary that specializes in them. The most common types of sanctuaries welcome horses (and sometimes their close relatives) and tropical birds.

Research suggests that these three types of facilities, especially animal retirement homes, are rare to non-existent in countries other than the United States. Non-U.S. residents may have to consult with veterinarians, special interest groups, animal shelters or welfare organizations to find out what is available locally.

For the United States, the following organizations are categorized and arranged alphabetically by state. These will provide a starting point for your own research and will give you an idea of the types of organizations and services that are available – as well as their costs. You can compare the retirement homes listed here with those that you find on your own.

Remember, however, these facilities are listed for your information only. A listing here is not a recommendation. You must make contact with any home in which you have an interest and do the research needed to determine if it is suitable for your pet. Costs are given for those facilities that have made them readily public; otherwise, you will have to contact the retirement homes yourself.

Remember, you do not have to restrict yourself to facilities in your home state but, no matter where you are thinking of placing your animals, investigate thoroughly and make sure you visit the facility. There have been cases where the owners of pet retirement homes have run into financial or other difficulties and authorities had to step in to rescue the animals in their care. If you can, make periodic visits to be sure that the facility is maintained properly on an ongoing basis.

Facilities for mixed species

Most of these facilities are geared to dogs and cats, although some will accept other animals as well.

Illinois

Assisi Animal Foundation
Continuing Pet Care Program
PO Box 143
Crystal Lake,
IL 60039-0143
Tel: 815-455-9411
Fax: 815-455-9417
www.assisi.org

This is a no-kill, not-for-profit, cage-less shelter for dogs and cats. It is named after St. Francis of Assisi, an early champion of animals.

From the website:

"If arrangements are made in advance, senior citizen pet owners can enjoy the company of their pet until their situation changes, and not worry about what will happen to their beloved companion afterward."

"…we established a program of continuing care that assures a pet's future here in our cheerful facility. The program provides peace of mind for the guardian and a comfortable natural lifetime for the pet if and when it is needed."

Kansas

Office of Development
K-State College of Veterinary
Medicine
103 Trotter Hall
Manhattan, KS 66506
Tel: 785-5324378
Fax: 785-532-5999
www.vet.ksu.edu/depts/
development/perpet/index.htm

From the website

"Established in 1996, the Perpetual
Pet Care Program is a comprehensive
program designed to provide animals
with loving homes once an owner
is no longer able to provide daily
care. Enrollment benefits include:

- Performing an extensive search
  to locate a loving home;
- Providing for your pet's lifelong
  medical needs;
- Monitoring of the adoptive home; and
- Designating your charitable interest.

"For more than a century, the College
of Veterinary Medicine has provided
care for animals. This expansive network will support every aspect of
your pet's adoption and life."

Minnesota

Home For Life
P.O. Box 847
Stillwater, MN 55082
Tel: 1-800-252-5918
Fax: 651-993-1512
E-mail: info@homeforlife.org
www.homeforlife.org

From the website:

"A typical family home is not appropriate for every animal. Those who are old,
or who have disabilities, health, or temperament problems may do better in
another setting. Home For Life® believes
that these special animals deserve an
alternative that will meet their needs."

"We believe that animals should live
in a setting that is appropriately scaled
to allow for individual attention and
specialized care."

"At Home for Life®, our animals are
not offered for adoption. Once an animal comes to us, it truly has a home
for life."

"Through our example, we hope to discourage an acceptance of euthanasia
for animals who can still live a quality
life. Just as apathy can become a way
of life, so can empathy."

The facility itself is located in Star
Prairie, Wisconsin. You will need to
contact them for costs.

New York

North Shore Animal League
25 Davis Avenue
Port Washington, NY 11050
Tel: 516-883-7575
www.NSAL.org

From the website:

"The plan is simple. Complete one enrollment form for each of your pets, which
we will keep on file here at the League.
If you are no longer able to care for your
pets or if they should outlive you, we will
immediately finalize arrangements with
your representative, family member, or

executor to have your pets transported to our facilities (transportation costs are separate and are your responsibility). This program is available to your pets regardless of where you reside."

"We will provide food, shelter, and state-of-the-art medical care for your pets until they can be adopted into new loving homes."

"To ensure that we do not have to divert funds from our other life- saving programs, we require a modest enroll-ment fee ($10,000 for your first pet, $5,000 per additional pet). No money is required up front to enroll but is instead paid when your pets are ready to be taken into our care. The enroll-ment fee can be paid through a bequest in your will or trust document, by making the League a beneficiary of a life insurance or retirement policy, or an up-front payment if you so choose."

Oklahoma

Oklahoma State University Development Office
308 McElroy Hall
Stillwater, OK 74078-2011
Tel: 405-744-5630
www.cvm.okstate.edu/development/CohnFamilyShelter.asp

From the website:

"The Oklahoma State University College of Veterinary Medicine has constructed a facility and developed a program to assure lifelong care for beloved family pets. Pet owners can feel secure in the knowledge that their pets will receive the love, care, and attention they had always enjoyed at home. A generous donation from the

estate of Ms. Leah Cohn Arendt along with matching funds from the University has enabled the OSU College of Veterinary Medicine to con-struct a life-care center for companion animals. In 1998 the Cohn family dream was brought to life through the establishment of the Cohn Family Shelter for Small Animals."

"Funds to operate the program come from the earnings from invested gifts. Minimum gift amounts are $15,000 for each cat, $25,000 for each dog and $50,000 for each large animal (pony, llama, or horse). Most people choose to provide necessary funding through a bequest in their wills. A 5 % non-refundable reservation fee assures your animal a place in the center."

For a full explanation of the program and photos of the facilities, search *life-care center* when you get to the website.

Texas

Texas A&M University Stevenson Companion Animal Life-Care Center
College Station, TX 77843-4461
Tel: 979-845-1188
www.cvm.tamu.edu/petcare

From the website:

"The Stevenson Companion Animal Life-Care Center provides the physical, emotional, and medical needs of com-panion animals whose owners are no longer able to provide that care. Clients of the center include pet owners who want to assure their pet's future prior to entering a retirement home, being hospitalized for an extended period, or predeceasing a pet."

"The center was established by the Texas A&M College of Veterinary Medicine in 1993."

"Enrollees at the center include dogs, cats, birds, horses, and even a donkey."

"An enrollment fee of $1000 per small animal and $2000 per large animal is due at the time of enrollment. The minimum endowment requirements vary depending upon the age of the owner at the time of the enrollment. For specific information about enrollment, please contact an administrator at the center."

"Our residents feel at home in the Center. It is designed in a relaxed fashion. The animals have freedom to roam and explore at will, while also having space for themselves during quiet times. There are five separate yard areas for the dogs to get plenty of sunshine and exercise. The cats have access in and out of their rooms through upper windows in the doors, but the dogs do not have access to the cat rooms."

"Residents receive daily exercise in their large fenced yard areas. There are Frisbees, rope tugs, balls, and an array of toys to keep the dogs and staff occupied and happy. All resident pets receive regularly scheduled bathing and grooming. Nutritional concerns are also monitored and special diets are developed for residents with special needs."

You can tour the center through a video on the website.

Facilities for birds

Arizona

The Oasis Sanctuary
PO Box 30502
Phoenix, AZ 85046-0502
Tel: 520) 212-4737
Fax: 520-212-0123
www.the-oasis.org

From the website:

"The Oasis Sanctuary is a rescue and retirement facility for exotic birds, predominantly CITES I and II endangered birds. We offer birds a stable and loving home for the duration of their natural lives. We do not sell or breed birds. Nor do we offer birds for adoption."

Colorado

The Gabriel Foundation
PO Box 11477
Aspen, CO 81612
Tel: 970-963-2620
www.thegabrielfoundation.org

From the website:

"The Foundation provides sanctuary and permanently cares for birds that are not suitable for adoption or foster care or for persons that have specifically requested that their birds remain in permanent sanctuary. All sanctuary birds receive the same high level of care as the birds available for adoption and foster care. Sanctuary birds are housed in species-specific rooms at the Foundation and have access to outdoor flights, abundant enrichment, and psychological and environmental support on a daily basis."

"The Gabriel Foundation has 3 programs for relinquishment – Adoption, Long Term Foster, and Sanctuary. To begin the process we require completion of the Client Bird History and the Parrot Acquisition Contract. The demand for incoming birds is high and the wait list time will vary by species and circumstances. The completed Client Bird History and Parrot Acquisition Contract returned to the Relinquishment Coordinator will put your bird(s) on the waiting list. Once the paperwork is received, you will be contacted and given an estimate of when you might expect an opening in Quarantine. Quarantine opens to take in new birds approximately 4 times a year. Exceptions and special arrangements for emergency situations can be discussed directly with the Director of Relinquishments."

Georgia

Feathered Friends Forever
2547 Misty Road
Appling, GA 30802
Tel: 706-541-9316
www.featheredfriendsforever.org

From the website:

"At Feathered Friends Forever we provide a loving, life long, care home for tropical birds. We take in all types, for any reason the bird cannot be cared for, in any situation. Feathered Friends Forever Rescue/Refuge, Inc. is the largest privately owned rescue/refuge in Georgia and one of the largest in the nation."

"Feathered Friends Forever is an organization dedicated to improving the lives of parrots, as pets. We are located in Harlem, Georgia. The goals of Feathered Friends Forever are:

1. To rescue abused or unwanted parrots from both retail and private situations. For example, birds that have been given from owner to owner because of behavioral problems.

2. To act as a placement service for friendly or tame birds whose owners have had to give up their bird's for any reason.

3. To serve as an educational resource on the care and responsibilities of owning tropical parrots as pets and advice service for: prospective and current bird owners via E-mail, schools, and retail pet stores.

4. To serve as a permanent sanctuary for birds not suitable for adoption.

5. Our long-term goals include building full flight areas for our birds."

Massachusetts

Foster Parrots Ltd.
PO Box 650
Rockland, MA 02370
Tel: 781-878-3733
www.fosterparrots.com

From the website:

"Foster Parrots, Ltd. is a non-profit organization dedicated to the rescue and sanctuary of unwanted, languishing, and abused captive parrots and other displaced exotics. Through educational initiatives we seek to bring wider public awareness to captive parrot issues and to help raise standards of care for domestically kept parrots. A staunch advocate for parrots as wild animals, Foster Parrots has established a conservation project in the South American country of Guyana that has helped protect parrots and other wildlife since 2004."

Minnesota

Midwest Avian Adoption & Revenue Services (MAARS)
PO Box 821
Stillwater, MN 55082
Tel: 651-275-0568
www.maars.org

From the website:

"MAARS' first function is to educate the public and people who already live with birds about proper bird care. We feel that education about bird care and behavior helps people to provide the best homes possible for the birds already in captivity. Our second function is to accept and rescue surrendered, abandoned, neglected, and abused parrots and other captive exotic birds for health care, behavioral therapy, and placement in a new home or sanctuary."

Facilities for cats only

Alaska

Alaska Humane Society Adopt-A-Cat
PO Box 240587
Anchorage, AK 99524
Tel: 907-344-8808
www.adopt-a-cat.org

This is a no-kill, non-profit cat shelter that tries to find homes for cats that do not have one. If necessary, it will provide a permanent home for cats that cannot be adopted. If you live in Anchorage and have no other options

should you be unable to care for your cat due to illness or death, you might be able to arrange to have it placed with the AHS Adopt-A-Cat program.

Arizona

The Hermitage No-Kill Cat Shelter
PO Box 13508
Tucson, AZ 85732
Tel: 520-571-7839
www.hermitagecats.org

Like the AHS Adopt-A-Cat program, this one tries to find homes for the cats under its protection and is not a dedicated retirement facility.

From the website:

"We are dedicated to the shelter, protection, and care of homeless cats, especially those that are often not considered adoptable by other organizations."

"We currently provide care for over 400 cats and kittens in clean, yet homey conditions. Our facility comprises approximately 4,000 square feet under roof, with an additional 4,000 square feet of entirely fenced-in outdoor areas. Our free-roaming felines have access to fresh air and sunlight without being in any danger from predators, vehicles, nasty people, or other vagaries of civilization."

California

Volunteers for Inter-Valley Animals
Sylvester House
PO Box 896
Lompoc, CA 93438
Tel: 805-735-6741
www.viva-animal-shelter.org

"The residents of Sylvester House are cats whose people have passed away or can no longer take care of them. Your cats will receive comprehensive, loving care for the rest of their days for a single lifetime fee of just $5,000 per cat. A cat's average stay at Sylvester House is ten years. Ten years worth of food, litter, and vaccines, as well as annual medical and dental checkups, totals approximately $3,652 at today's prices. When you add in overhead for shelter, maintenance, and utilities, and consider that a cat's medical needs increase as she ages, you can see that our rates are very reasonable."

NatCat – The National Cat Protection Society Retirement Centers

6904 W. Coast Hwy
Newport Beach, CA 92663
Tel: 949-650-1232
and
9031 Birch St
Spring Valley, CA 91977
Tel: 619-469-8871
www.natcat.org

This is another organization that does not provide permanent retirement facilities for cats, but is a no-kill organization that attempts to find homes for animals left with them.

From the website:

"Our state-of-the-art facilities with protected access to the outdoors in large enclosed patio areas let them enjoy themselves without compromising their safety."

Pet Pride

PO Box 1055
Pacific Palisades, CA 90272
Tel: (310) 836-5427
www.petpride.org

From the website:

"Please contact us for information as to how you can provide the GIFT of LIFE by remembering PET PRIDE in your will. You may also provide for the future care of your cat(s) to be entrusted to our care in our "Home for Cats.""

California Cat Center, Inc.

Nancy Smith, J.D.
& Andrea S. Mullen, D.V.M.

Van Nuys location
7048 Sophia Ave.
Van Nuys, CA 91406

**Mar Vista location
(above Centinela Feed & Pet Store)**
3860 S. Centinela Ave., Second Floor
Los Angeles, CA 90066
Tel: toll free 866-780-2287
www.californiacatcenter.com

From the website:

- We provide luxurious, cats-only, living for the remainder of your cat's healthful life. Our facilities provide lifetime veterinary care and treatment including weekly vet visits and annual physical examinations.

- California Cat Center provides health maintenance diets, needed medicines for any ailments that may develop, such as daily insulin injections or fluids for kidney failure.

- We offer a stimulating feline environment with playful catwalks, music, bird-watching, and lots of love. Our facility offers a peace of mind for the cat lover who can no longer care for their precious pet.

New York

The Sunshine Home at This Old Cat
P.O. Box 320
Honeoye, NY 14471
Tel: 585-229-4790
www.thesunshinehome.com

From the website:

"Our property offers a retirement community exclusively for felines – where disabled and geriatric cats are able to live out the balance of their lives with respect, dignity, love, and care."

See the website or contact them by phone for information on how to have your cat admitted. Fees are based on the cat's age and medical condition as well as your ability to pay.

Kent Animal Shelter
2259 River Road
Calverton, NY 11933
Tel: 631-727-5731
www.kentanimalshelter.com

From the website:

"Kent provides an alternative for cats who survive their owners. A simple clause in a person's will can provide long term care for a pet that otherwise may not have an alternative place to live. The kitties live in a homelike atmosphere and are never caged. Veterinary care is always available if necessary. An outdoor screened cattery allows the residents to enjoy the warmer summer months outside. A donation in the amount of $5,000 is required for lifetime care regardless of the age of the pet."

Australia

Animal Welfare League of South Australia (AWLSA)
Wingfield Branch
1-19 Cormack Road
Wingfield, SA 5013
Tel: (08) 8348 1300
www.animalwelfare.com.au

From the website

"The cat retirement home in *purrrfect* surroundings!"

"The pampered cats that choose this facility as their new home will enjoy expert and committed attention from the League's dedicated staff. They enjoy air conditioned comfort, an opportunity to bask in the fresh air and sunshine, food to tempt the fussiest palate, and the ability to stroll outside in the security of enclosed pergolas, making this 'Cat Heaven.' This purpose built home provides luxury not normally associated with pet care, providing you with peace of mind."

"All the cats have the services of the League's full time vet with bi-annual vaccinations, dental checks, and weekly weight assessments. Their continuing good health is our primary concern."

"Peppertree Cottage is one of the best facilities of its type in Australia. A number of well cared-for cats see out their remaining years in comfortable and pleasing surroundings, removing the worry for those who are no longer able to care for their feline friend."

"Peppertree Cottage provides ongoing care for cats whose owners have provided a legacy from their estate for their cats. Cats must be 8 years or older."

"Your legacy will enable the AWL to ensure that your much loved cat lives out its days in comfort and security."

"Peppertree Cottage is open for inspection by appointment seven days a week, between 10am and 4pm. For more information please call the League at 8348 1300."

Facilities for dogs only

There are few retirement facilities devoted solely to dogs. Compared with cats, dogs are generally larger, noisier, cost more to maintain and are more demanding in terms of human time and attention.

New York

Silver Streak Kennels
Terry & Don Vought
129 Bourne Rd.
Morris, NY 13808
Tel: 607-263-2007
www.dogretirement.com

From the website:

"Silver Streak Kennels is an Upstate New York dog boarding kennel and life on a farm in the country for your dog. This is not a conventional kennel. These dogs are treated as our own."

"Dogs spend quality time – months or years – surrounded by trees, grass, and rolling hills – in comfort and love. In essence, your dog becomes a loving member of our family."

There is no onsite information for the cost of their services.

Facilities for horses

Arizona

Horse Rescue of North Scottsdale,
Arizona
6631 E Montgomery Rd.
Cave Creek, AZ 85331
Tel: 602-689-8825
www.rescueahorse.com

From the website:

"We are a non-profit animal rescue. We will provide a safe home for your animal, full of love, kindness, and food. We do provide medical and farrier care as needed."

"If you have an unwanted horse, mule, or donkey – PLEASE contact The Horse Rescue of North Scottsdale. We are a NON-KILL, PRO-ANIMAL Rescue! We care for ALL breeds – from Arabs, Saddlebreds, Quarter Horses, T-Breds, Morgans, Mustangs, Appys, Ex-Police horses, and many more."

"We are committed to placing the horses in very kind, knowledgeable, and loving homes while trying to place them in environments that are lasting and loving."

This is a rescue organization committed to finding good homes for the animals in its care rather than serving as a retirement facility. But for some people who can no longer look after their animal(s), it may be a good alternative to more painful options.

Maryland

HorseNet Horse Rescue
2504 Arthur Avenue
Eldersburg, MD 21784
Tel: 301-922-7029 (Skype link)
www.horsenethorserescue.org

Note: At the time of writing this facility was closed to incoming horses due to lack of funding, although emergencies were being considered on a case-by-case basis. This situation may change, so check the website.

Michigan

Hugs2Horses
P.O. Box 71
Fowlerville, MI 48836
Tel: 517-223-3263
www.hugs2horses.com

From the website:

"We want to offer an alternative to slaughter for older, abused, neglected, and abandoned horses. We provide a safe sanctuary until we can find them homes where they will be loved and cared for."

"We offer a place of sanctuary and a retirement home for aged and unwanted horses. We bring sanity to an insane situation. We give horse lovers an alternative to putting down their beloved animals."

"We are located just outside of Fowlerville on over 100 acres where we offer a sanctuary. Our facility provides a heaven for older, neglected, and abused horses, however, not all of our horses are abused and abandoned. We house several that have been turned into us by owners that for one reason or another are no longer able to care of them. They pay (this is not a free service if their horse is healthy, but it is a cost efficient one) for their loved one. They care enough about their horses to see that they are cared for until placement can be made. This can take up to six months, but most take only a couple of months to place. The healthy ones are the easy ones to find a good home for."

Note:

There is a webpage that lists a large number of horse rescue groups in the U.S., state-by-state. Remember, however, most of these organizations are dedicated to rescuing horses in bad situations, not providing retirement services for horses whose owners can no longer care for them. You might, however, check them out. Some are desperately short of funds and might be willing to provide permanent retirement spaces for animals with generous owners. Any profits could be directed to their disadvantaged animals.

For the U.S. listing, go to: www.netpets.com/horses/horsresc/horsgrp.html

For a list of horse rescue groups in Canada and the U.K., go to: www.netpets.com/horses/horsresc/internatgrp.html

Australia

Second Chance Horse Rescue & Rehabilitation
PO Box 120
Kalamunda,
WA6926
Tel: 045 858 9007
info@schrar.org
www.schrar.org

From the website

"We are a small horse welfare organization based in Western Australia. We aim to promote and educate the public on horse welfare throughout Western Australia to help reduce neglect, abandonment, and abuse of these animals. We also aim to provide sanctuary and all necessary care, training, and medical attention required to as many abused, neglected, and abandoned horses and ponies as possible."

Although the website does not specifically mention the acceptance of retired animals, this and similar organizations may well consider such requests if the animal(s) is accompanied by money sufficient for its care and perhaps extra to help offset the facility's operating costs.

Facilities for exotic animals

Indiana

Black Pine Animals Park
1426 W. 300 N.
P.O. Box 02
Albion, IN 45701

©2006 Professional Animal Retirement Center, Inc.
www.blackpineanimalpark.com

From the website

"Black Pine Animal Park in Albion, Indiana, is more than a zoo; it's a 'last chance' refuge for exotic animals in need. We exist to give rescued and retired animals a safe haven, as well as educate people on responsible pet ownership and enhance their knowledge of exotic and endangered species.

"We believe that by allowing you to look into our world, where we care on a daily basis for over 80 big cats, bears, primates, birds, reptiles, and more, we can plant a seed of awareness that can positively impact the conservation and preservation of exotic and endangered species around the world, and help ensure future generations will make informed decisions about how to live in harmony with them."

Leaving a legacy

Some of the ways to leave a legacy include:

Make a memorial cash contribution to an animal care organization

The Humane Society of the United States (HSUS) has established the Kindred Spirits Program, which allows anyone to make a memorial donation in honor of a pet, friend, or relative. Making a donation to the HSUS is a personal way to honor the memory of a pet or person – a kindred spirit. The idea is to let the gesture keep the spirit of a lost loved one alive, while helping all animals.

Once you have made a donation, the HSUS will send a card of sympathy to the person or family you designate, acknowledging your thoughtful donation. As a lasting tribute, the HSUS adds the name of the deceased to a *Book of Kindred Spirits*, located at its national operations center in Gaithersburg, Maryland.

The American Society for the Prevention of Cruelty to Animals (ASPCA) also offers you an opportunity to make a memorial gift to support its work.

In the words of the ASPCA:

"Give a gift to remember the lives of individuals who celebrated the human-animal bond, or a four-legged family member who changed the lives of those he or she loved, by giving an ASPCA Memorial Gift. The ASPCA will notify the recipient of your gift in 10 days, unless otherwise specified."

Bury your pet (or its ashes) in a special place

You can likely think of a suitable spot to bury your pet – your dog's favorite place to lie in the garden; a shady nook at the back of your yard for your cat. If you live in an apartment or condo, or if the law precludes you burying your pet on your property, you can opt for cremation and deal with the ashes in some manner that has meaning to you and your family. You could also bury the body or ashes in one of the many animal cemeteries that have sprung up over the past decade. Special caskets, urns, headstones and markers are available to memorialize your pet. (See *Appendix J*.)

Honor your pet with a memorial service

This little ceremony can be particularly helpful when young children are among the bereaved. It offers a structured opportunity for you to explain that most pet animals have shorter lives than humans but, in this case, their pet had a good and happy life to which they contributed. Such a ceremony provides everyone with an opportunity to say goodbye to the pet and to reach closure more smoothly.

Set up a living memorial

Some people dedicate a spot in their garden or plant a special tree or shrub in memory of their pet, setting it off with a marker or plaque with the pet's name and dates of birth and death.

Create a photo album

It should be self-evident that to carry out this idea, you must have taken photos of your pet when it was alive and active. If you did, pull them together and get busy while memories are still fresh. Don't be afraid to annotate your photos so that in a few years you won't be scratching your head wondering where they were taken or why. You could also put a number of photos together in a framed collage as a reminder of your beloved companion.

Make a video

Many people start when their pet is a youngster and record at various times throughout its life. Make sure you get lots of footage of you and your family members with the pet – playing with it, training it, feeding it, and so on. If, at the end of your pet's life, you hold a memorial service, you can end your video with this tribute.

Maintain a good estate plan

There can be no greater tribute to your pet, or pets, than an estate plan that provides for you, your family, your pets and organizations, such as the Humane Society, SPCA and others that benefit animals in general.

Surveys and research about pets

Pets rule the roost in the U.S.A. and Canada

2004 U.S. and Canadian survey by the American Animal Hospital Association (AAHA)

The American Animal Hospital Association is an international organization of more than 33,000 veterinary care providers who treat companion animals. It was established in 1933. For pet care information or a referral to an AAHA hospital, pet owners can visit the AAHA website at www.healthypet.com or call (800) 883-6301.

This 2004 survey looked at the growing importance of pets in today's society. Some 1,238 pet owners who take pets to AAHA-accredited veterinary hospitals in the United States and Canada were surveyed.

The results indicate that pets are getting preferential treatment as they become more important as members of the household.

Of the survey respondents:

- When asked, "Who listens to you best?" 45% chose their pet, while 30% chose their spouse or significant other.

- 82% thought of their pet more than once while away from it during the day.

- 53% spent more on their pets in 2004 than they did three years before.

- If they were deserted on an island and could choose only one companion, 50% would pick a dog or cat rather than a human.

- 93% were likely to risk their own life for their pet, while 64% of owners expected their pet to come to their rescue if they were in distress.

- When traveling without their pet, 61% left their pet in the care of friends or family.

- 55% had an emergency preparedness plan that included their pet in case of natural disasters such as fire, flood or earthquake.

- 94% thought their pet had human-like personality traits, such as being emotional or sensitive, outgoing, inquisitive or stubborn.

- 94% took their pet for regular veterinary checkups to ensure its quality of life.

"Pet owners are going to great lengths to keep their pets happy and healthy," said Dr. Daniel S. Aja of the AAHA. "From daily exercise and regular veterinary checkups to making arrangements for pets in case of emergency, this survey shows that pet owners are extremely dedicated to their beloved pets."

Source: American Animal Hospital Association (AAHA)
www.aahanet.org/media/s_pos2004.aspx

Who owns what kind of pet and how much do they spend?

2007-08 U.S. survey by the *American Pet Products Association, Inc. (APPA)*.

APPA is the leading not-for-profit trade association made up of more than 1,000 pet product manufacturers, their representatives, importers, and livestock suppliers. Membership consists of a diverse group representing both large corporations and growing business enterprises worldwide.

This survey analyzed American pet ownership from the standpoint of the types and numbers of pets kept and the amount of money spent on them for various products and services.

In the 2007-08 survey, APPA found:

- 63% of U.S. households own a pet, which equates to 71.1 million homes.

- In 1988, the first year the survey was conducted, 56% of U.S. households owned a pet compared to 63% of households today.

Breakdown of pet ownership in the United States

Number of U.S. households that own a pet (millions)

Bird	6.4	
Cat	38.4	
Dog	44.8	
Equine	4.3	
Freshwater fish	14.2	
Saltwater fish	.8	
Reptile	4.8	
Small animal	6.0	

Note: some households have more than one type of pet.

Total number of pets owned in the United States (millions)

Bird	16.0	
Cat	88.3	
Dog	74.8	
Equine	13.8	
Freshwater fish	142.0	
Saltwater fish	9.6	
Reptile	13.4	
Small animal	24.3	

* Ownership statistics are gathered from APPA's 2007/2008 National Pet Owners Survey.

Spending

These spending statistics are gathered by APPA from various market research sources, but are not included in the organization's bi-annual National Pet Owners Survey. The spending statistics do appear on the industry statistics and trends section of the website.

Total U.S. expenditures on pets (billions)

2009	$45.4 (est.)	
2008	$43.2	
2007	$41.2	
2006	$38.5	
2005	$36.3	
2004	$34.4	
2003	$32.4	
2002	$29.5	
2001	$28.5	
1998	$23	
1996	$21	
1994	$17	

Estimated 2009 sales within the U.S. market

In 2009, it is estimated that $45.4 billion will be spent on pets in the United States.

Breakdown (billions):

Food	$17.4	
Vet care	$12.2	
Supplies/OTC medicine	$10.2	
Live animal purchases	$2.2	
Pet services: grooming & boarding	$3.4	

Actual sales within the U.S. market in 2008

In 2008, $43.2 billion was spent on pets in the United States.

Breakdown (billions):

Food	$16.8	
Vet care	$11.1	
Supplies/OTC medicine	$10.0	
Live animal purchases	$2.1	
Pet services: grooming & boarding	$3.2	

According to the 2007-2008 APPA National Pet Owners Survey, basic annual expenses for dog and cat owners in dollars include:

	Dogs	Cats
Surgical vet visits	$453	$363
Food	$217	$188
Kennel boarding	$225	$149
Routine vet	$219	$175
Groomer/ grooming aids	$127	$18
Vitamins	$77	$31
Treats	$66	$40
Toys	$41	$26

Note: APPA does not ask survey participants how much in total they spend on their dog or cats annually. The expenses listed above are not all inclusive and each category was asked separately of the survey participant.

Source: American Pet Products Association, Inc. (APPA)
http://americanpetproducts.org/press_industrytrends.asp

What are the top 10 reasons people take their dogs and cats to the vet (aside from routine checkups and inoculations)?

Veterinary Pet Insurance (VPI) is the oldest and largest health insurance plan for pets in the United States.

A review of policyholder claims by VPI identifies the top reasons why dog and cat owners with VPI Pet Insurance took their pets to the veterinarian in 2008.

The complete list of top conditions/ illnesses follows:

2008	Top 10 claims by incident	
	Dogs	Cats
1.	Ear infections	Lower urinary tract disease
2.	Skin allergies	Gastritis/ Stomach upsets
3.	Pyoderma/ Hot spots	Chronic renal failure
4.	Gastritis/ Vomiting	Enteritis/ Diarrhea
5.	Enteritis/ Diarrhea	Diabetes mellitus
6.	Urinary tract infections	Skin allergies
7.	Benign skin tumors	Hyperthyroidism
8.	Osteoarthritis	Ear infections
9.	Eye inflammation	Upper respiratory virus
10.	Hypothyroidism	Eye inflammation

Source: VPI Pet Insurance Company
http://press.petinsurance.com/pressroom/211.aspx

Why do people give their pets to shelters?

National Council on Pet Population Study and Policy (NCPPSP) study identifying the top 10 reasons why people relinquish their pets to animal shelters.

The NCPPSP gathers and analyzes data concerning the number, origin, and disposition of pet dogs and cats in the United States, promoting responsible stewardship of these companion animals, and recommending programs to reduce the number of unwanted pets in the country.

Top 10 reasons people give pets to shelters in the United States

	Dogs	Cats
1.	Moving	Too many in house
2.	Landlord issues	Allergies
3.	Cost of maintenance	Moving
4.	No time for pet	Cost of maintenance
5.	Inadequate facilities	Landlord issues
6.	Too many pets in home	No homes for littermates
7.	Pet illness	House soiling
8.	Personal problems	Personal problems
9.	Biting	Inadequate facilities
10.	No homes for littermates	Doesn't get along with other pets

Source: National Council on Pet Population Study and Policy (NCPPSP)
www.petpopulation.org

Another survey conducted by the NCPPSP in the United States between 1994 and 1997 showed that 64% of all pets that entered participating animal shelters for any reason were destroyed.

Boarding kennel of the future

2003 survey, conducted by Best Friends Pet Resorts, on what pet owners want in a boarding kennel

Best Friends Pet Care is a leading boarding and grooming service provider in the United States, operating 39 centers in 19 states across the country.

The third annual "Kennel of the Future" survey, conducted by Best Friends Pet Resorts and Salons during 2003 included feedback from a total of 1,400 dog and cat owners. It concluded that American pet lovers want full-service pet care centers that provide not only quality care, but one-stop shopping for all of their pet care needs.

The survey found that today's pet owners want the convenience of having a variety of services – boarding, grooming, training, and even vet checkups – available all under one roof. Survey respondents who board their pets when they travel indicate that they would like additional services including:

- More than 70% of survey respondents say they want grooming services offered by the facility where they board their pets.

- Nearly half of all respondents want their pet to attend Doggie Day Camp or Play Group.

- Almost 35% want dog training while their pets are boarding.

- More than 30% would like their pets to have vet checkups when they board.

The percent of respondents choosing each of those service areas increased by at least 10% since the original survey conducted in 2001, and interest in dog training grew by more than 50%.

A growing number of pet owners also want to be able to book their pets' boarding reservations online. More than 40% of the 2003 survey respondents indicated that they would like to make reservations online, compared with just 25% two years ago. However, 50% say they still want to make their pets' reservations with a real person – either on the phone or face-to-face.

More amenities

Consistent with the finding of the 2003 survey, pet owners want the best care money can buy.

The survey found that 40% of cat owners and 38% of dog owners would like luxury suites with raised beds and rugs for their pets.

Even those pet owners not looking for luxury accommodations said they would pay extra for special amenities:

- 50% would like a video monitoring service that would allow them to look in on their pets via the internet while they are away.
- 33% would like a radio or television in their pets' room.
- 14% would like massage or water therapy.

Source: Best Friends Pet Care
www.bestfriendspetcare.com

What bothers neighbors about dog owners?

2005 survey by the American Kennel Club on responsible dog ownership in the United States

The American Kennel Club is dedicated to upholding the integrity of its registry, promoting the sport of purebred dogs, and breeding for type and function. Founded in 1884, the AKC® and its affiliated organizations advocate for the purebred dog as a family companion, advance canine health and well-being, work to protect the rights of all dog owners, and promote responsible dog ownership.

The survey of 500 dog owners and 500 non-dog owners, conducted in August 2005, aimed to gain a better understanding of the concerns of the two groups in order to mark the third annual AKC Responsible Dog Ownership Day.

What bothers non-dog owners about their canine-loving neighbors when they stroll with their pets in the community? A 2005 American Kennel Club survey revealed that the top issues bothering non-dog owners include jumping, barking, and owners not obeying pooper-scooper laws.

Of the non-dog owners surveyed:

- 47% said "a lack of picking up after their dogs" was their number one complaint with dog owners.
- 25% cited, "not controlling their dog" or "letting the dog jump on you."
- 13% said "allowing a dog to bark incessantly" was their number one grievance.

- 4% said "the way dog owners fawn over their pooches or use baby talk to address their dogs" was the most annoying trait of dog owners.

The survey of 500 dog owners and 500 non-dog owners aimed to gain a better understanding of the concerns of the two groups.

Why doesn't everyone have a dog? Of the non-dog owners surveyed:

- 22% cited "too much responsibility."
- 16% said they didn't have enough time.
- 5% said dogs were too messy.
- 4% said cost was the main factor.
- 3% were concerned about allergies.

Source: The American Kennel Club
www.akc.org

Stressed and unhappy? Get a pet

2004 research findings of the U.K. firm Benenden Healthcare

Benenden Healthcare is a mutual not-for-profit Friendly Society run by members for members.

The research, which polled people in the U.K., revealed that 55% of pet owners are happy and that 71% do not feel stressed. The figures for non-pet owners are 45% and 29% respectively.

The survey, which questioned respondents on various aspects related to pet ownership and well-being, also looked at whether pet ownership should be encouraged. Two-thirds of respondents felt that it should be, with just 32% believing that we are better off without animal companionship.

Some 56% of people questioned said pets are most beneficial for people over 50 who are heading into retirement. Nevertheless, many people felt that animals can also benefit youngsters, with 37% stating that children can profit most from owning a pet.

Furthermore, more than 97% of respondents believe that owning a pet later in life can help reduce loneliness in old age. In contrast, only 38% believed that owning a pet would speed up a person's recovery if they were ill. But when this percentage was split between the pet-owners and non-pet owners, 77% of those in agreement owned animals.

Some 67% of pet owners said they kept an animal "for company." Friendship, relaxation, and entertainment were also popular reasons with 62%, 40%, and 19% of respondents, respectively.

Jill Gardiner, Marketing Manager at Benenden Healthcare commented:

"The results of the survey show that pet-owners are much happier and less stressed than non-pet owners. Being overly stressed or unhappy can have very adverse affects on our overall wellbeing and health, both physically and mentally. In addition, feelings of loneliness which cannot be cured medically can often be a cause of upset for people young and old. Owning a pet can't completely resolve these problems but as the results of the survey prove animal ownership can improve our overall quality of life."

Source: Benenden Healthcare.
www.benenden.org.uk
(Survey no longer posted on the website.)

Indoor cats live much longer

Statistics from the Canadian Federation of Humane Societies

The Canadian Federation of Humane Societies is the national voice of humane societies and SPCAs. It supports its member animal welfare organizations across Canada in promoting respect and humane treatment toward all animals.

Here are some statistics about cats in Canada:

- 52% of Canadians own pets.
- Of these pet owners, 49% have cats.
- Over 50,000 cats are euthanized in Canadian animal shelters every year.
- 43% of cats that come into animal shelters are euthanized.
- Fewer than 4% of cats in shelters are reclaimed by their owners.
- The average lifespan of cats that roam free outside is 2-5 years.
- The average lifespan of indoor cats is 12.5 years.

Unfortunately, too many cat owners think it is best for their beloved *Whiskers* to prowl the neighborhood, making good use of her nine lives. However, with all the risks faced by outdoor cats, these owners are playing Russian roulette.

Some of the dangers that outdoor cats face are:

- Vehicles;
- unfriendly dogs;
- predators, such as coyotes and raccoons;
- other cats defending their territory;
- angry neighbors who dislike cats digging and defecating in their garden;
- diseases such as feline leukemia or immunodeficiency viruses;
- fleas, ticks and other parasites;
- sickness from eating garbage or other contaminated morsels;
- harsh weather that can cause frostbite in winter or dehydration in summer;
- getting lost.

Another reason to keep your cat indoors is to stop her from killing wild animals, particularly birds. Several studies suggest that domestic cats kill millions of songbirds every year. Besides, your neighbors will appreciate not having *Whiskers* traipsing through or relieving herself in their gardens or children's sandboxes. Indoor cats live longer, are healthier, and suffer fewer injuries and health complications than outdoor cats.

Source: Canadian Federation of Humane Societies
http://cfhs.ca/athome/happy_indoor_cat/

Pets – an integral part of Canadian families

Recent survey of pet owners in Canada by the Ontario Veterinary Medical Association (OVMA)

The Ontario Veterinary Medical Association is a professional association representing veterinarians in the province of Ontario, working in private practice, government, academia, industry and public service.

This study by the OVMA showed that:

- More than 50% of Canadian households own pets of some kind. Dogs, cats, birds, and other companion animals are living in more than five million homes.

- These animals are more than pets – they are part of the family.

- Each year, Canadian families spend about three billion dollars on their pets, exceeding spending on children's toys, footwear, eye care and dental plans.

- Nearly 80% of respondents gave their pets holiday or birthday presents.

- More than 60% signed their pets' names on cards or letters.

- 51% gave their pets human names.

- While all pet owners talk to their pets, an astounding 94% spoke to them as though they were human.

- One-third of respondents spoke to their pets on the telephone or via the answering machine.

- 90% of pet owners believed their pets were aware of their moods and emotions.

Source: The Ontario Veterinary Medical Association (OVMA)
www.ovma.org/search.html

In the U.K., a dog brings more happiness than a partner

2006 U.K. Ipsos MORI survey on the relationship between dog ownership and happiness

Ipsos MORI is the largest independently owned market research company in Great Britain.

The MORI poll of 2,000 people, commissioned by Pedigree® Dog Food, reveals that owning a dog beats other feel-good factors in life, including the weather, job satisfaction, and even being in a steady relationship.

Money came firmly at the bottom of what makes people really happy.

Indeed, the benefits of owning a dog extends to far more than general happiness – not only have more than one-fifth (21%) of people expanded their social network through their four-legged friends, but as many as 36% met a partner while walking their dog.

Furthermore, one-quarter of dog owners confess to sometimes loving their dog more than their partners. While it was once important to get along with your partner's parents, the same now applies to your partner's dog – more than half of respondents admitted that their relationship becomes strained if their partner dislikes their dog.

The study also shows how man's best friend has considerably grown in stature to take an even more significant role in modern life. Consider the fact that 96% of respondents consider their dog to be a member of the family, with 55% believing them to be great substitutes for children.

Source: *Good News Blog*
www.goodnewsblog.com/2006/07/10
/a-dog-brings-more-happiness-than-a-
partner

Brits neglecting canines' canines

2006 U.K. Ipsos MORI survey on how dog owners regard tooth care for their pets

The MORI survey, commissioned by Pedigree, questioned dog owners about how they cared for (or ignored) the health of their pets' teeth.

The survey suggested that about three million dog owners in Britain are harming their dogs by neglecting their oral health.

The survey found that, although 77% of dog owners consider their dogs' health important, when it comes to dental hygiene, 50% of owners never clean their dog's teeth.

More than 80% of dogs over the age of three currently suffer from gum disease, says the survey.

The research shows the neglect of dogs' teeth is in sharp contrast to that of the owners. While 60% of dog owners brush their own teeth twice a day and visit a dentist at least once every six months, only 24% of dog owners claim they have ever cleaned their dog's teeth, and a mere 7% say they would ever consider taking their dog to the vet for a thorough teeth cleaning.

Some 18% of Britons believe they are sufficiently cleaning their dog's teeth by feeding their dogs dry or crunchy food like biscuits.

The reasons cited by owners for not looking after their dog's teeth varied.

- 65% were either not aware that they needed to, or thought that it was unnecessary.
- 23% claimed that their dog would simply not let its teeth be cleaned.
- 5% said that their dog's breath or dribble was too off-putting to go anywhere near their mouths.

Source: *Petsitting*

People and pets in Australia

1995 national People and Pets Study done in Australia for the Urban Animal Management Coalition

The coalition draws its representatives from the major institutional interests concerned with the well-being, health and safety of people and pets, the scientific community, animal welfare agencies and the pet industry.

This survey is the group's first major project. The research builds on findings from the seminal Australian study, *Pets As A Social Phenomenon*, conducted in the mid-1970s.

The recent study found that:

Pets are the norm for most people, more so in their developmental years. During childhood, for example, pets were part of the family for more than four out of five Australians.

Households with pet membership are still the norm. Of Australia's 6.2 million households, 60% have a pet and of these:

- 68% care for one or more dogs.
- 45% care for one or more cats.
- 25% own birds.

Of those who do not presently own a pet, 53% would like one in the future. Most want a dog. The mitigating factors are mainly:

- Living in accommodations not suited to a pet, e.g.,
  - rental accommodations with no provision for pets
  - no yard for the pet's mental stimulation, play, and leisure.
- The absence of someone at home to care for the pet.

The total number of companion animals in Australia has remained fairly stable over the last five years. Looking to the near future, however, dogs may become even more significant as the preferred pet species.

Source: Urban Animal Management Coalition

12 million Aussies associated with pets

2002 pet ownership survey in Australia by PetNet [Petcare Information and Advisory Service Australia Pty Ltd (PIAS)]

The Petcare Information and Advisory Service Australia Pty Ltd (PIAS) was established in 1966 as an autonomous, non-commercial organization committed to promoting socially responsible pet ownership.

Funding is provided by Masterfoods Petcare as a community service.

The survey measured the number and types of pets in Australian households and their economic impact on the country.

The survey found that:

- 12 million (of a total 20 million) Australians are associated with pets.
- 64% of the 7.5 million households in Australia own pets.
- Australia has one of the highest rates of pet ownership in the world.
- Typically, the major caregiver of the pet is female, married with children, living in the suburbs, and most likely employed.
- 91% of pet owners report feeling "very close" to their pet, reinforcing that pets are an integral member of the family unit, however constituted.
- Pets were a normal part of childhood for more than 83% of Australians.

Other findings

Estimated number of Australian households with pets 2002

Dogs	2.8 million
Cats	1.7 million
Dog and/or cat	3.9 million

Proportion of Australian households with pets

Dogs	37 %
Cats	23 %
Dog and/or cat	52 %
Any kind of pet	64 %

Australian pet ownership statistics 2002 ('000)

Species	Total	NSW	VIC	QLD	WA	SA	TAS	ACT	NT
Dogs	3,972	1,332	913	815	367	318	129	49	49
Cats	2,466	769	616	436	256	228	95	29	38
Birds	8,700	2,765	1,978	1,657	1,088	725	249	93	145
Fish	12,200	4,203	2,973	2,153	1,230	1,025	308	123	185
Other*	2,102	735	525	368	210	158	53	53	negl

* Other includes pleasure horses, rabbits, guinea pigs, etc.

The economic benefits of pets in Australia

The pet care industry is one of the largest in Australia, contributing about AUS$4 billion to the economy annually and employing 40,200 people.

In aggregated terms, the pet care industry is among the largest in Australia – both in terms of turnover and employment.

Of the total expenditure on pets, 66% is spent on dogs and 25% on cats.

2002 Australian expenditure on pet care (AUS$ million)

State	Dogs	Cats	Other Pets*	Total	Total %
New South Wales	884	316	116	1,316	33
Victoria	607	254	82	943	24
Queensland	541	180	63	783	20
South Australia	211	94	29	334	8
Western Australia	244	105	38	388	10
Tasmania	86	39	9	134	3
Northern Territories	33	12	4	49	1
Australian Capital Territory	33	16	5	54	1
Total	2,640	1,015	345	4,000	100

* Other includes pleasure horses, rabbits, guinea pigs, etc.

Health benefits of Australia's pets

Compared to non-pet owners:

- People who own pets typically visit the doctor less often and use less medication.
- Pet owners, on average, have lower cholesterol and lower blood pressure.
- Pet owners recover more quickly from illness and surgery.
- Pet owners deal better with stressful situations.
- Pet owners are less likely to report feeling lonely.

It is estimated that Australian cats and dogs saved $3.86 billion of national health expenditure in 1999–2000.

Source: PetNet [Petcare Information and Advisory Service Australia Pty Ltd (PIAS)]
www.petnet.com.au/pet-statistics

The perils of pet ownership in Australia: a new fall-injury risk factor

Study by Susan E. Kurrle, Robert Day and Ian D. Cameron on fall-related injuries in Sydney, Australia, due to pets in an older population

While much is made of the positive aspects of having a pet, there can be a downside too. The November–December 2004 issue of the Medical Journal of Australia published a study by Susan E. Kurrle, Robert Day and Ian D. Cameron on fall-related injuries due to pets in an older population.

Participants were people 75 years and older who arrived at the emergency department of a metropolitan hospital in northern Sydney over 18 months with a fracture directly related to their pet.

Source: The Medical Journal of Australia
www.mja.com.au/public/issues/
181_11_061204/kur10720_fm.html

Summary of case series of pet-related fracture

Patient no.	Age (years)	Sex	Fracture	Pet	Circumstances of fracture
1.	78	Female	Femoral neck	Goat	Climbing stile over fence to feed mohair goats, slipped and fell to ground.
2,	83	Female	Pelvis	Cat	Tripped over cat, landed on cat. Cat deceased.
3.	84	Male	Neck of humerus	Dog	Taking Jack Russell terrier for walk using retractable leash. Dog ran round and round patient's legs and pulled him over.
4.	81	Female	Pelvis	Donkey	Feeding donkey from bucket. Donkey nudged patient, pushing her over backwards.

Table continues on next page

Summary of case series of pet-related fracture

Patient no.	Age (years)	Sex	Fracture	Pet	Circumstances of fracture
5.	79	Male	Wrist	Bird	Budgerigar escaped from cage, perched on curtain rail. Patient stood on chair to reach bird and fell.
6.	78	Female	Ribs	Dog	Slipped on puddle of urine from new Labrador pup. Fell against wooden arm of armchair.
7.	88	Female	3rd cervical vertebra	Cat	Fell backwards over cat, landing on back with impact on posterior skull.
8.	76	Female	Nasal bones	Dog	Fell forwards while trying to prevent young puppy from diving into fish tank.
9.	81	Female	Ankle	Bird	Tripped down steps while carrying bird cage (containing canary) outside to clean it.
10.	75	Male	Ribs	Dog	Walking two greyhounds on leashes along street. Dogs pulled and patient slipped and fell against fence.
11.	80	Female	Neck of humerus	Cat	Reaching down to pick up cat's food dish. Cat leant against legs and patient fell forwards over cat.
12.	83	Female	Wrist	Cat	Fell sideways in garden while trying to stop cat catching a blue tongue lizard.
13.	82	Female	Femoral neck	Cat	Tripped over black cat in darkened hallway.
14.	86	Female	Pelvis	Dog	Bringing garbage bin in from street while having golden retriever on leash. Became caught between garbage bin and dog, and fell.
15.	83	Female	Neck of humerus	Dog	Carrying small dog on veranda, tripped and fell onto tiled stairs.
16.	80	Female	Pelvis	Cat	Fall while attempting to move quickly out back door as cat carried live snake in through side door.

Online pet magazines

There are hundreds of online pet and animal magazines (ezines) and many are well-written and informative; others are really marketing tools for the manufacturers of pet products. Some of these are actually quite good. Manufacturers of pet products have the resources to put together well-researched articles and information. Here is a short list of ezines with which to begin your own exploration:

All Our Pets. Online magazine with articles on dogs, cats, health, nutrition, travel, and activities with pets. *All Our Pets* magazine emerged from a project in electronic marketing for the web and markets natural dog and cat food.

www.allourpets.com

Birdlife Online. The information on the site states: "If you are new to being a bird owner this is a great place to find info and links to sites that will help you bond with your new pet. If you are thinking about buying a pet bird we have listing[s] for breeders across the US and Canada. Information is available on different common pet birds from finches and parakeets to large parrots like Macaws and Cockatoos and everything in between!"

www.birdlife.com

Cyberdogs Magazine. International ezine with news, vets, trainers, and groomers on line, animated GIF and photographic contests, humor, art, and poetry. There is also an Italian language version.

www.cyberdogsmagazine.com/head-line.htm

Dogs In Canada. Devoted to dogs and their Canadians. An online newsletter originating in Canada, all about – you guessed it – dogs.

www.dogsincanada.com/newsletter

Dr. Dog Paw Prints Newsletter. A bi-monthly newsletter aimed at providing information and tips for one's cat or dog.

www.doctordog.com/Drdognewsletter/newletter.html

Golden News. Training tips, stories, and questions and answers for golden retrievers, from Wilsonia.

www3.ns.sympatico.ca/goldens/new.htm

K9 Magazine. This appears to be the online newsletter associated with K9, a British dog magazine. It has links to a lot of information and a large number of sites and videos associated with dogs. There is much to explore here, and you may even want to subscribe to K9.

www.dogmagazine.net/

Pawprints and Purrs. Includes a monthly newsletter, pet health care related sources, spay and neuter campaign, and information about pet loss and animal abuse. This is an extensive site.

www.sniksnak.com

PetMag. A U.K. online pet magazine that covers a variety of pets.

www.petmag.co.uk

Pet Peoples Place. Every week there are new columns, advice, pictures, and lots more – thousands of pages of useful tools and resources.

www.petpeoplesplace.com

Pura Pets Pourri. An online bimonthly magazine for dog, cat and bird lovers, with informative articles on pet health and various activities you can do with your pet.

www.petspourri.com

Things for Horses – For Horse Lovers: Saddles, Browbands, Tips, and Tack. This is a commercial site that has more than the usual number of articles and tips.

http://thingsforhorses.com

Winged Wisdom Pet Bird Magazine. A pet bird ezine for exotic birds and pet parrots. It includes articles on the care and breeding of pet birds.

www.birdsnways.com/wisdom/

Woofer Pages. Another ezine about dogs – this one from New Zealand. Doglinks is a directory that contains a plethora of information about sources of products and services available to dog owners in New Zealand. The information is so comprehensive you need to visit the site yourself.

www.doglinks.co.nz/woof/woof.htm

Additional pet resources

General interest & information

Adopt-a-pet.com

This is an extensive site with links to public and private animal shelters around the world. These shelters offer animals for adoption, and some that are privately operated will accept animals from owners who cannot look after them. The site also offers advice to animal shelters that need help, provides animal health and safety tips, and more.

www.adoptapet.com

Directgov

For pet owners in the U.K., this site offers a wealth of information on pets, pet ownership, pet loss, and more.

www.direct.gov.uk/en/HomeAndCommunity/InYourHome/AnimalsAndPets/index.htm

Dog Scouts of America

A vast Internet site dedicated to providing information on how to be a responsible dog owner. The site includes articles on training, raising a new puppy, preventing or eliminating behavior problems, and more. There is also information on pet micro chipping and tattooing for positive identification.

www.dogscouts1.com

Doris Day Animal League

A useful site, because it provides links to a variety of relevant pet sites.

www.ddal.org/pettrust/resources

HandicappedPets.com

You can purchase a wide variety of products for ill and handicapped pets at this site, including wheelchairs, harnesses, boots, strollers, therapeutic vests, and more. The site also lists a host of services for people who own handicapped animals.

www.handicappedpets.com

Pampered Pets

This is an excellent all-round resources site with information on all types of pets including dogs, cats, reptiles, amphibians, fish, birds, and more. Not only does it have informative articles, but the site also references other Internet sites, books, magazines, and so on.

www.pamper-pets.com

After death

APCS (Accredited Pet Cemetery Society)

This website outlines the organization's guidelines, standards, and code of ethics for members. It also lists its member cemeteries.

www.allbusiness.com/membership-organizations/business-associations-business/4034528-1.html

Association of Private Pet Cemeteries and Crematoria (APPCC)

This site lists pet cemeteries and crematoria around the United Kingdom and Ireland, including the island of Jersey. The APPCC is the only organization in the U.K. setting standards for cremation and burial of pets "such that owners can understand the service being provided."

www.appcc.org.uk

Cherished Memories

Directory of pet cemeteries state-by-state in the United States plus Canada and the United Kingdom, but does not give affiliations with APCS or IAOPCC.

www.nepanetwork.com/keepsakes/petcem1.htm

IAOPCC (International Association of Pet Cemeteries and Crematoria)

This is a not-for-profit organization dedicated to advancing pet cemeteries through public awareness programs. Founded in 1971 in West Chicago, its member pet cemeteries are expected to maintain the highest business and ethical standards.

www.iaopc.com

Pets 2 Rest

This U.K. Internet site provides a lot of practical information on how to deal with the loss of a pet. Information on how to properly bury a pet on your property would be of interest to anyone anywhere. Indeed, much of the information on this site could be considered universal.

www.pets2rest.co.uk

Planet Pets – Pet Cemeteries/ Mortuaries Directory

This site lists pet cemeteries in the United States state by state, but by no means includes all of them. Use this as a supplemental directory if you can't find a pet cemetery in your area any other place.

www.planetpets.com/petcemeteries.htm

Legal services and information

Dog Law

This U.S. site is a resource that spans the entire range of law as it relates to dogs, including strategies for taking care of dogs when their owners die or become incapable of looking after them.

http://doglaw.hugpug.com/doglaw_075.html

LegalScholar.com

As the name suggests, this is an extensive online site listing legal resources around much of the English-speaking world.

www.legalscholar.com

Michigan State University College of Law: Animal Legal & Historical Web Center

This is an excellent resource for anyone wanting U.S. and international animal law information.

www.animallaw.info

Estate planning

ProfessorBeyer.com

This is the website of co-author Professor Gerry W. Beyer. In addition to a plethora of authoritative and detailed information, this site also maintains an up-to-date list of the states that have enacted pet trust legislation and the associated statutes.

www.professorbeyer.com/Articles/Animals.htm

National Network of Estate Planning Attorneys (U.S.)

By typing in your address, you can obtain a list of estate planning attorneys in your area of the United States.

www.netplanning.com.

PetGuardian

This company creates pet trusts for dogs, cats, birds, and horses. For a fee, it enrolls its clients in a program that includes a pet trust document, an estimate of how much money to set aside for your pet's care, plus emergency ID cards for pet owners to post at home and carry in their wallets. You can use the services of this organization in conjunction with your lawyer and set up a trust for your pet. There are forms to fill out that cover every eventuality.

As part of the program, the Best Friends Animal Society, a large no-kill shelter in Utah finds homes for pets, no matter where in the United States they reside, should the caregiver(s) named in the trust be no longer willing or able to fulfill their duties.

www.petguardian.com

Pet Trust Lawyer

This is the site of Rachael Hirschfeld, attorney at law, who will draft a pet trust agreement or "The Hirschfeld Pet Protection Agreement" if you need someone to care for your pets during your lifetime. Hirschfeld has offices in Manhattan, Brooklyn, Nassau, Suffolk, Rockland and Westchester Counties, and a toll free telephone number at 1-877-PET-TRUST.

www.pettrustlawyer.com

Lost pets

National Dog Registry (NDR)

Founded in 1966, NDR claims to be America's largest pet recovery organization, registering tattooed animals of all types – dogs, cats, horses, goats, ferrets, and more.

www.nationaldogregistry.com

PetRescue.com

This is an extensive Internet site that offers pet owners a wealth of information on a large number of topics from how to find a lost pet to health and safety information.

www.petrescue.com/home.htm

The UK National Missing Pets Register

This is a free pet registry whereby pet owners can register up to three pets by creating an account at the UK National Pet Register and then add these pets to the database. Each pet is issued its own unique Pet ID, allowing a pet owner and other members to instantly know that the pet is missing, and on the UK National Pet Register, pet owners can include photos of their pets.

www.nationalpetregister.org

Veterinary Diagnostics Center – DDC Veterinary

This company provides DNA services for humans and some animals, including DNA profiling for dogs, cats, horses and birds. It will send you a special kit with instructions on how to collect a DNA sample. A mailer is included so you can send your sample to them. It offers service to customers worldwide.

www.vetdnacenter.com

Animal protection and shelter

Humane Society International (HSI)

HSI is the international arm of the Humane Society of the United States, addressing animal issues that cross many borders and impact millions of animals worldwide. HSI states that it "works with national and jurisdictional governments, humane organizations, and individual animal protectionists in countries around the world to find practical, culturally sensitive, and long-term solutions to common animal issues, and to share an ethic of respect and compassion for all life."

www.hsus.org/hsi

Humane Society International – Australia Office

(See *Humane Society International for the mission statement.*)

www.hsi.org.au

Humane Society of Canada (HSC)

HSC has the following mission: "The Humane Society of Canada works to protect dogs, cats, horses, birds, livestock, lab animals, wildlife, and the environment. They carry out hands on programs to help animals and nature, mount rescue operations, expose cruelty through hard hitting undercover investigations, work to pass laws to protect animals, fund non-invasive scientific research, support animal shelters and wildlife rehabilitation centers, and spread the word about how to help animals and nature through humane education."

www.humanesociety.com

Humane Society of the United States (HSUS)

The HSUS says it is the nation's largest animal protection organization – backed by 10 million Americans, or one in every 30. Established in 1954, it seeks a humane and sustainable world for all animals – a world that will also benefit people. It is America's mainstream force against cruelty, exploitation and neglect, as well as the most trusted voice extolling the human-animal bond.

Its mission statement: Celebrating Animals, Confronting Cruelty.

www.hsus.org

Humane Society of New Zealand

The Humane Society of New Zealand helps place dogs and cats in good homes, financially assists in the neutering of pets, runs a telephone advisory service on pet care, and promotes the humane treatment of animals. Additionally, it promotes better legislation for the humane treatment of animals and tries to improve people's attitudes and sense of responsibility towards animals.

www.petsonthenet.co.nz/humane society.htm

Miscellaneous

Pet Friendly Canada Accommodations Directory

This site lists places to stay in Canada with pets.

www.petfriendly.ca

Petswelcome.com

This site lists pet-friendly U.S. and Canadian lodgings, as well as pet-friendly beaches, bed-and-breakfast units, and other facilities in the U.S.

www.petswelcome.com

PetTravel.com

This site allows you to search the world for pet-friendly accommodations. Find hotels from Alaska to Yemen (the Sofitel Al Saeed Taiz hotel, located on a mountaintop in Taiz). Sorry, no pet-friendly hotels at the time of writing in Zambia or Zimbabwe. And the site was still under the impression that the now – extinct country of Yugoslavia still exists.

www.pettravel.com

Senior Dogs Project

This site offers a state by state listing of rescue groups and shelters that pay special attention to older dogs.

www.srdogs.com/Pages/agencies.html

GLOSSARY

Administrator/Administratrix.
This is a person appointed by a court
to settle the financial and legal affairs
of a person who dies without having
made a valid will. The term administrator is used if the person is male and
administratrix if the person is female.

Agent. The person named in a power
of attorney to handle a person's financial or health care matters when the
person is unable to do so.

Beneficiary. A beneficiary is a person
or organization named in a will or
trust to receive or use some or all
of the assets of a decedent's estate
or trust.

Bequest. This term refers to a transfer of personal property by will.

Codicil. A codicil is a supplement to
a will, adding, subtracting or altering
the will's provisions. Normally, it
must be executed with the same
formalities as a will.

Common disaster. This occurs when
two or more persons (usually husband
and wife) die in the same accident
and when the death of each follows
within a relatively short period of time.

**Durable or enduring power of
attorney.** Also called a continuing
power of attorney or a power of
attorney for property, this is a
written, legal instrument to deal
with personal possessions and
finances. It allows one person to
authorize another to take specific
actions for him or her, as stated in
the document. Usually, the authority
is triggered by periods of disability
and/or incompetence. The document
becomes void upon the death of the
person who authorized it.

(A power of attorney for personal
care or a medical power of attorney
is a separate instrument dealing with
personal health care decisions, such
as hygiene, shelter and consenting
to medical treatment.)

Endowment. This is a bequest, gift
or a set of funds intended to be kept
and invested to generate income for
an organization, foundation or charity.

Estate. An estate includes everything
an individual owns, both real and
personal. The term also refers to the
property which is being held in trust.

Estate plan. This is a plan for disposing of one's property during one's lifetime and at death, including the handling of property in the event of the incompetence or total disability of the estate owner. An estate plan can be accomplished by a will, trusts, gifts made during life, or a combination of these.

Executor, executrix. Sometimes used synonymously with the term "personal representative," this is a person or agency named in a will to administer the estate of a deceased person. The term executor is used if the person is male and executrix if the person is female.

Guardian. A guardian is someone who has the legal duty and power to take care of the person and property of another. A guardian is usually required for someone who is considered incapable of administering his or her own affairs due to age, incompetence or disability.

Holographic will. This is a will written entirely in the maker's own handwriting, and is valid in some jurisdictions even without subscribing witnesses.

Honorary pet trust. This type of trust is not legally enforceable and thus depends on the trustee's 'honor' to carry out.

Incompetent. This is a person declared incapable of managing his or her affairs by a judge.

Inheritance tax. A tax levied on the right to receive property from a deceased person. This tax should be distinguished from the estate tax that is levied on the right to transmit property, not the right to receive it.

Inter vivos. This is a term used in law to describe agreements made while living. (See *living trust*.)

Intestate. A person who dies intestate, dies without having made a valid will.

Irrevocable. This is a term in law meaning incapable of being retracted, revoked or taken back.

Living trust. Also called an *inter vivos* or lifetime trust, it is a trust that is created and takes effect during the trustmaker's lifetime. It may be revocable or irrevocable.

Personal representative. A person or agency named in a will to administer the estate of a deceased person. (Often used synonymously with administrator/administratrix/executor/executrix.)

Pet trust. This is a trust which has the end result of providing for a pet when the owner is incompetent or dead.

Power of attorney. (See *durable or enduring power of attorney*.)

Principal. The person who designates an agent to make decisions in a durable or enduring power of attorney.

Probate. The action of proving before a competent judicial authority that a document offered for official recognition and registration as the last will and testament of a deceased person is genuine.

Property. Property is anything that may be owned, real and personal, tangible and intangible. It is that which belongs exclusively to a person, with full rights to enjoy and dispose of it. Real property is land, or any estate in land. It generally includes whatever is built or growing upon the land. It may be defined to include anything that is immovable. *Personal property* is all property other than *real property*. It generally refers to property that is movable.

Revocable. Something that is revocable can be retracted or taken back.

§ Section. Represents the section number of a legal reference.

Successor trustee. This is a trustee who follows the original or prior trustee.

Statutory pet trust. This is a trust for the benefit of a pet. It is enforceable because of a statute which has authorized the creation of this type of trust.

Testamentary trust. A trust created in a will. It takes effect after the will-maker dies and the will is probated.

Traditional pet trust. This is a trust which ultimately benefits a pet, but is created with a human beneficiary so that it is has a greater chance of being enforceable in court. The pet's caregiver is the beneficiary conditioned on the person taking proper care of the pet.

Trust. A trust is a legal relationship in which one person (a "trustee") holds property for the benefit of another (the "beneficiary"). The person placing property in the trust is known as the "settlor." With most lifetime trusts, the settlors are the trustees during their lifetimes, as long as they remain competent. Normally, settlors name successor trustees to take over if they become incompetent or die, and to distribute the property after they die or promise a mechanism to do so.

Will. A legal declaration that makes provisions for the distribution of property at death.

NOTES

NOTES

NOTES

NOTES

NOTES

NOTES

NOTES